TEX BY TOPIC
A TEXnician's Reference

TEX BY TOPIC
A TEXnician's Reference

Victor Eijkhout
University of Illinois at Urbana-Champaign

ADDISON-WESLEY PUBLISHING COMPANY

Wokingham, England • Reading, Massachusetts
Menlo Park, California • New York • Don Mills, Ontario
Amsterdam • Bonn • Sydney • Singapore • Tokyo • Madrid
San Juan • Milan • Paris • Mexico City • Seoul • Taipei

© 1992 Addison-Wesley Publishers Ltd.
© 1992 Addison-Wesley Publishing Company Inc.

All rights reserved. No part of this publication may be reproduced, stored in a retrieval system, or transmitted in any form or by any means, electronic, mechanical, photocopying, recording or otherwise, without prior written permission of the publisher.

The programs in this book have been included for their instructional value. They have been tested with care but are not guaranteed for any particular purpose. The publisher does not offer any warranties or representations, nor does it accept any liabilities with respect to the programs.

Many of the designations used by manufacturers and sellers to distinguish their products are claimed as trademarks. Addison-Wesley has made every attempt to supply trademark information about manufacturers and their products mentioned in this book. A list of the trademark designations and their owners appears on page viii.

Cover designed by Chris Eley and
printed by The Riverside Printing Co. (Reading) Ltd.
Typeset by T$_E$XTECHNIQUE using Baskerville and Gill Sans typefaces; typographic design by Merry Obrecht.
Printed in Great Britain by Mackays of Chatham PLC.

First printed 1991.

British Library Cataloguing in Publication Data
A catalogue record for this book is available from the British Library.

Library of Congress Cataloging in Publication Data available.

Preface

To the casual observer, TeX is not a state-of-the-art typesetting system. No flashy multilevel menus and interactive manipulation of text and graphics dazzle the onlooker. On a less superficial level, however, TeX is a very sophisticated program, first of all because of the ingeniousness of its built-in algorithms for such things as paragraph breaking and make-up of mathematical formulas, and second because of its almost complete programmability. The combination of these factors makes it possible for TeX to realize almost every imaginable layout in a highly automated fashion.

Unfortunately, it also means that TeX has an unusually large number of commands and parameters, and that programming TeX can be far from easy. Anyone wanting to program in TeX, and maybe even the ordinary user, would seem to need two books: a tutorial that gives a first glimpse of the many nuts and bolts of TeX, and after that a systematic, complete reference manual. This book tries to fulfil the latter function. A TeXer who has already made a start (using any of a number of introductory books on the market) should be able to use this book indefinitely thereafter.

In this volume the universe of TeX is presented as about forty different subjects, each in a separate chapter. Each chapter starts out with a list of control sequences relevant to the topic of that chapter and proceeds to treat the theory of the topic. Most chapters conclude with remarks and examples.

Globally, the chapters are ordered as follows. The chapters on basic mechanisms are first, the chapters on text treatment and mathematics are next, and finally there are some chapters on output and aspects of TeX's connections to the outside world.

The book also contains a glossary of TeX commands, tables, and indexes by example, by control sequence, and by subject. The subject index refers for most concepts to only one page, where most of the information on that topic can be found, as well as references to the locations of related information.

This book does not treat any specific TeX macro package. Any parts of the plain format that are treated are those parts that belong to the 'core' of plain TeX: they are also present in, for instance, LaTeX. Therefore, most remarks about the plain format are true for LaTeX, as well as most other formats. Putting it differently, if the text refers to the plain format, this should be taken as a contrast to pure IniTeX, not to LaTeX. By way of illustration, occasionally macros from plain TeX are explained that do not belong to the core.

Acknowledgment

I am indebted to Barbara Beeton, Karl Berry, and Nico Poppelier, who read previous versions of this book. Their comments helped to improve the presentation. Also I would like to thank the participants of the discussion lists TeXhax, TeX-nl, and `comp.text.tex`. Their questions and answers gave me much food for thought. Finally, any acknowledgement in a book about TeX ought to include Donald Knuth for inventing TeX in the first place. This book is no exception.

Victor Eijkhout
Urbana, Illinois, August 1991

Contents

    Preface   *v*
1. The Structure of the TeX Processor   *1*
2. Category Codes and Internal States   *8*
3. Characters   *24*
4. Fonts   *33*
5. Boxes   *38*
6. Horizontal and Vertical Mode   *55*
7. Numbers   *62*
8. Dimensions and Glue   *70*
9. Rules and Leaders   *82*
10. Grouping   *89*
11. Macros   *94*
12. Expansion   *111*
13. Conditionals   *127*
14. Token Lists   *140*
15. Baseline Distances   *145*
16. Paragraph Start   *150*
17. Paragraph End   *155*
18. Paragraph Shape   *159*
19. Line Breaking   *165*
20. Spacing   *175*
21. Characters in Math Mode   *180*
22. Fonts in Formulas   *186*
23. Mathematics Typesetting   *190*
24. Display Math   *201*
25. Alignment   *206*
26. Page Shape   *215*
27. Page Breaking   *217*
28. Output Routines   *225*
29. Insertions   *231*
30. File Input and Output   *236*
31. Allocation   *242*
32. Running TeX   *245*
33. TeX and the Outside World   *248*
34. Tracing   *258*
35. Errors, Catastrophes, and Help   *263*
36. The Grammar of TeX   *268*
37. Glossary of TeX Primitives   *272*
38. References   *286*
39. Tables   *288*
    Indexes   *302*

Trademark notice
IBM^{TM} is a trademark of International Business Machines Corporation.
Metafont^{TM} is a trademark of Addison-Wesley Publishing Company.
PostScript^{TM} is a trademark of Adobe Systems Incorporated.
TeX^{TM} and $\mathcal{A}_{\mathcal{M}}\mathcal{S}$-TeX^{TM} are trademarks of the American Mathematical Society.
Unix^{TM} is a trademark of AT&T.

CHAPTER 1

The Structure of the TeX Processor

This book treats the various aspects of TeX in chapters that are concerned with relatively small, well-delineated, topics. In this chapter, therefore, a global picture of the way TeX operates will be given. Of necessity, many details will be omitted here, but all of these are treated in later chapters. On the other hand, the few examples given in this chapter will be repeated in the appropriate places later on; they are included here to make this chapter self-contained.

1.1 FOUR TeX PROCESSORS

The way TeX processes its input can be viewed as happening on four levels. One might say that the TeX processor is split into four separate units, each one accepting the output of the previous stage, and delivering the input for the next stage. The input of the first stage is then the .tex input file; the output of the last stage is a .dvi file.

For many purposes it is most convenient, and most insightful, to consider these four levels of processing as happening after one another, each one accepting the *completed* output of the previous level. In reality this is not true: all levels are simultaneously active, and there is interaction between them.

The four levels are (corresponding roughly to the 'eyes', 'mouth', 'stomach', and 'bowels' respectively in Knuth's original terminology) as follows.

1. The input processor. This is the piece of TeX that accepts input lines from the file system of whatever computer TeX runs on, and turns them into tokens. Tokens are the internal objects of TeX: there are character tokens that constitute the typeset text, and control sequence tokens that are commands to be processed by the next two levels.
2. The expansion processor. Some but not all of the tokens generated in the first level – macros, conditionals, and a number of primitive TeX commands – are subject to expansion. Expansion is the process that replaces some (sequences of) tokens by other (or no) tokens.
3. The execution processor. Control sequences that are not expandable are executable, and this execution takes place on the third level of the TeX processor.
    One part of the activity here concerns changes to TeX's internal state: assignments (including macro definitions) are typical activities in this category.

The other major thing happening on this level is the construction of horizontal, vertical, and mathematical lists.
4. The visual processor. In the final level of processing the visual part of TeX processing is performed. Here horizontal lists are broken into paragraphs, vertical lists are broken into pages, and formulas are built out of math lists. Also the output to the `dvi` file takes place on this level. The algorithms working here are not accessible to the user, but they can be influenced by a number of parameters.

1.2 THE INPUT PROCESSOR

The input processor of TeX is that part of TeX that translates whatever characters it gets from the input file into tokens. The output of this processor is a stream of tokens: a token list. Most tokens fall into one of two categories: character tokens and control sequence tokens. The remaining category is that of the parameter tokens; these will not be treated in this chapter.

1.2.1 Character input

For simple input text, characters are made into character tokens. However, TeX can ignore input characters: a row of spaces in the input is usually equivalent to just one space. Also, TeX itself can insert tokens that do not correspond to any character in the input, for instance the space token at the end of the line, or the `\par` token after an empty line.

Not all character tokens signify characters to be typeset. Characters fall into sixteen categories – each one specifying a certain function that a character can have – of which only two contain the characters that will be typeset. The other categories contain such characters as {, }, &, and #. A character token can be considered as a pair of numbers: the character code – typically the ASCII code – and the category code. It is possible to change the category code that is associated with a particular character code.

When the escape character (by default \ ) appears in the input, TeX's behaviour in forming tokens is more complicated. Basically, TeX builds a control sequence by taking a number of characters from the input and lumping them together into a single token.

The behaviour with which TeX's input processor reacts to category codes can be described as a machine that switches between three internal states: N, new line; M, middle of line; S, skipping spaces. These states and the transitions between them are treated in Chapter 2.

1.2.2 Two-level input processing

TeX's input processor is in fact itself a two-level processor. Because of limitations of the terminal, the editor, or the operating system, the user may not be able to input certain desired characters. Therefore, TeX provides a mechanism to access with two superscript characters all of the available character positions. This may be considered a separate stage of TeX processing, taking place prior to the three-state machine mentioned above.

For instance, the sequence `^^+` is replaced by k because the ASCII codes of k and + differ by 64. Since this replacement takes place before tokens are formed, writing `\vs^^+ip 5cm` has the same effect as `\vskip 5cm`. Examples more useful than this exist.

Note that this first stage is a transformation from characters to characters, without considering category codes. These come into play only in the second phase of input processing where characters are converted to character tokens by coupling the category code to the character code.

1.3 THE EXPANSION PROCESSOR

TeX's expansion processor accepts a stream of tokens and, if possible, expands the tokens in this stream one by one until only unexpandable tokens remain. Macro expansion is the clearest example of this: if a control sequence is a macro name, it is replaced (together possibly with parameter tokens) by the definition text of the macro.

Input for the expansion processor is provided mainly by the input processor. The stream of tokens coming from the first stage of TeX processing is subject to the expansion process, and the result is a stream of unexpandable tokens which is fed to the execution processor.

However, the expansion processor comes into play also when (among others) an `\edef` or `\write` is processed. The parameter token list of these commands is expanded very much as if the lists had been on the top level, instead of the argument to a command.

1.3.1 The process of expansion

Expanding a token consists of the following steps:
1. See whether the token is expandable.
2. If the token is unexpandable, pass it to the token list currently being built, and take on the next token.
3. If the token is expandable, replace it by its expansion. For macros without parameters, and a few primitive commands such as `\jobname`, this is indeed a simple replacement. Usually, however, TeX needs to absorb some argument tokens from the stream in order to be able to form the replacement of the current token. For instance, if the token was a macro with parameters, sufficiently many tokens need to be absorbed to form the arguments corresponding to these parameters.
4. Go on expanding, starting with the first token of the expansion.

Deciding whether a token is expandable is a simple decision. Macros and active characters, conditionals, and a number of primitive TeX commands (see the list on page 111) are expandable, other tokens are not. Thus the expansion processor replaces macros by their expansion, it evaluates conditionals and eliminates any irrelevant parts of these, but tokens such as \vskip and character tokens, including characters such as dollars and braces, are passed untouched.

1.3.2 Special cases: \expandafter, \noexpand, and \the

As stated above, after a token has been expanded, TeX will start expanding the resulting tokens. At first sight the \expandafter command would seem to be an exception to this rule, because it expands only one step. What actually happens is that the sequence

\expandafter⟨token$_1$⟩⟨token$_2$⟩

is replaced by

⟨token$_1$⟩⟨*expansion of token$_2$*⟩

and this replacement is in fact reexamined by the expansion processor.

Real exceptions do exist, however. If the current token is the \noexpand command, the next token is considered for the moment to be unexpandable: it is handled as if it were \relax, and it is passed to the token list being built.

For example, in the macro definition

\edef\a{\noexpand\b}

the replacement text \noexpand\b is expanded at definition time. The expansion of \noexpand is the next token, with a temporary meaning of \relax. Thus, when the expansion processor tackles the next token, the \b, it will consider that to be unexpandable, and just pass it to the token list being built, which is the replacement text of the macro.

Another exception is that the tokens resulting from \the⟨token variable⟩ are not expanded further if this statement occurs inside an \edef macro definition.

1.3.3 Braces in the expansion processor

Above, it was said that braces are passed as unexpandable character tokens. In general this is true. For instance, the \romannumeral command is handled by the expansion processor; when confronted with

\romannumeral1\number\count2 3{4 ...

TeX will expand until the brace is encountered: if \count2 has the value of zero, the result will be the roman numeral representation of 103.

As another example,

\iftrue {\else }\fi

is handled by the expansion processor completely analogous to

\iftrue *a*\else *b*\fi

The result is a character token, independent of its category.

However, in the context of macro expansion the expansion processor will recognize braces. First of all, a balanced pair of braces marks off a group of tokens to be passed as one argument. If a macro has an argument

    \def\macro#1{ ... }

one can call it with a single token, as in

    \macro 1 \macro \$

or with a group of tokens, surrounded by braces

    \macro {abc} \macro {d{ef}g}

Secondly, when the arguments for a macro with parameters are read, no expressions with unbalanced braces are accepted. In

    \def\a#1\stop{ ... }

the argument consists of all tokens up to the first occurrence of \stop that is not in braces: in

    \a bc{d\stop}e\stop

the argument of \a is bc{d\stop}e. Only balanced expressions are accepted here.

1.4 THE EXECUTION PROCESSOR

The execution processor builds lists: horizontal, vertical, and math lists. Corresponding to these lists, it works in horizontal, vertical, or math mode. Of these three modes 'internal' and 'external' variants exist. In addition to building lists, this part of the TeX processor also performs mode-independent processing, such as assignments.

Coming out of the expansion processor is a stream of unexpandable tokens to be processed by the execution processor. From the point of view of the execution processor, this stream contains two types of tokens:

- Tokens signalling an assignment (this includes macro definitions), and other tokens signalling actions that are independent of the mode, such as \show and \aftergroup.
- Tokens that build lists: characters, boxes, and glue. The way they are handled depends on the current mode.

Some objects can be used in any mode; for instance boxes can appear in horizontal, vertical, and math lists. The effect of such an object will of course still depend on the mode. Other objects are specific for one mode. For instance, characters (to be more precise: character tokens of categories 11 and 12), are intimately connected to horizontal mode: if the execution processor is in vertical mode when it encounters a character, it will switch to horizontal mode.

Not all character tokens signal characters to be typeset: the execution processor can also encounter math shift characters (by default $) and beginning/end of group characters (by default { and }). Math shift characters let TeX enter or exit math mode, and braces let it enter or exit a new level of grouping.

One control sequence handled by the execution processor deserves special mention: `\relax`. This control sequence is not expandable, but the execution is to do nothing. Compare the effect of `\relax` in

```
\count0=1\relax 2
```

with that of `\empty` defined by

```
\def\empty{}
```

in

```
\count0=1\empty 2
```

In the first case the expansion process that is forming the number stops at `\relax` and the number 1 is assigned; in the second case `\empty` expands to nothing, so 12 is assigned.

1.5 THE VISUAL PROCESSOR

TeX's output processor encompasses those algorithms that are outside direct user control: paragraph breaking, alignment, page breaking, math typesetting, and `dvi` file generation. Various parameters control the operation of these parts of TeX.

Some of these algorithms return their results in a form that can be handled by the execution processor. For instance, a paragraph that has been broken into lines is added to the main vertical list as a sequence of horizontal boxes with intermediate glue and penalties. Also, the page breaking algorithm stores its result in `\box255`, so output routines can dissect it. On the other hand, a math formula can not be broken into pieces, and, naturally, shipping a box to the `dvi` file is irreversible.

1.6 EXAMPLES

1.6.1 Skipped spaces

Skipped spaces provide an illustration of the view that TeX's levels of processing accept the completed input of the previous level. Consider the commands

```
\def\a{\penalty200}
\a 0
```

This is *not* equivalent to

```
\penalty200 0
```

which would place a penalty of 200, and typeset the digit 0. Instead it expands to

>   \penalty2000

because the space after \a is skipped in the input processor. Later stages of processing then receive the sequence

>   \a0

1.6.2 Internal quantities and their representations

TeX uses various sorts of internal quantities, such as integers and dimensions. These internal quantities have an external representation, which is a string of characters, such as 4711 or 91.44cm.

Conversions between the internal value and the external representation take place on two different levels, depending on what direction the conversion goes. A string of characters is converted to an internal value in assignments such as

>   \pageno=12 \baselineskip=13pt

or statements such as

>   \vskip 5.71pt

and all of these statements are handled by the execution processor.

On the other hand, the conversion of the internal values into a representation as a string of characters is handled by the expansion processor. For instance,

>   \number\pageno \romannumeral\year
>   \the\baselineskip

are all processed by expansion.

As a final example, suppose \count2=45, and consider the statement

>   \count0=1\number\count2 3

The expansion processor tackles \number\count2 to give the characters 45, and the space after the 2 does not end the number being assigned: it only serves as a delimiter of the number of the \count register. In the next stage of processing, the execution processor will then see the statement

>   \count0=1453

and execute this.

CHAPTER

2

Category Codes and Internal States

When characters are read, TeX assigns them category codes. The reading mechanism has three internal states, and transitions between these states are effected by category codes of characters in the input. This chapter describes how TeX reads its input and how the category codes of characters influence the reading behaviour. Spaces and line ends are discussed.

\endlinechar   The character code of the end-of-line character appended to input lines. IniTeX default: 13.
\par   Command to close off a paragraph and go into vertical mode. Is generated by empty lines.
\ignorespaces   Command that reads and expands until something is encountered that is not a ⟨space token⟩.
\catcode   Query or set category codes.
\ifcat   Test whether two characters have the same category code.
\␣   Control space. Insert the same amount of space that a space token would when \spacefactor = 1000.
\obeylines   Macro in plain TeX to make line ends significant.
\obeyspaces   Macro in plain TeX to make (most) spaces significant.

2.1   INTRODUCTION

TeX's input processor scans input lines from a file or terminal, and makes tokens out of the characters. The input processor can be viewed as a simple finite state automaton with three internal states; depending on the state its scanning behaviour may differ. This automaton will be treated here both from the point of view of the internal states and of the category codes governing the transitions.

2.2   INITIAL PROCESSING

Input from a file (or from the user terminal, but this will not be mentioned specifically most of the time) is handled one line at a time. Here follows a discussion of what exactly is an input line for TeX.

Computer systems differ with respect to the exact definition of an input line. The carriage return/line feed sequence terminating a line is most common, but some systems use just a line feed, and some systems with fixed record length (block) storage do not have a line terminator at all. Therefore TeX has its own way of terminating an input line.

1. An input line is read from an input file (minus the line terminator, if any).
2. Trailing spaces are removed (this is for the systems with block storage, and it prevents confusion because these spaces are hard to see in an editor).
3. The \endlinechar, by default ⟨return⟩ (code 13) is appended. If the value of \endlinechar is negative or more than 255 (this was 127 in versions of TeX older than version 3; see page 271 for more differences), no character is appended. The effect then is the same as if the line were to end with a comment character.

Computers may also differ in the character encoding (the most common schemes are ASCII and EBCDIC), so TeX converts the characters that are read from the file to its own character codes. These codes are then used exclusively, so that TeX will perform the same on any system. For more on this, see Chapter 3.

2.3 CATEGORY CODES

Each of the 256 character codes (0–255) has an associated category code, though not necessarily always the same one. There are 16 categories, numbered 0–15. When scanning the input, TeX thus forms character-code–category-code pairs. The input processor sees only these pairs; from them are formed character tokens, control sequence tokens, and parameter tokens. These tokens are then passed to TeX's expansion and execution processes.

A character token is a character-code–category-code pair that is passed unchanged. A control sequence token consists of one or more characters preceded by an escape character; see below. Parameter tokens are also explained below.

This is the list of the categories, together with a brief description. More elaborate explanations follow in this and later chapters.

0. Escape character; this signals the start of a control sequence. IniTeX makes the backslash \ (code 92) an escape character.
1. Beginning of group; such a character causes TeX to enter a new level of grouping. The plain format makes the open brace { a beginning-of-group character.
2. End of group; TeX closes the current level of grouping. Plain TeX has the closing brace } as end-of-group character.
3. Math shift; this is the opening and closing delimiter for math formulas. Plain TeX uses the dollar sign $ for this.
4. Alignment tab; the column (row) separator in tables made with \halign (\valign). In plain TeX this is the ampersand &.
5. End of line; a character that TeX considers to signal the end of an input line. IniTeX assigns this code to the ⟨return⟩, that is, code 13. Not coincidentally, 13 is also the value that IniTeX assigns to the \endlinechar parameter; see above.

6. Parameter character; this indicates parameters for macros. In plain TeX this is the hash sign #.
7. Superscript; this precedes superscript expressions in math mode. It is also used to denote character codes that cannot be entered in an input file; see below. In plain TeX this is the circumflex ^.
8. Subscript; this precedes subscript expressions in math mode. In plain TeX the underscore _ is used for this.
9. Ignored; characters of this category are removed from the input, and have therefore no influence on further TeX processing. In plain TeX this is the ⟨null⟩ character, that is, code 0.
10. Space; space characters receive special treatment. IniTeX assigns this category to the ASCII ⟨space⟩ character, code 32.
11. Letter; in IniTeX only the characters a..z, A..Z are in this category. Often, macro packages make some 'secret' character (for instance @) into a letter.
12. Other; IniTeX puts everything that is not in the other categories into this category. Thus it includes, for instance, digits and punctuation.
13. Active; active characters function as a TeX command, without being preceded by an escape character. In plain TeX this is only the tie character ~, which is defined to produce an unbreakable space; see page 177.
14. Comment character; from a comment character onwards, TeX considers the rest of an input line to be comment and ignores it. In IniTeX the per cent sign % is made a comment character.
15. Invalid character; this category is for characters that should not appear in the input. IniTeX assigns the ASCII ⟨delete⟩ character, code 127, to this category.

The user can change the mapping of character codes to category codes with the \catcode command (see Chapter 36 for the explanation of concepts such as ⟨equals⟩):

\catcode⟨number⟩⟨equals⟩⟨number⟩.

In such a statement, the first number is often given in the form

'⟨character⟩   or   '\⟨character⟩

both of which denote the character code of the character (see pages 24 and 63). The plain format defines

\chardef\active=13

so that one can write statements such as

\catcode'\{=\active

The \chardef command is treated on pages 26 and 64.
The LaTeX format has the control sequences

\def\makeatletter{\catcode'@=11 }
\def\makeatother{\catcode'@=12 }

in order to switch on and off the 'secret' character @ (see below).

The \catcode command can also be used to query category codes: in

\count255=\catcode'\{

it yields a number, which can be assigned.

Category codes can be tested by

\ifcat⟨token$_1$⟩⟨token$_2$⟩

TeX expands whatever is after \ifcat until two unexpandable tokens are found; these are then compared with respect to their category codes. Control sequence tokens are considered to have category code 16, which makes them all equal to each other, and unequal to all character tokens. Conditionals are treated further in Chapter 13.

2.4 FROM CHARACTERS TO TOKENS

The input processor of TeX scans input lines from a file or from the user terminal, and converts the characters in the input to tokens. There are three types of tokens.

- Character tokens: any character that is passed on its own to TeX's further levels of processing with an appropriate category code attached.
- Control sequence tokens, of which there are two kinds: an escape character – that is, a character of category 0 – followed by a string of 'letters' is lumped together into a *control word*, which is a single token. An escape character followed by a single character that is not of category 11, letter, is made into a *control symbol*. If the distinction between control word and control symbol is irrelevant, both are called *control sequences*.

  The control symbol that results from an escape character followed by a space character is called *control space*.
- Parameter tokens: a parameter character – that is, a character of category 6, by default # – followed by a digit 1..9 is replaced by a parameter token. Parameter tokens are allowed only in the context of macros (see Chapter 11).

  A macro parameter character followed by another macro parameter character (not necessarily with the same character code) is replaced by a single character token. This token has category 6 (macro parameter), and the character code of the second parameter character. The most common instance is of this is replacing ## by #$_6$, where the subscript denotes the category code.

2.5 THE INPUT PROCESSOR AS A FINITE STATE AUTOMATON

TeX's input processor can be considered to be a finite state automaton with three internal states, that is, at any moment in time it is in one of three states, and after transition to another state there is no memory of the previous states.

2.5.1 State N: new line

State N is entered at the beginning of each new input line, and that is the only time TeX is in this state. In state N all space tokens (that is, characters of category 10) are ignored; an end-of-line character is converted into a \par token. All other tokens bring TeX into state M.

2.5.2 State S: skipping spaces

State S is entered in any mode after a control word or control space (but after no other control symbol), or, when in state M, after a space. In this state all subsequent spaces or end-of-line characters in this input line are discarded.

2.5.3 State M: middle of line

By far the most common state is M, 'middle of line'. It is entered after characters of categories 1–4, 6–8, and 11–13, and after control symbols other than control space. An end-of-line character encountered in this state results in a space token.

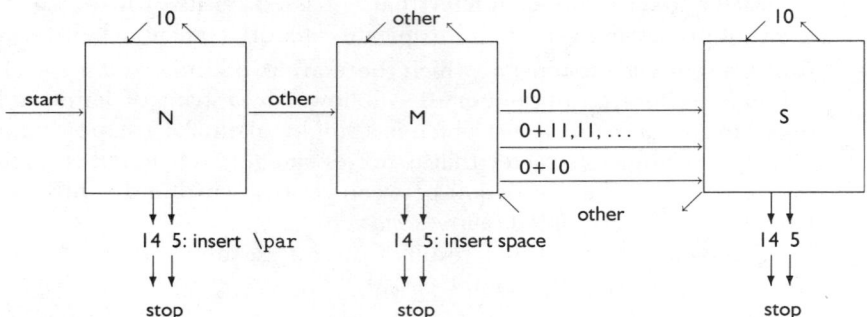

2.6 ACCESSING THE FULL CHARACTER SET

Strictly speaking, TeX's input processor is not a finite state automaton. This is because during the scanning of the input line all trios consisting of two *equal* superscript characters (category code 7) and a subsequent character (with character code < 128) are replaced by a single character with a character code in the range 0–127, differing by 64 from that of the original character.

This mechanism can be used, for instance, to access positions in a font corresponding to character codes that cannot be input, for instance because they are ASCII control characters. The most obvious examples are the ASCII ⟨return⟩ and ⟨delete⟩ characters; the corresponding positions 13 and 127 in a font are accessible as ^^M and ^^?. However, since the category of ^^? is 15, invalid, that has to be changed before character 127 can be accessed.

In TeX3 this mechanism has been modified and extended to access 256 characters: any quadruplet ^^xy where both x and y are lowercase hexadecimal digits 0–9, a–f, is replaced by a character in the range 0–255, namely the character the number of which is represented hexadecimally as xy. This imposes a slight restriction on the applicability of the earlier mechanism: if, for instance, ^^a is typed to produce character 33, then a following 0–9, a–f will be misunderstood.

While this process makes TeX's input processor somewhat more powerful than a true finite state automaton, it does not interfere with the rest of the scanning. Therefore it is conceptually simpler to pretend that such a replacement of triplets or quadruplets of characters, starting with ^^, is performed in advance. In actual practice this is not possible, because an input line may assign category code 7 to some character other than the circumflex, thereby influencing its further processing.

2.7 TRANSITIONS BETWEEN INTERNAL STATES

Let us now discuss the effects on the internal state of TeX's input processor when certain category codes are encountered in the input.

2.7.1 0: escape character

When an escape character is encountered, TeX starts forming a control sequence token. Three different types of control sequence can result, depending on the category code of the character that follows the escape character.

- If the character following the escape is of category 11, letter, then TeX combines the escape, that character and all following characters of category 11, into a control word. After that TeX goes into state S, skipping spaces.
- With a character of category 10, space, a control symbol called control space results, and TeX goes into state S.
- With a character of any other category code a control symbol results, and TeX goes into state M, middle of line.

The letters of a control sequence name have to be all on one line; a control sequence name is not continued on the next line if the current line ends with a comment sign, or if (by letting \endlinechar be outside the range 0–255) there is no terminating character.

2.7.2 1–4, 7–8, 11–13: non-blank characters

Characters of category codes 1–4, 7–8, and 11–13 are made into tokens, and TeX goes into state M.

2.7.3 5: end of line

Upon encountering an end-of-line character, TeX discards the rest of the line, and starts processing the next line, in state N. If the current state was N, that is, if the line so far contained at most spaces, a \par token is inserted; if the state was M, a space token is inserted, and in state S nothing is inserted.

Note that by 'end-of-line character' a character with category code 5 is meant. This is not necessarily the \endlinechar, nor need it appear at the end of the line. See below for further remarks on line ends.

2.7.4 6: parameter

Parameter characters – usually # – can be followed by either a digit 1..9 in the context of macro definitions or by another parameter character. In the first case a 'parameter token' results, in the second case only a single parameter character is passed on as a character token for further processing. In either case TeX goes into state M.

A parameter character can also appear on its own in an alignment preamble (see Chapter 25).

2.7.5 7: superscript

A superscript character is handled like most non-blank characters, except in the case where it is followed by a superscript character of the same character code. The process that replaces these two characters plus the following character (possibly two characters in TeX3) by another character was described above.

2.7.6 9: ignored character

Characters of category 9 are ignored; TeX remains in the same state.

2.7.7 10: space

A token with category code 10 – this is called a ⟨space token⟩, irrespective of the character code – is ignored in states N and S (and the state does not change); in state M TeX goes into state S, inserting a token that has category 10 and character code 32 (ASCII space), that is, the character code of the space token may change from the character that was actually input.

2.7.8 14: comment

A comment character causes TeX to discard the rest of the line, including the comment character. In particular, the end-of-line character is not seen, so even if the comment was encountered in state M, no space token is inserted.

2.7.9 15: invalid

Invalid characters cause an error message. TeX remains in the state it was in. However, in the context of a control symbol an invalid character is acceptable. Thus \^^? does not cause any error messages.

2.8 LETTERS AND OTHER CHARACTERS

In most programming languages identifiers can consist of both letters and digits (and possibly some other character such as the underscore), but control sequences in TeX are only allowed to be formed out of characters of category 11, letter. Ordinarily, the digits and punctuation symbols have category 12, other character. However, there are contexts where TeX itself generates a string of characters, all of which have category code 12, even if that is not their usual category code.

This happens when the operations \string, \number, \romannumeral, \jobname, \fontname, \meaning, and \the are used to generate a stream of character tokens. If any of the characters delivered by such a command is a space character (that is, character code 32), it receives category code 10, space.

For the extremely rare case where a hexadecimal digit has been hidden in a control sequence, TeX allows A_{12}–F_{12} to be hexadecimal digits, in addition to the ordinary A_{11}–F_{11} (here the subscripts denote the category codes).

For example,

\string\end   gives four character tokens $\backslash_{12}e_{12}n_{12}d_{12}$

Note that $\backslash_{12}$ is used in the output only because the value of \escapechar is the character code for the backslash. Another value of \escapechar leads to another character in the output of \string. The \string command is treated further in Chapter 3.

Spaces can wind up in control sequences:

\csname a b\endcsname

gives a control sequence token in which one of the three characters is a space. Turning this control sequence token into a string of characters

\expandafter\string\csname a b\endcsname

gives $\backslash_{12}a_{12}\sqcup_{10}b_{12}$.

As a more practical example, suppose there exists a sequence of input files file1.tex, file2.tex, and we want to write a macro that finds the number of the input file that is being processed. One approach would be to write

\newcount\filenumber   \def\getfilenumber file#1.{\filenumber=#1 }
\expandafter\getfilenumber\jobname.

where the letters file in the parameter text of the macro (see Section 11.5) absorb that part of the jobname, leaving the number as the sole parameter.

However, this is slightly incorrect: the letters file resulting from the \jobname command have category code 12, instead of 11 for the ones in the definition of \getfilenumber. This can be repaired as follows:

{\escapechar=-1
 \expandafter\gdef\expandafter\getfilenumber
     \string\file#1.{\filenumber=#1 }
}

Now the sequence `\string\file` gives the four letters f₁₂i₁₂l₁₂e₁₂; the `\expandafter` commands let this be executed prior to the macro definition; the backslash is omitted because we put `\escapechar=-1`. Confining this value to a group makes it necessary to use `\gdef`.

2.9 THE \par TOKEN

TeX inserts a `\par` token into the input after encountering a character with category code 5, end of line, in state N. It is good to realize when exactly this happens: since TeX leaves state N when it encounters any token but a space, a line giving a `\par` can only contain characters of category 10. In particular, it cannot end with a comment character. Quite often this fact is used the other way around: if an empty line is wanted for the layout of the input one can put a comment sign on that line.

Two consecutive empty lines generate two `\par` tokens. For all practical purposes this is equivalent to one `\par`, because after the first one TeX enters vertical mode, and in vertical mode a `\par` only exercises the page builder, and clears the paragraph shape parameters.

A `\par` is also inserted into the input when TeX sees a ⟨vertical command⟩ in unrestricted horizontal mode. After the `\par` has been read and expanded, the vertical command is examined anew (see Chapters 6 and 17).

The `\par` token may also be inserted by the `\end` command that finishes off the run of TeX; see Chapter 28.

It is important to realize that TeX does what it normally does when encountering an empty line (which is ending a paragraph) only because of the default definition of the `\par` token. By redefining `\par` the behaviour caused by empty lines and vertical commands can be changed completely, and interesting special effects can be achieved. In order to continue to be able to cause the actions normally associated with `\par`, the synonym `\endgraf` is available in the plain format. See further Chapter 17.

The `\par` token is not allowed to be part of a macro argument, unless the macro has been declared to be `\long`. A `\par` in the argument of a non-`\long` macro prompts TeX to give a 'runaway argument' message. Control sequences that have been `\let` to `\par` (such as `\endgraf`) are allowed, however.

2.10 SPACES

This section treats some of the aspects of space characters and space tokens in the initial processing stages of TeX. The topic of spacing in text typesetting is treated in Chapter 20.

2.10.1 Skipped spaces

From the discussion of the internal states of TeX's input processor it is clear that some spaces in the input never reach the output; in fact they never get past the input processor. These are for instance the spaces at the beginning of an input line, and the spaces following the one that lets TeX switch to state S.

On the other hand, line ends can generate spaces (which are not in the input) that may wind up in the output. There is a third kind of space: the spaces that get past the input processor, or are even generated there, but still do not wind up in the output. These are the ⟨optional spaces⟩ that the syntax of TeX allows in various places.

2.10.2 Optional spaces

The syntax of TeX has the concepts of 'optional spaces' and 'one optional space':

⟨one optional space⟩ ⟶ ⟨space token⟩ | ⟨empty⟩
⟨optional spaces⟩ ⟶ ⟨empty⟩ | ⟨space token⟩⟨optional spaces⟩

In general, ⟨one optional space⟩ is allowed after numbers and glue specifications, while ⟨optional spaces⟩ are allowed whenever a space can occur inside a number (for example, between a minus sign and the digits of the number) or glue specification (for example, between `plus` and `1fil`). Also, the definition of ⟨equals⟩ allows ⟨optional spaces⟩ before the = sign.

Here are some examples of optional spaces.

- A number can be delimited by ⟨one optional space⟩. This prevents accidents (see Chapter 7), and it speeds up processing, as TeX can detect more easily where the ⟨number⟩ being read ends. Note, however, that not every 'number' is a ⟨number⟩: for instance the 2 in `\magstep2` is not a number, but the single token that is the parameter of the `\magstep` macro. Thus a space or line end after this is significant. Another example is a parameter number, for example #1: since at most nine parameters are allowed, scanning one digit after the parameter character suffices.
- From the grammar of TeX it follows that the keywords `fill` and `filll` consist of `fil` and separate `l`s, each of which is a keyword (see page 269 for a more elaborate discussion), and hence can be followed by optional spaces. Therefore forms such as `fil L l` are also valid. This is a potential source of strange accidents. In most cases, appending a `\relax` token prevents such mishaps.
- The primitive command `\ignorespaces` may come in handy as the final command in a macro definition. As it gobbles up optional spaces, it can be used to prevent spaces following the closing brace of an argument from winding up in the output inadvertently. For example, in

```
\def\item#1{\par\leavevmode
    \llap{#1\enspace}\ignorespaces}
\item{a/}one line \item{b/} another line \item{c/}
yet another
```

the `\ignorespaces` prevents spurious spaces in the second and third item. An empty line after `\ignorespaces` will still insert a `\par`, however.

2.10.3 Ignored and obeyed spaces

After control words spaces are ignored. This is not an instance of optional spaces, but it is due to the fact that TeX goes into state S, skipping spaces, after control words. Similarly an end-of-line character is skipped after a control word.

Numbers are delimited by only ⟨one optional space⟩, but still

```
a\count0=3  b    gives   'ab',
```

because TeX goes into state S after the first space token. The second space is therefore skipped in the input processor of TeX; it never becomes a space token.

Spaces are skipped furthermore when TeX is in state N, newline. When TeX is processing in vertical mode space tokens (that is, spaces that were not skipped) are ignored. For example, the space inserted after the first box in

```
\par
\hbox{a}
\hbox{b}
```

has no effect.

Both plain TeX and LaTeX define a command \obeyspaces that makes spaces significant: after one space other spaces are no longer ignored. In both cases the basis is

```
\catcode`\ =13 \def {\space}
```

However, there is a difference between the two cases: in plain TeX

```
\def\space{ }
```

while in LaTeX

```
\def\space{\leavevmode{} }
```

although the macros bear other names there.

The difference between the two macros becomes apparent in the context of \obeylines: each line end is then a \par command, implying that each next line is started in vertical mode. An active space is expanded by the plain macro to a space token, which is ignored in vertical mode. The active spaces in LaTeX will immediately switch to horizontal mode, so that each space is significant.

2.10.4 More ignored spaces

There are three further places where TeX will ignore space tokens.

1. When TeX is looking for an undelimited macro argument it will accept the first token (or group) that is not a space. This is treated in Chapter 11.
2. In math mode space tokens are ignored (see Chapter 23).
3. After an alignment tab character spaces are ignored (see Chapter 25).

2.10.5 ⟨space token⟩

Spaces are anomalous in TeX. For instance, the \string operation assigns category code 12 to all characters except spaces; they receive category 10. Also, as was said above, TeX's input processor converts (when in state *M*) all tokens with category code 10 into real spaces: they get character code 32. Any character token with category 10 is called ⟨space token⟩. Space tokens with character code not equal to 32 are called 'funny spaces'.

Example
After giving the character Q the category code of a space character, and using it in a definition

```
\catcode`Q=10 \def\q{aQb}
```

we get

```
\show\q
macro:-> a b
```

because the input processor changes the character code of the funny space in the definition.

Space tokens with character codes other than 32 can be created using, for instance, \uppercase. However, 'since the various forms of space tokens are almost identical in behaviour, there's no point dwelling on the details'; see Knuth (1984a), p. 377.

2.10.6 Control space

The 'control space' command \␣ contributes the amount of space that a ⟨space token⟩ would when the \spacefactor is 1000. A control space is not treated like a space token, or like a macro expanding to one (which is how \space is defined in plain TeX). For instance, TeX ignores spaces at the beginning of an input line, but control space is a ⟨horizontal command⟩, so it makes TeX switch from vertical to horizontal mode (and insert an indentation box). See Chapter 20 for the space factor.

2.10.7 '␣'

The explicit symbol '␣' for a space is character 32 in the Computer Modern typewriter typeface. However, switching to \tt is not sufficient to get spaces denoted this way, because spaces will still receive special treatment in the input processor.
One way to let spaces be typeset by ␣ is to set

```
\catcode`\ =12
```

TeX will then take a space as the instruction to typeset character number 32. Moreover, subsequent spaces are not skipped, but also typeset this way: state *S* is only entered after a character with category code 10. Similarly, spaces after a control sequence are made visible by changing the category code of the space character.

2.11 MORE ABOUT LINE ENDS

TeX accepts lines from an input file, excluding any line terminator that may be used. Because of this, TeX's behaviour here is not dependent on the operating system and the line terminator it uses (CR-LF, LF, or none at all for block storage). From the input line any trailing spaces are removed. The reason for this is historic; it has to do with the block storage mode on IBM mainframe computers. For some computer-specific problems with end-of-line characters, see Beeton (1988).

A terminator character is then appended with a character code of \endlinechar, unless this parameter has a value that is negative or more than 255. Note that this terminator character need not have category code 5, end of line.

2.11.1 Obeylines

Every once in a while it is desirable that the line ends in the input correspond to those in the output. The following piece of code does the trick:

```
\catcode'\^^M=13 %
\def^^M{\par}%
```

The \endlinechar character is here made active, and its meaning becomes \par. The comment signs prevent TeX from seeing the terminator of the lines of this definition, and expanding it since it is active.

However, it takes some care to embed this code in a macro. The definition

```
\def\obeylines{\catcode'\^^M=13 \def^^M{\par}}
```

will be misunderstood: TeX will discard everything after the second ^^M, because this has category code 5. Effectively, this line is then

```
\def\obeylines{\catcode'\^^M=13 \def
```

To remedy this, the definition itself has to be performed in a context where ^^M is an active character:

```
{\catcode'\^^M=13 %
 \gdef\obeylines{\catcode'\^^M=13 \def^^M{\par}}%
}
```

Empty lines in the input are not taken into account in this definition: these disappear, because two consecutive \par tokens are (in this case) equivalent to one. A slightly modified definition for the line end as

```
\def^^M{\par\leavemode}
```

remedies this: now every line end forces TeX to start a paragraph. For empty lines this will then be an empty paragraph.

2.11.2 Changing the \endlinechar

Occasionally you may want to change the \endlinechar, or the \catcode of the ordinary line terminator ^^M, for instance to obtain special effects such as macros where the argument is terminated by the line end. See page 108 for a worked-out example.

There are a couple of traps. Consider the following:

```
{\catcode`\^^M=12 \endlinechar=`\^^J \catcode`\^^J=5
...
... }
```

This causes unintended output of both character 13 (^^M) and 10 (^^J), caused by the line terminators of the first and last line.

Terminating the first and last line with a comment works, but replacing the first line by the two lines

```
{\endlinechar=`\^^J \catcode`\^^J=5
\catcode`\^^M=12
```

is also a solution.

Of course, in many cases it is not necessary to substitute another end-of-line character; a much simpler solution is then to put

```
\endlinechar=-1
```

which treats all lines as if they end with a comment.

2.11.3 More remarks about the end-of-line character

The character that TeX appends at the end of an input line is treated like any other character. Usually one is not aware of this, as its category code is special, but there are a few ways to let it be processed in an unusual way.

Example
Terminating an input line with ^^ will (ordinarily, when \endlinechar is 13) give 'M' in the output, which is the ASCII character with code 13+64.

Example
If \^^M has been defined, terminating an input line with a backslash will execute this command. The plain format defines

```
\def\^^M{\ }
```

which makes a 'control return' equivalent to a control space.

2.12 MORE ABOUT THE INPUT PROCESSOR

2.12.1 The input processor as a separate process

TeX's levels of processing are all working at the same time and incrementally, but conceptually they can often be considered to be separate processes that each accept the completed output of the previous stage. The juggling with spaces provides a nice illustration for this.

Consider the definition

`\def\DoAssign{\count42=800}`

and the call

`\DoAssign 0`

The input processor, the part of TeX that builds tokens, in scanning this call skips the space before the zero, so the expansion of this call is

`\count42=8000`

It would be incorrect to reason '`\DoAssign` is read, then expanded, the space delimits the number 800, so 800 is assigned and the zero is printed'. Note that the same would happen if the zero appeared on the next line.

Another illustration shows that optional spaces appear in a different stage of processing from that for skipped spaces:

`\def\c.{\relax}`
`a\c.`␣`b`

expands to

`a\relax`␣`b`

which gives as output

'a b'

because spaces after the `\relax` control sequence are only skipped when the line is first read, not when it is expanded. The fragment

`\def\c.{\ignorespaces}`
`a\c. b`

on the other hand, expands to

`a\ignorespaces`␣`b`

Executing the `\ignorespaces` command removes the subsequent space token, so the output is

'ab'.

In both definitions the period after `\c` is a delimiting token; it is used here to prevent spaces from being skipped.

2.12.2 The input processor not as a separate process

Considering the tokenizing of TeX to be a separate process is a convenient view, but sometimes it leads to confusion. The line

`\catcode'\^^M=13{}`

makes the line end active, and subsequently gives an 'undefined control sequence' error for the line end of this line itself. Execution of the commands on the line thus influences the scanning process of that same line.

By contrast,

`\catcode`\^^M=13`

does not give an error. The reason for this is that TeX reads the line end while it is still scanning the number 13; that is, at a time when the assignment has not been performed yet. The line end is then converted to the optional space character delimiting the number to be assigned.

2.12.3 Recursive invocation of the input processor

Above, the activity of replacing a parameter character plus a digit by a parameter token was described as something similar to the lumping together of letters into a control sequence token. Reality is somewhat more complicated than this. TeX's token scanning mechanism is invoked both for input from file and for input from lists of tokens such as the macro definition. Only in the first case is the terminology of internal states applicable.

Macro parameter characters are treated the same in both cases, however. If this were not the case it would not be possible to write things such as

`\def\a{\def\b{\def\c####1{####1}}}`

See page 100 for an explanation of such nested definitions.

2.13 THE @ CONVENTION

Anyone who has ever browsed through either the plain format or the LaTeX format will have noticed that a lot of control sequences contain an 'at' sign: @. These are control sequences that are meant to be inaccessible to the ordinary user.

Near the beginning of the format files the instruction

`\catcode`@=11`

occurs, making the at sign into a letter, meaning that it can be used in control sequences. Somewhere near the end of the format definition the at sign is made 'other' again:

`\catcode`@=12`

Now why is it that users cannot call a control sequence with an at sign directly, although they can call macros that contain lots of those 'at-definitions'? The reason is that the control sequences containing an @ are internalized by TeX at definition time, after which they are a token, not a string of characters. Macro expansion then just inserts such tokens, and at that time the category codes of the constituent characters do not matter any more.

CHAPTER 3

Characters

Internally, TeX represents characters by their (integer) character code. This chapter treats those codes, and the commands that have access to them.

\char   Explicit denotation of a character to be typeset.
\chardef   Define a control sequence to be a synonym for a character code.
\accent   Command to place accent characters.
\if   Test equality of character codes.
\ifx   Test equality of both character and category codes.
\let   Define a control sequence to be a synonym of a token.
\uccode   Query or set the character code that is the uppercase variant of a given code.
\lccode   Query or set the character code that is the lowercase variant of a given code.
\uppercase   Convert the ⟨general text⟩ argument to its uppercase form.
\lowercase   Convert the ⟨general text⟩ argument to its lowercase form.
\string   Convert a token to a string of one or more characters.
\escapechar   Number of the character that is to be used for the escape character when control sequences are being converted into character tokens. IniTeX default: 92 (\).

3.1 CHARACTER CODES

Conceptually it is easiest to think that TeX works with characters internally, but in fact TeX works with integers: the 'character codes'.

The way characters are encoded in a computer may differ from system to system. Therefore TeX uses its own scheme of character codes. Any character that is read from a file (or from the user terminal) is converted to a character code according to the character code table. A category code is then assigned based on this (see Chapter 2). The character code table is based on the 7-bit ASCII table for numbers under 128 (see Chapter 39).

There is an explicit conversion between characters (better: character tokens) and character codes using the left quote (grave, back quote) character ': at all places where TeX expects a ⟨number⟩ you can use the left quote followed by a character token or a single-character control sequence. Thus both \count'a and \count'\a are synonyms for \count97. See also Chapter 7.

The possibility of a single-character control sequence is necessary in certain cases such as

`\catcode`\%=11` or `\def\CommentSign{\char`\%}`

which would be misunderstood if the backslash were left out. For instance

`\catcode`%=11`

would consider the =11 to be a comment. Single-character control sequences can be formed from characters with any category code.

After the conversion to character codes any connection with external representations has disappeared. Of course, for most characters the visible output will 'equal' the input (that is, an 'a' causes an 'a'). There are exceptions, however, even among the common symbols. In the Computer Modern roman fonts there are no 'less than' and 'greater than' signs, so the input '<>' will give '¡¿' in the output.

In order to make TeX machine independent at the output side, the character codes are also used in the `dvi` file: opcodes $n = 0 \ldots 127$ denote simply the instruction 'take character n from the current font'. The complete definition of the opcodes in a `dvi` file can be found in Knuth (1986a).

3.2 CONTROL SEQUENCES FOR CHARACTERS

There are a number of ways in which a control sequence can denote a character. The `\char` command specifies a character to be typeset; the `\let` command introduces a synonym for a character token, that is, the combination of character code and category code.

3.3 DENOTING CHARACTERS TO BE TYPESET: `\char`

Characters can be denoted numerically by, for example, `\char98`. This command tells TeX to add character number 98 of the current font to the horizontal list currently under construction.

Instead of decimal notation, it is often more convenient to use octal or hexadecimal notation. For octal the single quote is used: `\char'142`; hexadecimal uses the double quote: `\char"62`. Note that `\char''62` is incorrect; the process that replaces two quotes by a double quote works at a later stage of processing (the visual processor) than number scanning (the execution processor).

Because of the explicit conversion to character codes by the back quote character it is also possible to get a 'b' – provided that you are using a font organized a bit like the ASCII table – with `\char`b` or `\char`\b`.

The `\char` command looks superficially a bit like the `^^` substitution mechanism (Chapter 2). Both mechanisms access characters without directly denoting them. However, the `^^` mechanism operates in a very early stage of processing (in the input processor of TeX, but before category code assignment); the `\char` command, on the other hand, comes in the final stages of processing. In effect it says 'typeset character number so-and-so'.

There is a construction to let a control sequence stand for some character code: the \chardef command. The syntax of this is

\chardef⟨control sequence⟩⟨equals⟩⟨number⟩,

where the number can be an explicit representation or a counter value, but it can also be a character code obtained using the left quote command (see above; the full definition of ⟨number⟩ is given in Chapter 7). In the plain format the latter possibility is used in definitions such as

\chardef\%=`\%

which could have been given equivalently as

\chardef\%=37

After this command, the control symbol \% used on its own is a synonym for \char37, that is, the command to typeset character 37 (usually the per cent character).

A control sequence that has been defined with a \chardef command can also be used as a ⟨number⟩. This fact is used in allocation commands such as \newbox (see Chapters 7 and 31). Tokens defined with \mathchardef can also be used this way.

3.3.1 Implicit character tokens: \let

Another construction defining a control sequence to stand for (among other things) a character is \let:

\let⟨control sequence⟩⟨equals⟩⟨token⟩

with a character token on the right hand side of the (optional) equals sign. The result is called an implicit character token. (See page 102 for a further discussion of \let.)

In the plain format there are for instance synonyms for the open and close brace:

\let\bgroup={ \let\egroup=}

The resulting control sequences are called 'implicit braces' (see Chapter 10).

Assigning characters by \let is different from defining control sequences by \chardef, in the sense that \let makes the control sequence stand for the combination of a character code and category code.

As an example

```
\catcode`|=2 % make the bar an end of group
\let\b=|   % make \b a bar character
{\def\m{...}\b \m
```

gives an 'undefined control sequence \m' because the \b closed the group inside which \m was defined. On the other hand,

\let\b=| % make \b a bar character

```
\catcode'|=2  % make the bar character end of group
{\def\m{...}\b \m
```

leaves one group open, and it prints a vertical bar (or whatever is in position 124 of the current font). The first of these examples implies that even when the braces have been redefined (for instance into active characters for macros that format C code) the beginning-of-group and end-of-group functionality is available through the control sequences \bgroup and \egroup.

Here is another example to show that implicit character tokens are hard to distinguish from real character tokens. After the above sequence

```
\catcode'|=2 \let\b=|
```

the tests

```
\if\b|
```

and

```
\ifcat\b}
```

are both true.

Yet another example can be found in the plain format: the commands

```
\let\sp=^ \let\sb=_
```

allow people without an underscore or circumflex on their keyboard to make sub- and superscripts in mathematics. For instance:

```
x\sp2\sb{ij}
```
gives x_{ij}^2

If a person typing in the format itself does not have these keys, some further tricks are needed:

```
{\lccode',=94 \lccode'.=95 \catcode',=7 \catcode'.=8
\lowercase{\global\let\sp=, \global\let\sb=.}}
```

will do the job; see below for an explanation of lowercase codes. The ^^ method as it was in TeX version 2 (see page 12) cannot be used here, as it would require typing two characters that can ordinarily not be input. With the extension in TeX version 3 it would also be possible to write

```
{\catcode'\,=7
\global\let\sp=,,5e \global\let\sb=,,5f}
```

denoting the codes 94 and 95 hexadecimally.

Finding out just what a control sequence has been defined to be with \let can be done using \meaning: the sequence

```
\let\x=3 \meaning\x
```

gives 'the character 3'.

3.4 ACCENTS

Accents can be placed by the ⟨horizontal command⟩ \accent:

\accent⟨8-bit number⟩⟨optional assignments⟩⟨character⟩

where ⟨character⟩ is a character of category 11 or 12, a \char⟨8-bit number⟩ command, or a \chardef token. If none of these four types of ⟨character⟩ follows, the accent is taken to be a \char command itself; this gives an accent 'suspended in mid-air'. Otherwise the accent is placed on top of the following character. Font changes between the accent and the character can be effected by the ⟨optional assignments⟩.

An unpleasant implication of the fact that an \accent command has to be followed by a ⟨character⟩ is that it is not possible to place two accents on top of each other. In some languages, such as Hindi or Vietnamese, such double accents do occur. Positioning accents on top of each other is possible, however, in math mode.

The width of a character with an accent is the same as that of the unaccented character. TeX assumes that the accent as it appears in the font file is properly positioned for a character that is as high as the x-height of the font; for characters with other heights it correspondingly lowers or raises the accent.

No genuine under-accents exist in TeX. They are implemented as low placed over-accents. A way of handling them more correctly would be to write a macro that measures the following character, and raises or drops the accent accordingly. The cedilla macro, \c, in plain TeX does something along these lines. However, it does not drop the accent for characters with descenders.

The horizontal positioning of an accent is controlled by \fontdimen1, slant per point. Kerns are used for the horizontal movement. Note that, although they are inserted automatically, these kerns are classified as *explicit* kerns. Therefore they inhibit hyphenation in the parts of the word before and after the kern.

As an example of kerning for accents, here follows the dump of a horizontal list.

```
\setbox0=\hbox{\it \'l}
\showbox0
```

gives

```
\hbox(9.58334+0.0)x2.55554
.\kern -0.61803 (for accent)
.\hbox(6.94444+0.0)x5.11108, shifted -2.6389
..\tenit ^^R
.\kern -4.49306 (for accent)
.\tenit l
```

Note that the accent is placed first, so afterwards the italic correction of the last character is still available.

3.5 TESTING CHARACTERS

Equality of character codes is tested by \if:

\if⟨token$_1$⟩⟨token$_2$⟩

Tokens following this conditional are expanded until two unexpandable tokens are left. The condition is then true if those tokens are character tokens with the same character code, regardless of category code.

An unexpandable control sequence is considered to have character code 256 and category code 16 (so that it is unequal to anything except another control sequence), except in the case where it had been \let to a non-active character token. In that case it is considered to have the character code and category code of that character. This was mentioned above.

The test \ifcat for category codes was mentioned in Chapter 2; the test

\ifx⟨token$_1$⟩⟨token$_2$⟩

can be used to test for category code and character code simultaneously. The tokens following this test are not expanded. However, if they are macros, TeX tests their expansions for equality.

Quantities defined by \chardef can be tested with \ifnum:

\chardef\a=`x \chardef\b=`y \ifnum\a=\b % is false

based on the fact (see Chapter 7) that ⟨chardef token⟩s can be used as numbers.

3.6 UPPERCASE AND LOWERCASE

3.6.1 Uppercase and lowercase codes

To each of the character codes correspond an uppercase code and a lowercase code (for still more codes see below). These can be assigned by

\uccode⟨number⟩⟨equals⟩⟨number⟩

and

\lccode⟨number⟩⟨equals⟩⟨number⟩.

In IniTeX codes `a..`z, `A..`Z have uppercase code `A..`Z and lowercase code `a..`z. All other character codes have both uppercase and lowercase code zero.

3.6.2 Uppercase and lowercase commands

The commands \uppercase{...} and \lowercase{...} go through their argument lists, replacing all character codes of explicit character tokens by their uppercase and lowercase code respectively if these are non-zero, without changing the category codes.

The argument of \uppercase and \lowercase is a ⟨general text⟩, which is defined as

⟨general text⟩ ⟶ ⟨filler⟩{⟨balanced text⟩⟨right brace⟩

(for the definition of ⟨filler⟩ see Chapter 36) meaning that the left brace can be implicit, but the closing right brace must be an explicit character token with category code 2. TeX performs expansion to find the opening brace.

Uppercasing and lowercasing are executed in the execution processor; they are not 'macro expansion' activities like \number or \string. The sequence (attempting to produce \A)

```
\expandafter\csname\uppercase{a}\endcsname
```

gives an error (TeX inserts an \endcsname before the \uppercase because \uppercase is unexpandable), but

```
\uppercase{\csname a\endcsname}
```

works.

As an example of the correct use of \uppercase, here is a macro that tests if a character is uppercase:

```
\def\ifIsUppercase#1{\uppercase{\if#1}#1}
```

The same test can be performed by \ifnum`#1=\uccode`#1.

Hyphenation of words starting with an uppercase character, that is, a character not equal to its own \lccode, is subject to the \uchyph parameter: if this is positive, hyphenation of capitalized words is allowed. See also Chapter 19.

3.6.3 Uppercase and lowercase forms of keywords

Each character in TeX keywords, such as pt, can be given in uppercase or lowercase form. For instance, pT, Pt, pt, and PT all have the same meaning. TeX does not use the \uccode and \lccode tables here to determine the lowercase form. Instead it converts uppercase characters to lowercase by adding 32 – the ASCII difference between uppercase and lowercase characters – to their character code. This has some implications for implementations of TeX for non-roman alphabets; see page 370 of *The TeXbook*, Knuth (1984a).

3.6.4 Creative use of \uppercase and \lowercase

The fact that \uppercase and \lowercase do not change category codes can sometimes be used to create certain character-code–category-code combinations that would otherwise be difficult to produce. See for instance the explanation of the \newif macro in Chapter 13, and another example on page 27.

For a slightly different application, consider the problem (solved by Rainer Schöpf) of, given a counter \newcount\mycount, writing character number \mycount to the terminal. Here is a solution:

```
\lccode`a=\mycount
```

```
\lowercase{\write\terminal{a}}
```

The `\lowercase` command effectively changes the argument of the `\write` command from 'a' into whatever it should be.

3.7 CODES OF A CHARACTER

Each character code has a number of ⟨codename⟩s associated with it. These are integers in various ranges that determine how the character is treated in various contexts, or how the occurrence of that character changes the workings of TeX in certain contexts.

The code names are as follows:

`\catcode` ⟨4-bit number⟩ (0–15); the category to which a character belongs. This is treated in Chapter 2.
`\mathcode` ⟨15-bit number⟩ (0–"7FFF) or "8000; determines how a character is treated in math mode. See Chapter 21.
`\delcode` ⟨27-bit number⟩ (0–"7 FFF FFF); determines how a character is treated after `\left` or `\right` in math mode. See page 182.
`\sfcode` integer; determines how spacing is affected after this character. See Chapter 20.
`\lccode`, `\uccode` ⟨8-bit number⟩ (0-255); lowercase and uppercase codes – these were treated above.

3.8 CONVERTING TOKENS INTO CHARACTER STRINGS

The command `\string` takes the next token and expands it into a string of separate characters. Thus

```
\tt\string\control
```

will give \control in the output, and

```
\tt\string$
```

will give $, but, noting that the string operation comes after the tokenizing,

```
\tt\string%
```

will *not* give %, because the comment sign is removed by TeX's input processor. Therefore, this command will 'string' the first token on the next line.

The `\string` command is executed by the expansion processor, thus it is expanded unless explicitly inhibited (see Chapter 12).

3.8.1 Output of control sequences

In the above examples the typewriter font was selected, because the Computer Modern roman font does not have a backslash character. However, TeX need not have used the backslash character to display a control sequence: it uses character number \escapechar. This same value is also used when a control sequence is output with \write, \message, or \errmessage, and it is used in the output of \show, \showthe and \meaning. If \escapechar is negative or more than 255, the escape character is not output; the default value (set in IniTeX) is 92, the number of the backslash character.

For use in a \write statement the \string can in some circumstances be replaced by \noexpand (see page 121).

3.8.2 Category codes of a \string

The characters that are the result of a \string command have category code 12, except for any spaces in a stringed control sequence; they have category code 10. Since inside a control sequence there are no category codes, any spaces resulting from \string are of necessity only space *characters*, that is, characters with code 32. However, TeX's input processor converts all space tokens that have a character code other than 32 into character tokens with character code 32, so the chances are pretty slim that 'funny spaces' wind up in control sequences.

Other commands with the same behaviour with respect to category codes as \string, are \number, \romannumeral, \jobname, \fontname, \meaning, and \the.

CHAPTER 4

Fonts

In text mode TeX takes characters from a 'current font'. This chapter describes how fonts are identified to TeX, and what attributes a font can have.

\font   Declare the identifying control sequence of a font.
\fontname   The external name of a font.
\nullfont   Name of an empty font that TeX uses in emergencies.
\hyphenchar   Number of the hyphen character of a font.
\defaulthyphenchar   Value of \hyphenchar when a font is loaded. Plain TeX default: '\-.
\fontdimen   Access various parameters of fonts.
\/   Italic correction.
\noboundary   Omit implicit boundary character.

4.1   FONTS

In TeX terminology a font is the set of characters that is contained in one external font file. During processing, TeX decides from what font a character should be taken. This decision is taken separately for text mode and math mode.

When TeX is processing ordinary text, characters are taken from the 'current font'. External font file names are coupled to control sequences by statements such as

    \font\MyFont=myfont10

which makes TeX load the file `myfont10.tfm`. Switching the current font to the font described in that file is then done by

    \MyFont

The status of the current font can be queried: the sequence

    \the\font

produces the control sequence for the current font.

Math mode completely ignores the current font. Instead it looks at the 'current family', which can contain three fonts: one for text style, one for script style, and one for scriptscript style. This is treated in Chapter 21.

See Southall (1984) for a consistent terminology of fonts and typefaces.

With 'virtual fonts' (see Knuth (1990)) it is possible that what looks like one font to TeX resides in more than one physical font file. See further page 255.

4.2 FONT DECLARATION

Somewhere during a run of TeX or IniTeX the coupling between an internal identifying control sequence and the external file name of a font has to be made. The syntax of the command for this is

> \font⟨control sequence⟩⟨equals⟩⟨file name⟩⟨at clause⟩

where

> ⟨at clause⟩ ⟶ at ⟨dimen⟩ | scaled ⟨number⟩ | ⟨optional spaces⟩

Font declarations are local to a group.

By the ⟨at clause⟩ the user specifies that some magnified version of the font is wanted. The ⟨at clause⟩ comes in two forms: if the font is given scaled f TeX multiplies all its font dimensions for that font by $f/1000$; if the font has a design size $d$pt and the ⟨at clause⟩ is at $p$pt TeX multiplies all font data by p/d. The presence of an ⟨at clause⟩ makes no difference for the external font file (the .tfm file) that TeX reads for the font; it just multiplies the font dimensions by a constant.

After such a font declaration, using the defined control sequence will set the current font to the font of the control sequence.

4.2.1 Fonts and `tfm` files

The external file needed for the font is a `tfm` (TeX font metrics) file, which is taken independent of any ⟨at clause⟩ in the \font declaration. If the `tfm` file has been loaded already (for instance by IniTeX when it constructed the format), an assignment of that font file can be reexecuted without needing recourse to the `tfm` file.

Font design sizes are given in the font metrics files. The `cmr10` font, for instance, has a design size of 10 point. However, there is not much in the font that actually has a size of 10 points: the opening and closing parentheses are two examples, but capital letters are considerably smaller.

4.2.2 Querying the current font and font names

It was already mentioned above that the control sequence which set the current font can be retrieved by the command \the\font. This is a special case of

> \the⟨font⟩

where

> ⟨font⟩ ⟶ \font | ⟨fontdef token⟩ | ⟨family member⟩
> ⟨family member⟩ ⟶ ⟨font range⟩⟨4-bit number⟩
> ⟨font range⟩ ⟶ \textfont | \scriptfont | \scriptscriptfont

A ⟨fontdef token⟩ is a control sequence defined by \font, or the predefined control sequence \nullfont. The concept of ⟨family member⟩ is only relevant in math mode.

Also, the external name of fonts can be retrieved:

\fontname⟨font⟩

gives a sequence of character tokens of category 12 (but space characters get category 10) that spells the font file name, plus an ⟨at clause⟩ if applicable.

Example
After

\font\tenroman=cmr10 \tenroman

the calls \the\font and \the\tenroman both give \tenroman. The call \fontname\tenroman gives cmr10.

4.2.3 \nullfont

TeX always knows a font that has no characters: the \nullfont. If no font has been specified, or if in math mode a family member is needed that has not been specified, TeX will take its characters from the nullfont. This control sequence qualifies as a ⟨fontdef token⟩: it acts like any other control sequence that stands for a font; it just does not have an associated tfm file.

4.3 FONT INFORMATION

During a run of TeX the main information needed about the font consists of the dimensions of the characters. TeX finds these in the font metrics files, which usually have extension .tfm. Such files contain

- global information: the \fontdimen parameters, and some other information,
- dimensions and the italic corrections of characters, and
- ligature and kerning programs for characters.

Also, the design size of a font is specified in the tfm file; see above. The definition of the tfm format can be found in Knuth (1986a).

4.3.1 Font dimensions

Text fonts need to have at least seven \fontdimen parameters (but TeX will take zero for unspecified parameters); math symbol and math extension fonts have more (see page 198). For text fonts the minimal set of seven comprises the following:

1. the slant per point; this dimension is used for the proper horizontal positioning of accents;

2. the interword space: this is used unless the user specifies an explicit \spaceskip; see Chapter 20;
3. interword stretch: the stretch component of the interword space;
4. interword shrink: the shrink component of the interword space;
5. the x-height: the value of the ⟨internal unit⟩ ex, which is usually about the height of the lowercase letter 'x';
6. the quad width: the value of the ⟨internal unit⟩ em, which is approximately the width of the capital letter 'M'; and
7. the extra space: the space added to the interword space at the end of sentences (that is, when \spacefactor ≥ 2000) unless the user specifies an explicit \xspaceskip.

Parameters 1 and 5 are purely information about the font and there is no point in varying them. The values of other parameters can be changed in order to adjust spacing; see Chapter 20 for examples of changing parameters 2, 3, 4, and 7.

Font dimensions can be altered in a ⟨font assignment⟩, which is a ⟨global assignment⟩ (see page 90):

\fontdimen⟨number⟩⟨font⟩⟨equals⟩⟨dimen⟩

See above for the definition of ⟨font⟩.

4.3.2 Kerning

Some combinations of characters should be moved closer together than would be the case if their bounding boxes were to be just abutted. This fine spacing is called kerning, and a proper kerning is as essential to a font as the design of the letter shapes.

Consider as an example

'Vo' versus the unkerned variant 'Vo'

Kerning in TeX is controlled by information in the tfm file, and is therefore outside the influence of the user. The tfm file can be edited, however (see Chapter 33).

The \kern command has (almost) nothing to do with the phenomenon of kerning; it is explained in Chapter 8.

4.3.3 Italic correction

The primitive control symbol \/ inserts the 'italic correction' of the previous character or ligature. Such a correction may be necessary owing to the definition of the 'bounding box' of a character. This box always has vertical sides, and the width of the character as TeX perceives it is the distance between these sides. However, in order to achieve proper spacing for slanted or italic typefaces, characters may very well project outside their bounding boxes. The italic correction is then needed if such an overhanging character is followed by a character from a non-slanting typeface.

Compare for instance

'*TEX* has' to '*TEX* has',

where the second version was typed as

    {\italic\TeX\/} has

The size of the italic correction of each character is determined by font information in the font metrics file; for the Computer Modern fonts it is approximately half the 'overhang' of the characters; see Knuth (1986b). Italic correction is not the same as \fontdimen1, slant per point. That font dimension is used only for positioning accents on top of characters.

An italic correction can only be inserted if the previous item processed by TEX was a character or ligature. Thus the following solution for roman text inside an italic passage does not work:

    {\italic Some text {\/\roman not} emphasized}

The italic correction has no effect here, because the previous item is glue.

4.3.4 Ligatures

Replacement of character sequences by ligatures is controlled by information in the tfm file of a font. Ligatures are formed from ⟨character⟩ commands: sequences such as fi are replaced by 'fi' in some fonts.

Other ligatures traditionally in use are between ff, ffi, fl, and ffl; in some older works ft and st can be found, and similarly to the fl ligature fk and fb can also occur.

Ligatures in TEX can be formed between explicit character tokens, \char commands, and ⟨chardef token⟩s. For example, the sequence \char'f\char'i is replaced by the 'fi' ligature, if such a ligature is part of the font.

Unwanted ligatures can be suppressed in a number of ways: the unwanted ligature 'halflife' can for instance be prevented by

    half{}life, half{l}ife, half\/life, or half\hbox{}life

but the solution using italic correction is not equivalent to the others.

4.3.5 Boundary ligatures

Each word is surrounded by a left and a right boundary character (TEX3 only). This makes phenomena possible such as the two different sigmas in Greek: one at the end of a word, and one for every other position. This can be realized through a ligature with the boundary character. A \noboundary command immediately before or after a word suppresses the boundary character at that place.

In general, the ligature mechanism has become more complicated with the transition to TEX version 3; see Knuth (1989b).

CHAPTER 5

Boxes

The horizontal and vertical boxes of TeX are containers for pieces of horizontal and vertical lists. Boxes can be stored in box registers. This chapter treats box registers and such aspects of boxes as their dimensions, and the way their components are placed relative to each other.

\hbox   Construct a horizontal box.
\vbox   Construct a vertical box with reference point of the last item.
\vtop   Construct a vertical box with reference point of the first item.
\vcenter   Construct a vertical box vertically centred on the math axis; this command can only be used in math mode.
\vsplit   Split off the top part of a vertical box.
\box   Use a box register, emptying it.
\setbox   Assign a box to a box register.
\copy   Use a box register, but retain the contents.
\ifhbox \ifvbox   Test whether a box register contains a horizontal/vertical box.
\ifvoid   Test whether a box register is empty.
\newbox   Allocate a new box register.
\unhbox \unvbox   Unpack a box register containing a horizontal/vertical box, adding the contents to the current horizontal/vertical list, and emptying the register.
\unhcopy \unvcopy   The same as \unhbox / \unvbox, but do not empty the register.
\ht \dp \wd   Height/depth/width of the box in a box register.
\boxmaxdepth   Maximum allowed depth of boxes. Plain TeX default: \maxdimen.
\splitmaxdepth   Maximum allowed depth of boxes generated by \vsplit.
\badness   Badness of the most recently constructed box.
\hfuzz \vfuzz   Excess size that TeX tolerates before it considers a horizontal/vertical box overfull.
\hbadness \vbadness   Amount of tolerance before TeX reports an underfull or overfull horizontal/vertical box.
\overfullrule   Width of the rule that is printed to indicate overfull horizontal boxes.
\hsize   Line width used for text typesetting inside a vertical box.

`\vsize`   Height of the page box.
`\lastbox`   Register containing the last item added to the current list, if this was a box.
`\raise` `\lower`   Adjust vertical positioning of a box in horizontal mode.
`\moveleft` `\moveright`   Adjust horizontal positioning of a box in vertical mode.
`\everyhbox` `\everyvbox`   Token list inserted at the start of a horizontal/vertical box.

5.1 BOXES

In this chapter we shall look at boxes. Boxes are containers for pieces of horizontal or vertical lists. Boxes that are needed more than once can be stored in box registers.

When TeX expects a ⟨box⟩, any of the following forms is admissible:

- `\hbox`⟨box specification⟩{⟨horizontal material⟩}
- `\vbox`⟨box specification⟩{⟨vertical material⟩}
- `\vtop`⟨box specification⟩{⟨vertical material⟩}
- `\box`⟨8-bit number⟩
- `\copy`⟨8-bit number⟩
- `\vsplit`⟨8-bit number⟩`to`⟨dimen⟩
- `\lastbox`

A ⟨box specification⟩ is defined as

⟨box specification⟩ ⟶ ⟨filler⟩
  | `to` ⟨dimen⟩⟨filler⟩ | `spread` ⟨dimen⟩⟨filler⟩

An ⟨8-bit number⟩ is a number in the range 0–255.

The braces surrounding box material define a group; they can be explicit characters of categories 1 and 2 respectively, or control sequences `\let` to such characters; see also below.

A ⟨box⟩ can in general be used in horizontal, vertical, and math mode, but see below for the `\lastbox`. The connection between boxes and modes is explored further in Chapter 6.

The box produced by `\vcenter` – a command that is allowed only in math mode – is not a ⟨box⟩. For instance, it can not be assigned with `\setbox`; see further Chapter 23.

The `\vsplit` operation is treated in Chapter 27.

5.2 BOX REGISTERS

There are 256 box registers, numbered 0–255. Either a box register is empty ('void'), or it contains a horizontal or vertical box. This section discusses specifically box *registers*; the sizes of boxes, and the way material is arranged inside them, is treated below.

5.2.1 Allocation: \newbox

The plain TeX \newbox macro allocates an unused box register:

> \newbox\MyBox

after which one can say

> \setbox\MyBox=...

or

> \box\MyBox

and so on. Subsequent calls to this macro give subsequent box numbers; this way macro collections can allocate their own boxes without fear of collision with other macros.

The number of the box is assigned by \chardef (see Chapter 31). This implies that \MyBox is equivalent to, and can be used as, a ⟨number⟩. The control sequence \newbox is an \outer macro. Newly allocated box registers are initially empty.

5.2.2 Usage: \setbox, \box, \copy

A register is filled by assigning a ⟨box⟩ to it:

> \setbox⟨number⟩⟨equals⟩⟨box⟩

For example, the ⟨box⟩ can be explicit

> \setbox37=\hbox{...}   or   \setbox37=\vbox{...}

or it can be a box register:

> \setbox37=\box38

Usually, box numbers will have been assigned by a \newbox command.

The box in a box register is appended by the commands \box and \copy to whatever list TeX is building: the call

> \box38

appends box 38. To save memory space, box registers become empty by using them: TeX assumes that after you have inserted a box by calling \box*nn* in some mode, you do not need the contents of that register any more and empties it. In case you *do* need the contents of a box register more than once, you can \copy it. Calling \copy*nn* is equivalent to \box*nn* in all respects except that the register is not cleared.

It is possible to unwrap the contents of a box register by 'unboxing' it using the commands \unhbox and \unvbox, and their copying versions \unhcopy and \unvcopy. Whereas a box can be used in any mode, the unboxing operations can only be used in the appropriate mode, since in effect they contribute a partial horizontal or vertical list (see also Chapter 6). See below for more information on unboxing registers.

5.2.3 Testing: \ifvoid, \ifhbox, \ifvbox

Box registers can be tested for their contents:

\ifvoid⟨number⟩

is true if the box register is empty. Note that an empty, or 'void', box register is not the same as a register containing an empty box. An empty box is still either a horizontal or a vertical box; a void register can be used as both.

The test

\ifhbox⟨number⟩

is true if the box register contains a horizontal box;

\ifvbox⟨number⟩

is true if the box register contains a vertical box. Both tests are false for void registers.

5.2.4 The \lastbox

When TeX has built a partial list, the last box in this list is accessible as the \lastbox. This behaves like a box register, so you can remove the last box from the list by assigning the \lastbox to some box register. If the last item on the current list is not a box, the \lastbox acts like a void box register. It is not possible to get hold of the last box in the case of the main vertical list. The \lastbox is then always void.

As an example, the statement

{\setbox0=\lastbox}

removes the last box from the current list, assigning it to box register 0. Since this assignment occurs inside a group, the register is cleared at the end of the group. At the start of a paragraph this can be used to remove the indentation box (see Chapter 16). Another example of \lastbox can be found on page 53.

Because the \lastbox is always empty in external vertical mode, it is not possible to get hold of boxes that have been added to the page. However, it is possible to dissect the page once it is in \box255, for instance doing

\vbox{\unvbox255{\setbox0=\lastbox}}

inside the output routine.

If boxes in vertical mode have been shifted by \moveright or \moveleft, or if boxes in horizontal mode have been raised by \raise or lowered by \lower, any information about this displacement due to such a command is lost when the \lastbox is taken from the list.

5.3 NATURAL DIMENSIONS OF BOXES

5.3.1 Dimensions of created horizontal boxes

Inside an \hbox all constituents are lined up next to each other, with their reference points on the baseline of the box, unless they are moved explicitly in the vertical direction by \lower or \raise.

The resulting width of the box is the sum of the widths of the components. Thus the width of

>   \hbox{\hskip1cm}

is positive, and the width of

>   \hbox{\hskip-1cm}

is negative. By way of example,

>   a\hbox{\kern-1em b}--

gives as output

>   ba-

which shows that a horizontal box can have negative width.

The height and depth of an \hbox are the maximum amount that constituent boxes project above and below the baseline of the box. They are non-negative when the box is created.

The commands \lower and \raise are the only possibilities for vertical movement inside an \hbox (other than including a \vbox inside the \hbox, of course); a ⟨vertical command⟩ – such as \vskip – is not allowed in a horizontal box, and \par, although allowed, does not do anything inside a horizontal box.

5.3.2 Dimensions of created vertical boxes

Inside a \vbox vertical material is lined up with the reference points on the vertical line through the reference point of the box, unless components are moved explicitly in the horizontal direction by \moveleft or \moveright.

The reference point of a vertical box is always located at the left boundary of the box. The width of a vertical box is then the maximal amount that any material in the box sticks to the right of the reference point. Material to the left of the reference point is not taken into account in the width. Thus the result of

>   a\vbox{\hbox{\kern-1em b}}--

is

>   ba–

This should be contrasted with the above example.

The calculation of height and depth is different for vertical boxes constructed by \vbox and \vtop. The ground rule is that a \vbox has a reference point that lies on the baseline of its last component, and a \vtop has its reference point on the baseline of the first component. In general, the depth (height) of a \vbox (\vtop) can be non-zero if the last (first) item is a box or rule.

The height of a \vbox is then the sum of the heights and depths of all components except the last, plus the height of that last component; the depth of the \vbox is the depth of its last component. The depth of a \vtop is the sum of the depth of the first component and the heights and depths of all subsequent material; its height is the height of the first component.

However, the actual rules are a bit more complicated when the first component of a \vtop or the last component of a \vbox is not a box or rule. If the last component of a \vbox is a kern or a glue, the depth of that box is zero; a \vtop's height is zero unless its first component is a box or rule. (Note the asymmetry in these definitions; see below for an example illustrating this.) The depth of a \vtop, then, is equal to the total height plus depth of all enclosed material minus the height of the \vtop.

There is a limit on the depth of vertical boxes: if the depth of a \vbox or \vtop calculated by the above rules would exceed \boxmaxdepth, the reference point of the box is moved down by the excess amount. More precisely, the excess depth is added to the natural height of the box. If the box had a to or spread specification, any glue is set anew to take the new height into account.

Ordinarily, \boxmaxdepth is set to the maximum dimension possible in TeX. It is for instance reduced during some of the calculations in the plain TeX output routine; see Chapter 28.

5.3.3 Examples

Horizontal boxes are relatively straightforward. Their width is the distance between the 'beginning' and the 'end' of the box, and consequently the width is not necessarily positive. With

```
\setbox0=\hbox{aa} \setbox1=\hbox{\copy0 \hskip-\wd0}
```

the \box1 has width zero;

/\box1/   gives   '/aa'

The height and depth of a horizontal box cannot be negative: in

```
\setbox0=\hbox{\vrule height 5pt depth 5pt}
\setbox1=\hbox{\raise 10pt \box0}
```

the \box1 has depth 0pt and height 15pt

Vertical boxes are more troublesome than horizontal boxes. Let us first treat their width. After

```
\setbox0=\hbox{\hskip 10pt}
```

the box in the \box0 register has a width of 10pt. Defining

```
\setbox1=\vbox{\moveleft 5pt \copy0}
```

the \box1 will have width 5pt; material to the left of the reference point is not accounted for in the width of a vertical box. With

    \setbox2=\vbox{\moveright 5pt \copy0}

the \box2 will have width 15pt.

The depth of a \vbox is the depth of the last item if that is a box, so

    \vbox{\vskip 5pt \hbox{\vrule height 5pt depth 5pt}}

has height 10pt and depth 5pt, and

    \vbox{\vskip -5pt \hbox{\vrule height 5pt depth 5pt}}

has height 0pt and depth 5pt. With a glue or kern as the last item in the box, the resulting depth is zero, so

    \vbox{\hbox{\vrule height 5pt depth 5pt}\vskip 5pt}

has height 15pt and depth 0pt;

    \vbox{\hbox{\vrule height 5pt depth 5pt}\vskip -5pt}

has height 5pt and depth 0pt.

The height of a \vtop behaves (almost) the same with respect to the first item of the box, as the depth of a \vbox does with respect to the last item. Repeating the above examples with a \vtop gives the following:

    \vtop{\vskip 5pt \hbox{\vrule height 5pt depth 5pt}}

has height 0pt and depth 15pt, and

    \vtop{\vskip -5pt \hbox{\vrule height 5pt depth 5pt}}

has height 0pt and depth 5pt;

    \vtop{\hbox{\vrule height 5pt depth 5pt} \vskip 5pt}

has height 5pt and depth 10pt, and

    \vtop{\hbox{\vrule height 5pt depth 5pt} \vskip -5pt}

has height 5pt and depth 0pt.

5.4 MORE ABOUT BOX DIMENSIONS

5.4.1 Predetermined dimensions

The size of a box can be specified in advance with a ⟨box specification⟩; see above for the syntax. Any glue in the box is then set in order to reach the required size. Prescribing the size of the box is done by

    \hbox to ⟨dimen⟩ {...}, \vbox to ⟨dimen⟩ {...}

If stretchable or shrinkable glue is present in the box, it is stretched or shrunk in order to give the box the specified size. Associated with this glue setting is a badness value (see Chapter 8). If no stretch or shrink – whichever is necessary – is present, the resulting box will be underfull or overfull respectively. Error reporting for over/underfull boxes is treated below.

Another command to let a box have a size other than the natural size is

`\hbox spread` ⟨dimen⟩ `{...}`, `\vbox spread` ⟨dimen⟩ `{...}`

which tells TeX to set the glue in such a way that the size of the box is a specified amount more than the natural size.

Box specifications for `\vtop` vertical boxes are somewhat difficult to interpret. TeX constructs a `\vtop` by first making a `\vbox`, including glue settings induced by a ⟨box specification⟩; then it computes the height and depth by the above rules. Glue setting is described in Chapter 8.

5.4.2 Changes to box dimensions

The dimensions of a box register are accessible by the commands `\ht`, `\dp`, and `\wd`; for instance `\dp13` gives the depth of box 13. However, not only can boxes be measured this way; by assigning values to these dimensions TeX can even be fooled into thinking that a box has a size different from its actual. However, changing the dimensions of a box does not change anything about the contents; in particular it does not change the way the glue is set.

Various formats use this in 'smash' macros: the macro defined by

`\def\smash#1{{\setbox0=\hbox{#1}\dp0=0pt \ht0=0pt \box0\relax}}`

places its argument but annihilates its height and depth; that is, the output does show the whole box, but further calculations by TeX act as if the height and depth were zero.

Box dimensions can be changed only by setting them. They are ⟨box dimen⟩s, which can only be set in a ⟨box size assignment⟩, and not, for instance changed with `\advance`.

Note that a ⟨box size assignment⟩ is a ⟨global assignment⟩: its effect transcends any groups in which it occurs (see Chapter 10). Thus the output of

`\setbox0=\hbox{---} {\wd0=0pt} a\box0b`

is 'ab—'.

The limits that hold on the dimensions with which a box can be created (see above) do not hold for explicit changes to the size of a box: the assignment `\dp0=-2pt` for a horizontal box is perfectly admissible.

5.4.3 Moving boxes around

In a horizontal box all constituent elements are lined up with their reference points at the same height as the reference point of the box. Any box inside a horizontal box can be lifted or dropped using the macros `\raise` and `\lower`.

Similarly, in a vertical box all constituent elements are lined up with their reference points underneath one another, in line with the reference point of the box. Boxes can now be moved sideways by the macros \moveleft and \moveright.

Only boxes can be shifted thus; these operations cannot be applied to, for instance, characters or rules.

5.4.4 Box dimensions and box placement

TeX places the components of horizontal and vertical lists by maintaining a reference line and a current position on that line. For horizontal lists the reference line is the baseline of the surrounding \hbox; for vertical lists it is the vertical line through the reference point of the surrounding \vbox.

In horizontal mode a component is placed as follows. The current position coincides initially with the reference point of the surrounding box. After that, the following actions are carried out.

1. If the component has been shifted by \raise or \lower, shift the current position correspondingly.
2. If the component is a horizontal box, use this algorithm recursively for its contents; if it is a vertical box, go up by the height of this box, putting a new current position for the enclosed vertical list there, and place its components using the algorithm for vertical lists below.
3. Move the current position (on the reference line) to the right by the width of the component.

For the list in a vertical box TeX's current position is initially at the upper left corner of that box, as explained above, and the reference line is the vertical line through that point; it also runs through the reference point of the box. Enclosed components are then placed as follows.

1. If a component has been shifted using \moveleft or \moveright, shift the current position accordingly.
2. Put the component with its upper left corner at the current position.
3. If the component is a vertical box, use this algorithm recursively for its contents; if it is a horizontal box, its reference point can be found below the current position by the height of the box. Put the current position for that box there, and use the above algorithm for horizontal lists.
4. Go down by the height plus depth of the box (that is, starting at the upper left corner of the box) on the reference line, and continue processing vertically.

Note that the above processes do not describe the construction of boxes. That would (for instance) involve for vertical boxes the insertion of baselineskip glue. Rather, it describes the way the components of a finished box are arranged in the output.

5.4.5 Boxes and negative glue

Sometimes it is useful to have boxes overlapping instead of lined up. An easy way to do this is to use negative glue. In horizontal mode

```
{\dimen0=\wd8 \box8 \kern-\dimen0}
```

places box 8 without moving the current location.

More versatile are the macros `\llap` and `\rlap`, defined as

```
\def\llap#1{\hbox to 0pt{\hss #1}}
```

and

```
\def\rlap#1{\hbox to 0pt{#1\hss}}
```

that allow material to protrude left or right from the current location. The `\hss` glue is equivalent to `\hskip 0pt plus 1fil minus 1fil`, which absorbs any positive or negative width of the argument of `\llap` or `\rlap`.

Example
The sequence

```
\llap{\hbox to 10pt{a\hfil}}
```

is effectively the same as

```
\hbox{\hskip-10pt \hbox to 10pt{a\hfil}}
```

which has a total width of 0pt.

5.5 OVERFULL AND UNDERFULL BOXES

If a box has a size specification TeX will stretch or shrink glue in the box. For glue with only finite stretch or shrink components the *badness* (see Chapter 19) of stretching or shrinking is computed. In TeX version 3 the badness of the box most recently constructed is available for inspection by the user through the `\badness` parameter. Values for badness range 0–10 000, but if the box is overfull it is 1 000 000.

When TeX considers the badness too large, it gives a diagnostic message. Let us first consider error reporting for horizontal boxes.

Horizontal boxes of which the glue has to stretch are never reported if `\hbadness` $\geq$ 10 000; otherwise TeX reports them as 'underfull' if their badness is more than `\hbadness`.

Glue shrinking can lead to 'overfull' boxes: a box is called overfull if the available shrink is less than the shrink necessary to meet the box specification. An overfull box is only reported if the difference in shrink is more than `\hfuzz`, or if `\hbadness` $<$ 100 (and it turns out that using all available shrinkability has badness 100).

Example
Setting `\hfuzz=1pt` will let TeX ignore boxes that can not shrink enough if they lack less than 1pt. In

```
\hbox to 1pt{\hskip3pt minus .5pt}
```

```
\hbox to 1pt{\hskip3pt minus 1.5pt}
```

only the first box will give an error message: it is `1.5pt` too big, whereas the second lacks `.5pt` which is less than `\hfuzz`.

Also, boxes that shrink but that are not overfull can be reported: if a box is 'tight', that is, if it uses at least half its shrinkability, TeX reports this fact if the computed badness (which is between 13 and 100) is more than `\hbadness`.

For horizontal and vertical boxes this error reporting is almost the same, with parameters `\vbadness` and `\vfuzz`. The difference is that for horizontal overfull boxes TeX will draw a rule to the right of the box that has the same height as the box, and width `\overfullrule`. No overfull rule ensues if the `\tabskip` glue in an `\halign` cannot be shrunk enough.

5.6 OPENING AND CLOSING BOXES

The opening and closing braces of a box can be either explicit, that is, character tokens of category 1 and 2, or implicit, a control sequence `\let` to such a character. After the opening brace the `\everyhbox` or `\everyvbox` tokens are inserted. If this box appeared in a `\setbox` assignment any `\afterassignment` token is inserted even before the 'everybox' tokens.

Example

```
\everyhbox{b}
\afterassignment a
\setbox0=\hbox{c}
\showbox0
```

gives

```
> \box0=
\hbox(6.94444+0.0)x15.27782
.\tenrm a
.\tenrm b
.\kern0.27779
.\tenrm c
```

Implicit braces can be used to let a box be opened or closed by a macro, for example:

```
\def\openbox#1{\setbox#1=\hbox\bgroup}
\def\closebox#1{\egroup\DoSomethingWithBox#1}
\openbox0 ... \closebox0
```

This mechanism can be used to scoop up paragraphs:

```
\everypar{\setbox\parbox=
    \vbox\bgroup
```

```
\everypar{}
\def\par{\egroup\UseBox\parbox}}
```

Here the `\everypar` opens the box and lets the text be set in the box: starting for instance

```
Begin a text ...
```

gives the equivalent of

```
\setbox\parbox=\vbox{Begin a text ...
```

Inside the box `\par` has been redefined, so

```
... a text ends.\par
```

is equivalent to

```
... a text ends.}\Usebox\parbox
```

In this example, the `\UseBox` command can only treat the box as a whole; if the elements of the box should somehow be treated separately another approach is necessary. In

```
\everypar{\setbox\parbox=
  \vbox\bgroup\everypar{}%
      \def\par{\endgraf\HandleLines
              \egroup\box\parbox}}
\def\HandleLines{ ... \lastbox ... }
```

the macro `\HandleLines` can have access to successive elements from the vertical list of the paragraph. See also the example on page 53.

5.7 UNBOXING

Boxes can be unwrapped by the commands `\unhbox` and `\unvbox`, and by their copying versions `\unhcopy` and `\unvcopy`. These are horizontal and vertical commands (see Chapter 6), considering that in effect they contribute a partial horizontal or vertical list. It is not possible to `\unhbox` a register containing a `\vbox` or vice versa, but a void box register can both be `\unhboxed` and `\unvboxed`.

Unboxing takes the contents of a box in a box register and appends them to the surrounding list; any glue can then be set anew. Thus

```
\setbox0=\hbox to 1cm{\hfil} \hbox to 2cm{\unhbox0}
```

is completely equivalent to

```
\hbox to 2cm{\hfil}
```

and not to

```
\hbox to 2cm{\kern1cm}
```

The intrinsically horizontal nature of \unhbox is used to define

```
\def\leavevmode{\unhbox\voidb@x}
```

This command switches from vertical mode to horizontal without adding anything to the horizontal list. However, the subsequent \indent caused by this transition adds an indentation box. In horizontal mode the \leavevmode command has no effect. Note that here it is not necessary to use \unhcopy, because the register is empty anyhow.

Beware of the following subtlety: unboxing in vertical mode does not add interline glue between the box contents and any preceding item. Also, the value of \prevdepth is not changed, so glue between the box contents and any following item will occur only if there was something preceding the box; interline glue will be based on the depth of that preceding item. Similarly, unboxing in horizontal mode does not influence the \spacefactor.

5.8   TEXT IN BOXES

Both horizontal and vertical boxes can contain text. However, the way text is treated differs. In horizontal boxes the text is placed in one straight line, and the width of the box is in principle the natural width of the text (and other items) contained in it. No ⟨vertical command⟩s are allowed inside a horizontal box, and \par does nothing in this case.

For vertical boxes the situation is radically different. As soon as a character, or any other ⟨horizontal command⟩ (see page 57), is encountered in a vertical box, TeX starts building a paragraph in unrestricted horizontal mode, that is, just as if the paragraph were directly part of the page. At the occurrence of a ⟨vertical command⟩ (see page 57), or at the end of the box, the paragraph is broken into lines using the current values of parameters such as \hsize.

Thus

```
\hbox to 3cm{\vbox{some reasonably long text}}
```

will *not* give a paragraph of width 3 centimetres (it gives an overfull horizontal box if \hsize > 3cm). However,

```
\vbox{\hsize=3cm some reasonably long text}
```

will be 3 centimetres wide.

A paragraph of text inside a vertical box is broken into lines, which are packed in horizontal boxes. These boxes are then stacked in internal vertical mode, possibly with \baselineskip and \lineskip separating them (this is treated in Chapter 15). This process is also used for text on the page; the boxes are then stacked in outer vertical mode.

If the internal vertical list is empty, no \parskip glue is added at the start of a paragraph.

Because text in a horizontal box is not broken into lines, there is a further difference between text in restricted and unrestricted horizontal mode. In restricted horizontal mode no discretionary nodes and whatsit items changing the value of the current language are inserted. This may give problems if the text is subsequently unboxed to form part of a paragraph.

See Chapter 19 for an explanation of these items, and Downes (1990) for a way around this problem.

5.9 ASSORTED REMARKS

5.9.1 Forgetting the \box

After `\newcount\foo`, one can use `\foo` on its own to get the `\foo` counter. For boxes, however, one has to use `\box\foo` to get the `\foo` box. The reason for this is that there exists no separate `\boxdef` command, so `\chardef` is used (see Chapter 31).

Example
Suppose `\newbox\foo` allocates box register 25; then typing `\foo` is equivalent to typing `\char25`.

5.9.2 Special-purpose boxes

Some box registers have a special purpose:
- `\box255` is by used TeX internally to give the page to the output routine.
- `\voidb@x` is the number of a box register allocated in `plain.tex`; it is supposed to be empty always. It is used in the macro `\leavevmode` and others.
- when a new `\insert` is created with the plain TeX `\newinsert` macro, a `\count`, `\dimen`, `\skip`, and `\box` all with the same number are reserved for that insert. The numbers for these registers count down from 254.

5.9.3 The height of a vertical box in horizontal mode

In horizontal mode a vertical box is placed with its reference point aligned vertically with the reference point of the surrounding box. TeX then traverses its contents starting at the left upper corner; that is, the point that lies above the reference point by a distance of the height of the box. Changing the height of the box implies then that the contents of the box are placed at a different height.

Consider as an example

```
\hbox{a\setbox0=\vbox{\hbox{b}}\box0 c}
```

which gives

abc

and

```
\hbox{a\setbox0=\vbox{\hbox{b}}\ht0=0cm \box0 c}
```

which gives

$$\begin{matrix} a & & c \\ & b & \end{matrix}$$

By contrast, changing the width of a box placed in vertical mode has no effect on its placement.

5.9.4 More subtleties with vertical boxes

Since there are two kinds of vertical boxes, the \vbox and the \vtop, using these two kinds nested may lead to confusing results. For instance,

```
\vtop{\vbox{...}}
```

is completely equivalent to just

```
\vbox{...}
```

It was stated above that the depth of a \vbox is zero if the last item is a kern or glue, and the height of a \vtop is zero unless the first item in it is a box. The above examples used a kern for that first or last item, but if, in the case of a \vtop, this item is not a glue or kern, one is apt to overlook the effect that it has on the surrounding box. For instance,

```
\vtop{\write16{...}...}
```

has zero height, because the write instruction is packed into a 'whatsit' item that is placed on the current, that is, the vertical, list. The remedy here is

```
\vtop{\leavevmode\write16{...}...}
```

which puts the whatsit in the beginning of the paragraph, instead of above it.

Placement of items in a vertical list is sometimes a bit tricky. There is for instance a difference between how vertical and horizontal boxes are treated in a vertical list. Consider the following examples. After \offinterlineskip the first example

```
\vbox{\hbox{a}
      \setbox0=\vbox{\hbox{(}}
      \ht0=0pt \dp0=0pt \box0
      \hbox{ b}}
```

gives

$$\begin{matrix} a & \\ (& \\ b & \end{matrix}$$

while a slight variant

```
\vbox{\hbox{a}
      \setbox0=\hbox{(}
      \ht0=0pt \dp0=0pt \box0
      \hbox{ b}}
```

gives

$$\substack{a \\ b}$$

The difference is caused by the fact that horizontal boxes are placed with respect to their reference point, but vertical boxes with respect to their upper left corner.

5.9.5 Hanging the \lastbox back in the list

You can pick the last box off a vertical list that has been compiled in (internal) vertical mode. However, if you try to hang it back in the list the vertical spacing may go haywire. If you just hang it back,

```
\setbox\tmpbox=\lastbox
\usethetmpbox \box\tmpbox
```

baselineskip glue is added a second time. If you 'unskip' prior to hanging the box back,

```
\setbox\tmpbox=\lastbox \unskip
\usethetmpbox \box\tmpbox
```

things go wrong in a more subtle way. The ⟨internal dimen⟩ \prevdepth (which controls interline glue; see Chapter 15) will have a value based on the last box, but what you need for the proper interline glue is a depth based on one box earlier. The solution is not to unskip, but to specify \nointerlineskip:

```
\setbox\tmpbox=\lastbox
\usethetmpbox \nointerlineskip \box\tmpbox
```

5.9.6 Dissecting paragraphs with \lastbox

Repeatedly applying \last... and \un... macros can be used to take a paragraph apart. Here is an example of that.

In typesetting advertisement copy, a way of justifying paragraphs has become popular in recent years that is somewhere between flushright and raggedright setting. Lines that would stretch beyond certain limits are set with their glue at natural width. This paragraph exemplifies this procedure; the macros follow next.

```
\newbox\linebox \newbox\snapbox
\def\eatlines{
    \setbox\linebox\lastbox      % check the last line
    \ifvoid\linebox
    \else                        % if it's not empty
    \unskip\unpenalty            % take whatever is
    {\eatlines}                  % above it;
                                 % collapse the line
    \setbox\snapbox\hbox{\unhcopy\linebox}
```

```
                        % depending on the difference
\ifdim\wd\snapbox<.98\wd\linebox
        \box\snapbox % take the one or the other,
\else \box\linebox \fi
\fi}
```

This macro can be called as

```
\vbox{ ... some text ... \par\eatlines}
```

or it can be inserted automatically with `\everypar`; see Eijkhout (1990a).

In the macro `\eatlines`, the `\lastbox` is taken from a vertical list. If the list is empty the last box will test true on `\ifvoid`. These boxes containing lines from a paragraph are actually horizontal boxes: the test `\ifhbox` applied to them would give a true result.

CHAPTER

6

Horizontal and Vertical Mode

At any point in its processing TeX is in some mode. There are six modes, divided in three categories:

1. horizontal mode and restricted horizontal mode,
2. vertical mode and internal vertical mode, and
3. math mode and display math mode.

The math modes will be treated elsewhere (see page 191). Here we shall look at the horizontal and vertical modes, the kinds of objects that can occur in the corresponding lists, and the commands that are exclusive for one mode or the other.

\ifhmode   Test whether the current mode is (possibly restricted) horizontal mode.
\ifvmode   Test whether the current mode is (possibly internal) vertical mode.
\ifinner   Test whether the current mode is an internal mode.
\vadjust   Specify vertical material for the enclosing vertical list while in horizontal mode.
\showlists   Write to the log file the contents of the partial lists currently being built in all modes.

6.1   HORIZONTAL AND VERTICAL MODE

When not typesetting mathematics, TeX is in horizontal or vertical mode, building horizontal or vertical lists respectively. Horizontal mode is typically used to make lines of text; vertical mode is typically used to stack the lines of a paragraph on top of each other. Note that these modes are different from the internal states of TeX's input processor (see page 11).

6.1.1   Horizontal mode

The main activity in horizontal mode is building lines of text. Text on the page and text in a \vbox or \vtop is built in horizontal mode (this might be called 'paragraph mode'); if the text is in an \hbox there is only one line of text, and the corresponding mode is the restricted horizontal mode.

In horizontal mode all material is added to a horizontal list. If this list is built in unrestricted horizontal mode, it will later be broken into lines and added to the surrounding vertical list.

Each element of a horizontal list is one of the following:

- a box (a character, ligature, \vrule, or a ⟨box⟩),
- a discretionary break,
- a whatsit (see Chapter 30),
- vertical material enclosed in \mark, \vadjust, or \insert,
- glue or leaders, a kern, a penalty, or a math-on/off item.

The items in the last point are all discardable. Discardable items are called that, because they disappear in a break. Breaking of horizontal lists is treated in Chapter 19.

6.1.2 Vertical mode

Vertical mode can be used to stack items on top of one another. Most of the time, these items are boxes containing the lines of paragraphs.

Stacking material can take place inside a vertical box, but the items that are stacked can also appear by themselves on the page. In the latter case TeX is in vertical mode; in the former case, inside a vertical box, TeX operates in internal vertical mode.

In vertical mode all material is added to a vertical list. If this list is built in external vertical mode, it will later be broken when pages are formed.

Each element of a vertical list is one of the following:

- a box (a horizontal or vertical box or an \hrule),
- a whatsit,
- a mark,
- glue or leaders, a kern, or a penalty.

The items in the last point are all discardable. Breaking of vertical lists is treated in Chapter 27.

There are a few exceptional conditions at the beginning of a vertical list: the value of \prevdepth is set to -1000pt. Furthermore, no \parskip glue is added at the top of an internal vertical list; at the top of the main vertical list (the top of the 'current page') no glue or other discardable items are added, and \topskip glue is added when the first box is placed on this list (see Chapters 26 and 27).

6.2 HORIZONTAL AND VERTICAL COMMANDS

Some commands are so intrinsically horizontal or vertical in nature that they force TeX to go into that mode, if possible. A command that forces TeX into horizontal mode is called a ⟨horizontal command⟩; similarly a command that forces TeX into vertical mode is called a ⟨vertical command⟩.

However, not all transitions are possible: TeX can switch from both vertical modes to (unrestricted) horizontal mode and back through horizontal and vertical commands, but no transitions to or from restricted horizontal mode are possible (other than by enclosing horizontal boxes in vertical boxes or the other way around). A vertical command in restricted horizontal mode thus gives an error; the \par command in restricted horizontal mode has no effect.

The horizontal commands are the following:

- any ⟨letter⟩, ⟨otherchar⟩, \char, a control sequence defined by \chardef, or \noboundary;
- \accent, \discretionary, the discretionary hyphen \- and control space \⊔;
- \unhbox and \unhcopy;
- \vrule and the ⟨horizontal skip⟩ commands \hskip, \hfil, \hfill, \hss, and \hfilneg;
- \valign;
- math shift ($).

The vertical commands are the following:

- \unvbox and \unvcopy;
- \hrule and the ⟨vertical skip⟩ commands \vskip, \vfil, \vfill, \vss, and \vfilneg;
- \halign;
- \end and \dump.

Note that the vertical commands do not include \par; nor are \indent and \noindent horizontal commands.

The connection between boxes and modes is explored below; see Chapter 9 for more on the connection between rules and modes.

6.3 THE INTERNAL MODES

Restricted horizontal mode and internal vertical mode are the variants of horizontal mode and vertical mode that hold inside an \hbox and \vbox (or \vtop or \vcenter) respectively. However, restricted horizontal mode is rather more restricted in nature than internal vertical mode. The third internal mode is non-display math mode (see Chapter 23).

6.3.1 Restricted horizontal mode

The main difference between restricted horizontal mode, the mode in an \hbox, and unrestricted horizontal mode, the mode in which paragraphs in vertical boxes and on the page are built, is that you cannot break out of restricted horizontal mode: \par does nothing in this mode. Furthermore, a ⟨vertical command⟩ in restricted horizontal mode gives an error. In unrestricted horizontal mode it would cause a \par token to be inserted and vertical mode to be entered (see also Chapter 17).

6.3.2 Internal vertical mode

Internal vertical mode, the vertical mode inside a \vbox, is a lot like external vertical mode, the mode in which pages are built. A ⟨horizontal command⟩ in internal vertical mode, for instance, is perfectly valid: TeX then starts building a paragraph in unrestricted horizontal mode.

One difference is that the commands \unskip and \unkern have no effect in external vertical mode, and \lastbox is always empty in external vertical mode. See further pages 41 and 80.

The entries of alignments (see Chapter 25) are processed in internal modes: restricted horizontal mode for the entries of an \halign, and internal vertical mode for the entries of a \valign. The material in \vadjust and \insert items is also processed in internal vertical mode; furthermore, TeX enters this mode when processing the \output token list.

The commands \end and \dump (the latter exists only in IniTeX) are not allowed in internal vertical mode; furthermore, \dump is not allowed inside a group (see Chapter 33).

6.4 BOXES AND MODES

There are horizontal and vertical boxes, and there is horizontal and vertical mode. Not surprisingly, there is a connection between the boxes and the modes. One can ask about this connection in two ways.

6.4.1 What box do you use in what mode?

This is the wrong question. Both horizontal and vertical boxes can be used in both horizontal and vertical mode. Their placement is determined by the prevailing mode at that moment.

6.4.2 What mode holds in what box?

This is the right question. When an \hbox starts, TeX is in restricted horizontal mode. Thus everything in a horizontal box is lined up horizontally.

When a \vbox is started, TeX is in internal vertical mode. Boxes of both kinds and other items are then stacked on top of each other.

6.4.3 Mode-dependent behaviour of boxes

Any ⟨box⟩ (see Chapter 5 for the full definition) can be used in horizontal, vertical, and math mode. Unboxing commands, however, are specific for horizontal or vertical mode. Both \unhbox and \unhcopy are ⟨horizontal command⟩s, so they can make TeX switch from vertical to horizontal mode; both \unvbox and \unvcopy are ⟨vertical command⟩s, so they can make TeX switch from horizontal to vertical mode.

In horizontal mode the `\spacefactor` is set to 1000 after a box has been placed. In vertical mode the `\prevdepth` is set to the depth of the box placed. Neither statement holds for unboxing commands: after an `\unhbox` or `\unhcopy` the spacefactor is not altered, and after `\unvbox` or `\unvcopy` the `\prevdepth` remains unchanged. After all, these commands do not a add a box, but a piece of a (horizontal or vertical) list.

The operations `\raise` and `\lower` can only be applied to a box in horizontal mode; similarly, `\moveleft` and `\moveright` can only be applied in vertical mode.

6.5   MODES AND GLUE

Both in horizontal and vertical mode TeX can insert glue items the size of which is determined by the preceding object in the list.

For horizontal mode the amount of glue that is inserted for a space token depends on the `\spacefactor` of the previous object in the list. This is treated in Chapter 20.

In vertical mode TeX inserts glue to keep boxes at a certain distance from each other. This glue is influenced by the height of the current item and the depth of the previous one. The depth of items is recorded in the `\prevdepth` parameter (see Chapter 15).

The two quantities `\prevdepth` and `\spacefactor` use the same internal register of TeX. Thus the `\prevdepth` can be used or asked only in vertical mode, and the `\spacefactor` only in horizontal mode.

6.6   MIGRATING MATERIAL

The three control sequences `\insert`, `\mark`, and `\vadjust` can be given in a paragraph (the first two can also occur in vertical mode) to specify material that will wind up on the surrounding vertical list. Note that this need not be the main vertical list: it can be a vertical box containing a paragraph of text. In this case a `\mark` or `\insert` command will not reach the page breaking algorithm.

When several migrating items are specified in a certain line of text, their left-to-right order is preserved when they are placed on the surrounding vertical list. These items are placed directly after the horizontal box containing the line of text in which they were specified: they come before any penalty or glue items that are automatically inserted (see page 169).

6.6.1   \vadjust

The command

> `\vadjust`⟨filler⟩`{`⟨vertical mode material⟩`}`

is only allowed in horizontal and math modes (but it is not a ⟨horizontal command⟩). Vertical mode material specified by \vadjust is moved from the horizontal list in which the command is given to the surrounding vertical list, directly after the box in which it occurred.

- In the current line a \vadjust item was placed to put the bullet in the margin.

Any vertical material in a \vadjust item is processed in internal vertical mode, even though it will wind up on the main vertical list. For instance, the \ifinner test is true in a \vadjust, and at the start of the vertical material \prevdepth= -1000pt.

6.7 TESTING MODES

The three conditionals \ifhmode, \ifvmode, and \ifinner can distinguish between the four modes of TeX that are not math modes. The \ifinner test is true if TeX is in restricted horizontal mode or internal vertical mode (or in non-display math mode). Exceptional condition: during a \write TeX is in a 'no mode' state. The tests \ifhmode, \ifvmode, and \ifmmode are then all false.

Inspection of all current lists, including the 'recent contributions' (see Chapter 27), is possible through the command \showlists. This command writes to the log file the contents of all lists that are being built at the moment the command is given.

Consider the example

```
a\hfil\break b\par
c\hfill\break d
\hbox{e\vbox{f\showlists
```

Here the first paragraph has been broken into two lines, and these have been added to the current page. The second paragraph has not been concluded or broken into lines.

The log file shows the following. TeX was busy building a paragraph (starting with an indentation box 20pt wide):

```
### horizontal mode entered at line 3
\hbox(0.0+0.0)x20.0
\tenrm f
spacefactor 1000
```

This paragraph was inside a vertical box:

```
### internal vertical mode entered at line 3
prevdepth ignored
```

The vertical box was in a horizontal box,

```
### restricted horizontal mode entered at line 3
\tenrm e
spacefactor 1000
```

which was part of an as-yet unfinished paragraph:

```
### horizontal mode entered at line 2
\hbox(0.0+0.0)x20.0
\tenrm c
\glue 0.0 plus 1.0fill
\penalty -10000
\tenrm d
etc.
spacefactor 1000
```

Note how the infinite glue and the \break penalty are still part of the horizontal list.

Finally, the first paragraph has been broken into lines and added to the current page:

```
### vertical mode entered at line 0
### current page:
\glue(\topskip) 5.69446
\hbox(4.30554+0.0)x469.75499, glue set 444.75497fil
.\hbox(0.0+0.0)x20.0
.\tenrm a
.\glue 0.0 plus 1.0fil
.\penalty -10000
.\glue(\rightskip) 0.0
\penalty 300
\glue(\baselineskip) 5.05556
\hbox(6.94444+0.0)x469.75499, glue set 464.19943fil
.\tenrm b
.\penalty 10000
.\glue(\parfillskip) 0.0 plus 1.0fil
.\glue(\rightskip) 0.0
etc.
total height 22.0 plus 1.0
 goal height 643.20255
prevdepth 0.0
```

CHAPTER

7

Numbers

In this chapter integers and their denotations will be treated, the conversions that are possible either way, allocation and use of \count registers, and arithmetic with integers.

\number   Convert a ⟨number⟩ to decimal representation.
\romannumeral   Convert a positive ⟨number⟩ to lowercase roman representation.
\ifnum   Test relations between numbers.
\ifodd   Test whether a number is odd.
\ifcase   Enumerated case statement.
\count   Prefix for count registers.
\countdef   Define a control sequence to be a synonym for a \count register.
\newcount   Allocate an unused \count register.
\advance   Arithmetic command to add to or subtract from a ⟨numeric variable⟩.
\multiply   Arithmetic command to multiply a ⟨numeric variable⟩.
\divide   Arithmetic command to divide a ⟨numeric variable⟩.

7.1   NUMBERS AND ⟨number⟩S

An important part of the grammar of TeX is the rigorous definition of a ⟨number⟩, the syntactic entity that TeX expects when semantically an integer is expected. This definition will take the largest part of this chapter. Towards the end, \count registers, arithmetic, and tests for numbers are treated.

For clarity of discussion a distinction will be made here between integers and numbers, but note that a ⟨number⟩ can be both an 'integer' and a 'number'. 'Integer' will be taken to denote a mathematical number: a quantity that can be added or multiplied. 'Number' will be taken to refer to the printed representation of an integer: a string of digits, in other words.

7.2   INTEGERS

Quite a few different sorts of objects can function as integers in TeX. In this section they will all be treated, accompanied by the relevant lines from the grammar of TeX.

First of all, an integer can be positive or negative:

⟨number⟩ ⟶ ⟨optional signs⟩⟨unsigned number⟩
⟨optional signs⟩ ⟶ ⟨optional spaces⟩
  | ⟨optional signs⟩⟨plus or minus⟩⟨optional spaces⟩

A first possibility for an unsigned integer is a string of digits in decimal, octal, or hexadecimal notation. Together with the alphabetic constants these will be named here ⟨integer denotation⟩. Another possibility for an integer is an internal integer quantity, an ⟨internal integer⟩; together with the denotations these form the ⟨normal integer⟩s. Lastly an integer can be a ⟨coerced integer⟩: an internal ⟨dimen⟩ or ⟨glue⟩ quantity that is converted to an integer value.

⟨unsigned number⟩ ⟶ ⟨normal integer⟩ | ⟨coerced integer⟩
⟨normal integer⟩ ⟶ ⟨integer denotation⟩ | ⟨internal integer⟩
⟨coerced integer⟩ ⟶ ⟨internal dimen⟩ | ⟨internal glue⟩

All of these possibilities will be treated in sequence.

7.2.1 Denotations: integers

Anything that looks like a number can be used as a ⟨number⟩: thus 42 is a number. However, bases other than decimal can also be used:

    '123

is the octal notation for $1 \times 8^2 + 2 \times 8^1 + 3 \times 8^0 = 83$, and

    "123

is the hexadecimal notation for $1 \times 16^2 + 2 \times 16^1 + 3 \times 16^0 = 291$.

⟨integer denotation⟩ ⟶ ⟨integer constant⟩⟨one optional space⟩
  | '⟨octal constant⟩⟨one optional space⟩
  | "⟨hexadecimal constant⟩⟨one optional space⟩

The octal digits are 0–7; a digit 8 or 9 following an octal denotation is not part of the number: after

    \count0='078

the \count0 will have the value 7, and the digit 8 is typeset.

The hexadecimal digits are 0–9, A–F, where the A–F can have category code 11 or 12. The latter has a somewhat far-fetched justification: the characters resulting from a \string operation have category code 12. Lowercase a–f are not hexadecimal digits, although (in TeX3) they are used for hexadecimal notation in the 'circumflex method' for accessing all character codes (see Chapter 3).

7.2.2 Denotations: characters

A character token is a pair consisting of a character code, which is a number in the range 0–255, and a category code. Both of these codes are accessible, and can be used as a ⟨number⟩.

The character code of a character token, or of a single letter control sequence, is accessible through the left quote command: both `a and `\a denote the character code of a, which can be used as an integer.

⟨integer denotation⟩ ⟶ `⟨character token⟩⟨one optional space⟩

In order to emphasize that accessing the character code is in a sense using a denotation, the syntax of TeX allows an optional space after such a 'character constant'. The left quote must have category 12.

7.2.3 Internal integers

The class of ⟨internal integers⟩ can be split into five parts. The ⟨codename⟩s and ⟨special integer⟩s will be treated separately below; furthermore, there are the following.

- The contents of \count registers; either explicitly used by writing for instance \count23, or by referring to such a register by means of a control sequence that was defined by \countdef: after

    \countdef\MyCount=23

    \MyCount is called a ⟨countdef token⟩, and it is fully equivalent to \count23.
- All parameters of TeX that hold integer values; this includes obvious ones such as \linepenalty, but also parameters such as \hyphenchar⟨font⟩ and \parshape (if a paragraph shape has been defined for n lines, using \parshape in the context of a ⟨number⟩ will yield this value of n).
- Tokens defined by \chardef or \mathchardef. After

    \chardef\foo=74

    the control sequence \foo can be used on its own to mean \char74, but in a context where a ⟨number⟩ is wanted it can be used to denote 74:

    \count\foo

    is equivalent to \count74. This fact is exploited in the allocation routines for registers (see Chapter 31).

    A control sequence thus defined by \chardef is called a ⟨chardef token⟩; if it is defined by \mathchardef it is called a ⟨mathchardef token⟩.

Here is the full list:

⟨internal integer⟩ ⟶ ⟨integer parameter⟩
　| ⟨special integer⟩ | \lastpenalty
　| ⟨countdef token⟩ | \count⟨8-bit number⟩
　| ⟨chardef token⟩ | ⟨mathchardef token⟩
　| ⟨codename⟩⟨8-bit number⟩
　| \hyphenchar⟨font⟩ | \skewchar⟨font⟩ | \parshape
　| \inputlineno | \badness
⟨integer parameter⟩ ⟶ | \adjdemerits | \binoppenalty
　| \brokenpenalty | \clubpenalty | \day

```
| \defaulthyphenchar | \defaultskewchar
| \delimiterfactor | \displaywidowpenalty
| \doublehyphendemerits | \endlinechar | \escapechar
| \exhypenpenalty | \fam | \finalhyphendemerits
| \floatingpenalty | \globaldefs | \hangafter
| \hbadness | \hyphenpenalty | \interlinepenalty
| \linepenalty | \looseness | \mag
| \maxdeadcycles | \month
| \newlinechar | \outputpenalty | \pausing
| \postdisplaypenalty | \predisplaypenalty
| \pretolerance | \relpenalty | \showboxbreadth
| \showboxdepth | \time | \tolerance
| \tracingcommands | \tracinglostchars | \tracingmacros
| \tracingonline | \tracingoutput | \tracingpages
| \tracingparagraphs | \tracingrestores | \tracingstats
| \uchyph | \vbadness | \widowpenalty | \year
```

Any internal integer can function as an ⟨internal unit⟩, which – preceded by ⟨optional spaces⟩ – can serve as a ⟨unit of measure⟩. Examples of this are given in Chapter 8.

7.2.4 Internal integers: other codes of a character

The \catcode command (which was described in Chapter 2) is a ⟨codename⟩, and like the other code names it can be used as an integer.

⟨codename⟩ ⟶ \catcode | \mathcode | \uccode | \lccode
    | \sfcode | \delcode

A ⟨codename⟩ has to be followed by an ⟨8-bit number⟩.

Uppercase and lowercase codes were treated in Chapter 3; the \sfcode is treated in Chapter 20; the \mathcode and \delcode are treated in Chapter 21.

7.2.5 ⟨special integer⟩

One of the subclasses of the internal integers is that of the special integers.

⟨special integer⟩ ⟶ \spacefactor | \prevgraf
    | \deadcycles | \insertpenalties

An assignment to any of these is called an ⟨intimate assignment⟩, and is automatically global (see Chapter 10).

7.2.6 Other internal quantities: coersion to integer

TeX provides a conversion between dimensions and integers: if an integer is expected, a ⟨dimen⟩ or ⟨glue⟩ used in that context is converted by taking its (natural) size in scaled points. However, only ⟨internal dimen⟩s and ⟨internal glue⟩ can be used this way: no dimension or glue denotations can be coerced to integers.

7.2.7 Trailing spaces

The syntax of TeX defines integer denotations (decimal, octal, and hexadecimal) and 'back-quoted' character tokens to be followed by ⟨one optional space⟩. This means that TeX reads the token after the number, absorbing it if it was a space token, and backing up if it was not.

Because TeX's input processor goes into the state 'skipping spaces' after it has seen one space token, this scanning behaviour implies that integer denotations can be followed by arbitrarily many space characters in the input. Also, a line end is admissible. However, only one space token is allowed.

7.3 NUMBERS

TeX can perform an implicit conversion from a string of digits to an integer. Conversion from a representation in decimal, octal, or hexadecimal notation was treated above. The conversion the other way, from an ⟨internal integer⟩ to a printed representation, has to be performed explicitly. TeX provides two conversion routines, \number and \romannumeral. The command \number is equivalent to \the when followed by an internal integer. These commands are performed in the expansion processor of TeX, that is, they are expanded whenever expansion has not been inhibited.

Both commands yield a string of tokens with category code 12; their argument is a ⟨number⟩. Thus \romannumeral51, \romannumeral\year, and \number\linepenalty are valid, and so is \number13. Applying \number to a denotation has some uses: it removes leading zeros and superfluous plus and minus signs.

A roman numeral is a string of lowercase 'roman digits', which are characters of category code 12. The sequence

\uppercase\expandafter{\romannumeral ...}

gives uppercase roman numerals. This works because TeX expands tokens in order to find the opening brace of the argument of \uppercase. If \romannumeral is applied to a negative number, the result is simply empty.

7.4 INTEGER REGISTERS

Integers can be stored in \count registers:

\count⟨8-bit number⟩

is an ⟨integer variable⟩ and an ⟨internal integer⟩. As an integer variable it can be used in a ⟨variable assignment⟩:

⟨variable assignment⟩ ⟶ ⟨integer variable⟩⟨equals⟩⟨number⟩ | ...

As an internal integer it can be used as a ⟨number⟩:

⟨number⟩ → ⟨optional signs⟩⟨internal integer⟩ | ...

Synonyms for \count registers can be introduced by the \countdef command in a ⟨shorthand definition⟩:

\countdef⟨control sequence⟩⟨equals⟩⟨8-bit number⟩

A control sequence defined this way is called a ⟨countdef token⟩, and it serves as an ⟨internal integer⟩.

The plain TeX macro \newcount (which is declared \outer) uses the \countdef command to allocate an unused \count register. Counters 0–9 are scratch registers, like all registers with numbers 0–9. However, counters 0–9 are used for page identification in the dvi file (see Chapter 33), so they should be used as scratch registers only inside a group. Counters 10–22 are used for plain TeX's bookkeeping of allocation of registers. Counter 255 is also scratch.

7.5 ARITHMETIC

The user can perform some arithmetic in TeX, and TeX also performs arithmetic internally. User arithmetic is concerned only with integers; the internal arithmetic is mostly on fixed-point quantities, and only in the case of glue setting on floating-point numbers.

7.5.1 Arithmetic statements

TeX allows the user to perform some arithmetic on integers. The statement

\advance⟨integer variable⟩⟨optional by⟩⟨number⟩

adds the value of the ⟨number⟩ – which may be negative – to the ⟨integer variable⟩. Similarly,

\multiply⟨integer variable⟩⟨optional by⟩⟨number⟩

multiplies the value of the ⟨integer variable⟩, and

\divide⟨integer variable⟩⟨optional by⟩⟨number⟩

divides an ⟨integer variable⟩.

Multiplication and division are also available for any so-called ⟨numeric variable⟩: their most general form is

\multiply⟨numeric variable⟩⟨optional by⟩⟨number⟩

where

⟨numeric variable⟩ ⟶ ⟨integer variable⟩ | ⟨dimen variable⟩
  | ⟨glue variable⟩ | ⟨muglue variable⟩

The result of an arithmetic operation should not exceed 2^{30} in absolute value.

Division of integers yields an integer; that is, the remainder is discarded. This raises the question of how rounding is performed when either operand is negative. In such cases TeX performs the division with the absolute values of the operands, and takes the negative of the result if exactly one operand was negative.

7.5.2 Floating-point arithmetic

Internally some arithmetic on floating-point quantities is performed, namely in the calculation of glue set ratios. However, machine-dependent aspects of rounding cannot influence the decision process of TeX, so machine independence of TeX is guaranteed in this respect (sufficient accuracy of rounding is enforced by the `Trip` test of Knuth (1984c)).

7.5.3 Fixed-point arithmetic

All fractional arithmetic in TeX is performed in fixed-point arithmetic of 'scaled integers': multiples of 2^{-16}. This ensures the machine independence of TeX. Printed representations of scaled integers are rounded to 5 decimal digits.

In ordinary 32-bit implementations of TeX the largest integers are 2^{31} in absolute size. The user is not allowed to specify dimensions larger in absolute size than 2^{30}: two such dimensions can be added or subtracted without overflow on a 32-bit system.

7.6 NUMBER TESTING

The most general test for integers in TeX is

   `\ifnum`$\langle number_1\rangle\langle relation\rangle\langle number_2\rangle$

where $\langle relation\rangle$ is a <, >, or = character, all of category 12.

Distinguishing between odd and even numbers is done by

   `\ifodd`$\langle number\rangle$

A numeric case statement is provided by

   `\ifcase`$\langle number\rangle\langle case_0\rangle$`\or`$\ldots$`\or`$\langle case_n\rangle$`\else`$\langle other\ cases\rangle$`\fi`

where the `\else`-part is optional. The tokens for $\langle case_i\rangle$ are processed if the number turns out to be i; other cases are skipped, similarly to what ordinarily happens in conditionals (see Chapter 13).

7.7 REMARKS

7.7.1 Character constants

In formats and macro collections numeric constants are often needed. There are several ways to implement these in TeX.

Firstly,

```
\newcount\SomeConstant \SomeConstant=42
```

This is wasteful, as it uses up a `\count` register.
Secondly,

```
\def\SomeConstant{42}
```

Better but accident prone: TeX has to expand to find the number – which in itself is a slight overhead – and may inadvertently expand some tokens that should have been left alone.
Thirdly,

```
\chardef\SomeConstant=42
```

This one is fine. A ⟨chardef token⟩ has the same status as a `\count` register: both are ⟨internal integer⟩s. Therefore a number defined this way can be used everywhere that a `\count` register is feasible. For large numbers the `\chardef` can be replaced by `\mathchardef`, which runs to "7FFF = 32 767. Note that a ⟨mathchardef token⟩ can usually only appear in math mode, but in the context of a number it can appear anywhere.

7.7.2 Expanding too far / how far

It is a common mistake to write pieces of TeX code where TeX will inadvertently expand something because it is trying to compose a number. For example:

```
\def\par{\endgraf\penalty200}
...\par \number\pageno
```

Here the page number will be absorbed into the value of the penalty.
Now consider

```
\newcount\midpenalty \midpenalty=200
\def\par{\endgraf\penalty\midpenalty}
...\par \number\pageno
```

Here the page number is not scooped up by mistake: TeX is trying to locate a ⟨number⟩ after the `\penalty`, and it finds a ⟨countdef token⟩. This is *not* converted to a representation in digits, so there is never any danger of the page number being touched.

It is possible to convert a ⟨countdef token⟩ first to a representation in digits before assigning it:

```
\penalty\number\midpenalty
```

and this brings back again all previous problems of expansion.

CHAPTER 8

Dimensions and Glue

In TeX vertical and horizontal white space can have a possibility to adjust itself through 'stretching' or 'shrinking'. An adjustable white space is called 'glue'. This chapter treats all technical concepts related to dimensions and glue, and it explains how the badness of stretching or shrinking a certain amount is calculated.

\dimen   Dimension register prefix.
\dimendef   Define a control sequence to be a synonym for a \dimen register.
\newdimen   Allocate an unused dimen register.
\skip   Skip register prefix.
\skipdef   Define a control sequence to be a synonym for a \skip register.
\newskip   Allocate an unused skip register.
\ifdim   Compare two dimensions.
\hskip   Insert in horizontal mode a glue item.
\hfil   Equivalent to \hskip 0cm plus 1fil.
\hfilneg   Equivalent to \hskip 0cm minus 1fil.
\hfill   Equivalent to \hskip 0cm plus 1fill.
\hss   Equivalent to \hskip 0cm plus 1fil minus 1fil.
\vskip   Insert in vertical mode a glue item.
\vfil   Equivalent to \vskip 0cm plus 1fil.
\vfill   Equivalent to \vskip 0cm plus 1fill.
\vfilneg   Equivalent to \vskip 0cm minus 1fil.
\vss   Equivalent to \vskip 0cm plus 1fil minus 1fil.
\kern   Add a kern item to the current horizontal or vertical list.
\lastkern   If the last item on the current list was a kern, the size of it.
\lastskip   If the last item on the current list was a glue, the size of it.
\unkern   If the last item of the current list was a kern, remove it.
\unskip   If the last item of the current list was a glue, remove it.
\removelastskip   Macro to append the negative of the \lastskip.
\advance   Arithmetic command to add to or subtract from a ⟨numeric variable⟩.
\multiply   Arithmetic command to multiply a ⟨numeric variable⟩.
\divide   Arithmetic command to divide a ⟨numeric variable⟩.

8.1 DEFINITION OF ⟨glue⟩ AND ⟨dimen⟩

This section gives the syntax of the quantities ⟨dimen⟩ and ⟨glue⟩. In the next section the practical aspects of glue are treated.

Unfortunately the terminology for glue is slightly confusing. The syntactical quantity ⟨glue⟩ is a dimension (a distance) with possibly a stretch and/or shrink component. In order to add a glob of 'glue' (a white space) to a list one has to let a ⟨glue⟩ be preceded by commands such as `\vskip`.

8.1.1 Definition of dimensions

A ⟨dimen⟩ is what TeX expects to see when it needs to indicate a dimension; it can be positive or negative.

⟨dimen⟩ ⟶ ⟨optional signs⟩⟨unsigned dimen⟩

The unsigned part of a ⟨dimen⟩ can be

⟨unsigned dimen⟩ ⟶ ⟨normal dimen⟩ | ⟨coerced dimen⟩
⟨normal dimen⟩ ⟶ ⟨internal dimen⟩ | ⟨factor⟩⟨unit of measure⟩
⟨coerced dimen⟩ ⟶ ⟨internal glue⟩

That is, we have the following three cases:

- an ⟨internal dimen⟩; this is any register or parameter of TeX that has a ⟨dimen⟩ value:

  ⟨internal dimen⟩ ⟶ ⟨dimen parameter⟩
     | ⟨special dimen⟩ | `\lastkern`
     | ⟨dimendef token⟩ | `\dimen`⟨8-bit number⟩
     | `\fontdimen`⟨number⟩⟨font⟩
     | ⟨box dimension⟩⟨8-bit number⟩
  ⟨dimen parameter⟩ ⟶ `\boxmaxdepth`
     | `\delimitershortfall` | `\displayindent`
     | `\displaywidth` | `\hangindent`
     | `\hfuzz` | `\hoffset` | `\hsize`
     | `\lineskiplimit` | `\mathsurround`
     | `\maxdepth` | `\nulldelimiterspace`
     | `\overfullrule` | `\parindent`
     | `\predisplaysize` | `\scriptspace`
     | `\splitmaxdepth` | `\vfuzz`
     | `\voffset` | `\vsize`

- a dimension denotation, consisting of ⟨factor⟩⟨unit of measure⟩, for example `0.7\vsize`; or
- an ⟨internal glue⟩ (see below) coerced to a dimension by omitting the stretch and shrink components, for example `\parfillskip`.

A dimension denotation is a somewhat complicated entity:

- a ⟨factor⟩ is an integer denotation, a decimal constant denotation (a number with an integral and a fractional part), or an ⟨internal integer⟩

⟨factor⟩ ⟶ ⟨normal integer⟩ | ⟨decimal constant⟩
⟨normal integer⟩ ⟶ ⟨integer denotation⟩
    | ⟨internal integer⟩
⟨decimal constant⟩ ⟶ .₁₂ | ,₁₂
    | ⟨digit⟩⟨decimal constant⟩
    | ⟨decimal constant⟩⟨digit⟩

An internal integer is a parameter that is 'really' an integer (for instance, \count0), and not coerced from a dimension or glue. See Chapter 7 for the definition of various kinds of integers.

- a ⟨unit of measure⟩ can be a ⟨physical unit⟩, that is, an ordinary unit such as cm (possibly preceded by true), an internal unit such as em, but also an ⟨internal integer⟩ (by conversion to scaled points), an ⟨internal dimen⟩, or an ⟨internal glue⟩.

⟨unit of measure⟩ ⟶ ⟨optional spaces⟩⟨internal unit⟩
    | ⟨optional true⟩⟨physical unit⟩⟨one optional space⟩
⟨internal unit⟩ ⟶ em⟨one optional space⟩
    | ex⟨one optional space⟩ | ⟨internal integer⟩
    | ⟨internal dimen⟩ | ⟨internal glue⟩

Some ⟨dimen⟩s are called ⟨special dimen⟩s:

⟨special dimen⟩ ⟶ \prevdepth
    | \pagegoal | \pagetotal | \pagestretch
    | \pagefilstretch | \pagefillstretch
    | \pagefilllstretch | \pageshrink | \pagedepth

An assignment to any of these is called an ⟨intimate assignment⟩, and it is automatically global (see Chapter 10). The meaning of these dimensions is explained in Chapter 27, with the exception of \prevdepth which is treated in Chapter 15.

8.1.2 Definition of glue

A ⟨glue⟩ is either some form of glue variable, or a glue denotation with explicitly indicated stretch and shrink. Specifically,

⟨glue⟩ ⟶ ⟨optional signs⟩⟨internal glue⟩ | ⟨dimen⟩⟨stretch⟩⟨shrink⟩
⟨internal glue⟩ ⟶ ⟨glue parameter⟩ | \lastskip
    | ⟨skipdef token⟩ | \skip⟨8-bit number⟩
⟨glue parameter⟩ ⟶ \abovedisplayshortskip
    | \abovedisplayskip | \baselineskip
    | \belowdisplayshortskip | \belowdisplayskip
    | \leftskip | \lineskip | \parfillskip | \parskip
    | \rightskip | \spaceskip | \splittopskip | \tabskip
    | \topskip | \xspaceskip

The stretch and shrink components in a glue denotation are optional, but when both are specified they have to be given in sequence; they are defined as

⟨stretch⟩ ⟶ `plus` ⟨dimen⟩ | `plus`⟨fil dimen⟩ | ⟨optional spaces⟩
⟨shrink⟩ ⟶ `minus` ⟨dimen⟩ | `minus`⟨fil dimen⟩ | ⟨optional spaces⟩
⟨fil dimen⟩ ⟶ ⟨optional signs⟩⟨factor⟩⟨fil unit⟩⟨optional spaces⟩
⟨fil unit⟩ ⟶ | `fil` | `fill` | `filll`

The actual definition of ⟨fil unit⟩ is recursive (see Chapter 36), but these are the only valid possibilities.

8.1.3 Conversion of ⟨glue⟩ to ⟨dimen⟩

The grammar rule

⟨dimen⟩ ⟶ ⟨factor⟩⟨unit of measure⟩

has some noteworthy consequences, caused by the fact that a ⟨unit of measure⟩ need not look like a 'unit of measure' at all (see the list above).

For instance, from this definition we conclude that the statement

`\dimen0=\lastpenalty\lastpenalty`

is syntactically correct because `\lastpenalty` can function both as an integer and as ⟨unit of measure⟩ by taking its value in scaled points. After `\penalty8` the `\dimen0` thus defined will have a size of 64sp.

More importantly, consider the case where the ⟨unit of measure⟩ is an ⟨internal glue⟩, that is, any sort of glue parameter. Prefixing such a glue with a number (the ⟨factor⟩) makes it a valid ⟨dimen⟩ specification. Thus

`\skip0=\skip1`

is very different from

`\skip0=1\skip1`

The first statement makes `\skip0` equal to `\skip1`, the second converts the `\skip1` to a ⟨dimen⟩ before assigning it. In other words, the `\skip0` defined by the second statement has no stretch or shrink.

8.1.4 Registers for `\dimen` and `\skip`

TeX has registers for storing ⟨dimen⟩ and ⟨glue⟩ values: the `\dimen` and `\skip` registers respectively. These are accessible by the expressions

`\dimen`⟨number⟩

and

`\skip`⟨number⟩

As with all registers of TeX, these registers are numbered 0–255.

Synonyms for registers can be made with the `\dimendef` and `\skipdef` commands. Their syntax is

`\dimendef`⟨control sequence⟩⟨equals⟩⟨8-bit number⟩

and

`\skipdef`⟨control sequence⟩⟨equals⟩⟨8-bit number⟩

For example, after `\skipdef\foo=13` using `\foo` is equivalent to using `\skip13`.

Macros `\newdimen` and `\newskip` exist in plain TEX for allocating an unused dimen or skip register. These macros are defined to be `\outer` in the plain format.

8.1.5 Arithmetic: addition

As for integer variables, arithmetic operations exist for dimen, glue, and muglue (mathematical glue; see page 195) variables.

The expressions

`\advance`⟨dimen variable⟩⟨optional by⟩⟨dimen⟩
`\advance`⟨glue variable⟩⟨optional by⟩⟨glue⟩
`\advance`⟨muglue variable⟩⟨optional by⟩⟨muglue⟩

add to the size of a dimen, glue, or muglue.

Advancing a ⟨glue variable⟩ by ⟨glue⟩ is done by adding the natural sizes, and the stretch and shrink components. Because TEX converts between ⟨glue⟩ and ⟨dimen⟩, it is possible to write for instance

`\advance\skip1 by \dimen1`

or

`\advance\dimen1 by \skip1`

In the first case `\dimen1` is coerced to ⟨glue⟩ without stretch or shrink; in the second case the `\skip1` is coerced to a ⟨dimen⟩ by taking its natural size.

8.1.6 Arithmetic: multiplication and division

Multiplication and division operations exist for glue and dimensions. One may for instance write

`\multiply\skip1 by 2`

which multiplies the natural size, and the stretch and shrink components of `\skip1` by 2.

The second operand of a `\multiply` or `\divide` operation can only be a ⟨number⟩, that is, an integer. Introducing the notion of ⟨numeric variable⟩:

⟨numeric variable⟩ ⟶ ⟨integer variable⟩ | ⟨dimen variable⟩
　| ⟨glue variable⟩ | ⟨muglue variable⟩

these operations take the form

> \multiply⟨numeric variable⟩⟨optional by⟩⟨number⟩

and

> \divide⟨numeric variable⟩⟨optional by⟩⟨number⟩

Glue and dimen can be multiplied by non-integer quantities:

```
\skip1=2.5\skip2
\dimen1=.78\dimen2
```

However, in the first line the \skip2 is first coerced to a ⟨dimen⟩ value by omitting its stretch and shrink.

8.2 MORE ABOUT DIMENSIONS

8.2.1 Units of measurement

In TeX dimensions can be indicated in

centimetre denoted cm or
millimetre denoted mm; these are SI units (*Système International d'Unités*, the international system of standard units of measurements).
inch in; more common in the Anglo-American world. One inch is 2.54 centimetres.
pica denoted pc; one pica is 12 points.
point denoted pt; the common system for Anglo-American printers. One inch is 72.27 points.
didot point denoted dd; the common system for continental European printers. Furthermore, 1157 didot points are 1238 points.
cicero denoted cc; one cicero is 12 didot points.
big point denoted bp; one inch is 72 big points.
scaled point denoted sp; this is the smallest unit in TeX, and all measurements are integral multiples of one scaled point. There are 65 536 scaled points in a point.

Decimal fractions can be written using both the Anglo-American system with the decimal point (for example, 1in=72.27pt) and the continental European system with a decimal comma; 1in=72,27pt.

Internally TeX works with multiples of a smallest dimension: the scaled point. Dimensions larger (in absolute value) than 2^{30}sp, which is about 5.75 metres or 18.9 feet, are illegal.

Both the pica system and the didot system are of French origin: in 1737 the type founder Pierre Simon Fournier introduced typographical points based on the French foot. Although at first he introduced a system based on lines and points, he later took the point as unit: there are 72 points in an inch, which is one-twelfth of a foot. About 1770 another founder, François Ambroise Didot, introduced points based on the more common, and slightly longer, 'pied du roi'.

8.2.2 Dimension testing

Dimensions and natural sizes of glue can be compared with the `\ifdim` test. This takes the form

    `\ifdim`⟨dimen$_1$⟩⟨relation⟩⟨dimen$_2$⟩

where the relation can be an >, <, or = token, all of category 12.

8.2.3 Defined dimensions

`\z@`   `0pt`
`\maxdimen`   `16383.99999pt`; the largest legal dimension.

These ⟨dimen⟩s are predefined in the plain format; for instance

    `\newdimen\z@ \z@=0pt`

Using such abbreviations for commonly used dimensions has at least two advantages. First of all it saves main memory if such a dimension occurs in a macro: a control sequence is one token, whereas a string such as `0pt` takes three. Secondly, it saves time in processing, as TeX does not need to perform conversions to arrive at the correct type of object.

Control sequences such as `\z@` are only available to a user who changes the category code of the 'at' sign. Ordinarily, these control sequences appear only in the macros defined in packages such as the plain format.

8.3 MORE ABOUT GLUE

Glue items can be added to a vertical list with one of the commands `\vskip`⟨glue⟩, `\vfil`, `\vfill`, `\vss` or `\vfilneg`; glue items can be added to a horizontal list with one of the commands `\hskip`⟨glue⟩, `\hfil`, `\hfill`, `\hss` or `\hfilneg`. We will now treat the properties of glue.

8.3.1 Stretch and shrink

In the syntax given above, ⟨glue⟩ was defined as having
- a 'natural size', which is a ⟨dimen⟩, and optionally
- a 'stretch' and 'shrink' component built out of a ⟨fil dimen⟩.

Each list that TeX builds has amounts of stretch and shrink (possibly zero), which are the sum of the stretch and shrink components of individual pieces of glue in the list. Stretch and shrink are used if the context in which the list appears requires it to assume a size that is different from its natural size.

There is an important difference in behaviour between stretch and shrink components when they are finite – that is, when the ⟨fildimen⟩ is not fil(1(1)). A finite amount of shrink is indeed the maximum shrink that TeX will take: the amount of glue specified as

```
5pt minus 3pt
```

can shrink to 2pt, but not further. In contrast to this, a finite amount of stretch can be stretched arbitrarily far. Such arbitrary stretching has a large 'badness', however. Badness calculation is treated below.

Examples
The sequence with natural size 20pt

```
\hskip 10pt plus 2pt \hskip 10pt plus 3pt
```

has 5pt of stretch, but it has no shrink. In

```
\hskip 10pt minus 2pt \hskip 10pt plus 3pt
```

there is 3pt of stretch, and 2pt of shrink, so its minimal size is 18pt.
Positive shrink is not the same as negative stretch:

```
\hskip 10pt plus -2pt \hskip 10pt plus 3pt
```

looks a lot like the previous example, but it cannot be shrunk as there are no minus⟨dimen⟩ specifications. It does have 1pt of stretch, however.
This is another example of negative amounts of shrink and stretch. It is not possible to stretch glue (in the informal sense) by shrinking it (in the technical sense):

```
\hbox to 5cm{a\hskip 0cm minus -1fil}
```

is an underfull box, because TeX looks for a plus ⟨dimen⟩ specification when it needs to stretch the contents.
Finally,

```
\hskip 10pt plus -3pt \hskip 10pt plus 3pt
```

can neither stretch nor shrink. The fact that there is only stretch available means that the sequence cannot shrink. However, the stretch components cancel out: the total stretch is zero. Another way of looking at this is to consider that for each point that the second glue item would stretch, the first one would 'stretch back' one point.

Any amount of infinite stretch or shrink overpowers all finite stretch or shrink available:

```
\hbox to 5cm{\hskip 0cm plus 16384pt
             text\hskip 0cm plus 0.0001fil}
```

has the text at the extreme left of the box. There are three orders of 'infinity', each one infinitely stronger than the previous one:

```
\hbox to 5cm{\hskip 0cm plus 16384fil
```

```
                    text\hskip 0cm plus 0.0001fill}
```
and
```
\hbox to 5cm{\hskip 0cm plus 16384fill
                    text\hskip 0cm plus 0.0001filll}
```
both have the text at the left end of the box.

8.3.2 Glue setting

In the process of 'glue setting', the desired width (or height) of a box is compared with the natural dimension of its contents, which is the sum of all natural dimensions of boxes and globs of glue. If the two differ, any available stretchability or shrinkability is used to bridge the gap. To attain the desired dimension of the box only the glue of the highest available order is set: each piece of glue of that order is stretched or shrunk by the same ratio.

For example, in
```
\hbox to 6pt{\hskip 0pt plus 3pt \hskip 0pt plus 9pt}
```
the natural size of the box is 0pt, and the total stretch is 12pt. In order to obtain a box of 6pt each glue item is set with a stretch ratio of 1/2. Thus the result is equivalent to
```
\hbox {\hskip 1.5pt \hskip 4.5pt}
```
Only the highest order of stretch or shrink is used: in
```
\hbox to 6pt{\hskip 0pt plus 1fil \hskip 0pt plus 9pt}
```
the second glue will assume its natural size of 0pt, and only the first glue will be stretched.

TeX will never exceed the maximum value of a finite amount of shrink. A box that cannot be shrunk enough is called 'overfull'. Finite stretchability can be exceeded to provide an escape in difficult situations; however, TeX is likely to give an `Underfull \hbox` message about this (see page 47). For an example of infinite shrink see page 47.

8.3.3 Badness

When stretching or shrinking a list TeX calculates badness based on the ratio between actual stretch and the amount of stretch present in the line. See Chapter 19 for the application of badness to the paragraph algorithm.

The formula for badness of a list that is stretched (shrunk) is

$$b = \min\left(10\,000, 100 \times \left(\frac{\text{actual amount stretched (shrunk)}}{\text{possible amount of stretch (shrink)}}\right)^3\right)$$

In reality TeX uses a slightly different formula that is easier to calculate, but behaves the same. Since glue setting is one of the main activities of TeX, this must be performed as efficiently as possible.

This formula lets the badness be a reasonably small number if the glue set ratio (the fraction in the above expression) is reasonably small, but will let it grow rapidly once the ratio is more than 1. Badness is infinite if the glue would have to shrink more than the allotted amount; stretching glue beyond its maximum is possible, so this provides an escape for very difficult lines of text or pages.

In TeX3, the \badness parameter records the badness of the most recently formed box.

8.3.4 Glue and breaking

TeX can break lines and pages in several kinds of places. One of these places is before a glue item. The glue is then discarded. For line breaks this is treated in Chapter 19, for page breaks see Chapter 27.

There are two macros in plain TeX, \hglue and \vglue, that give non-disappearing glue in horizontal and vertical mode respectively. For the horizontal case this is accomplished by placing:

```
\vrule width 0pt \nobreak \hskip ...
```

Because TeX breaks at the front end of glue, this glue will always stay attached to the rule, and will therefore never disappear. The actual macro definitions are somewhat more complicated, because they take care to preserve the \spacefactor and the \prevdepth.

8.3.5 \kern

The \kern command specifies a kern item in whatever mode TeX is currently in. A kern item is much like a glue item without stretch or shrink. It differs from glue in that it is in general not a legal breakpoint. Thus in

```
.. text .. \hbox{a}\kern0pt\hbox{b}
```

TeX will not break lines in between the boxes; in

```
.. text .. \hbox{a}\hskip0pt\hbox{b}
```

a line can be broken in between the boxes.

However, if a kern is followed by glue, TeX can break at the kern (provided that it is not in math mode). In horizontal mode both the kern and the glue then disappear in the break. In vertical mode they are discarded when they are moved to the (empty) current page after the material before the break has been disposed of by the output routine (see Chapter 27).

8.3.6 Glue and modes

All horizontal skip commands are ⟨horizontal command⟩s and all vertical skip commands are ⟨vertical commands⟩s. This means that, for instance, an \hskip command makes TeX start a paragraph if it is given in vertical mode. The \kern command can be given in both modes.

8.3.7 The last glue item in a list: backspacing

The last glue item in a list can be measured, and it can be removed in all modes but external vertical mode. The internal variables \lastskip and \lastkern can be used to measure the last glob of glue in all modes; if the last glue was not a skip or kern respectively they give 0pt. In math mode the \lastskip functions as ⟨internal muglue⟩, but in general it classifies as ⟨internal glue⟩. The \lastskip and \lastkern are also 0pt if that was the size of the last glue or kern item on the list.

The operations \unskip and \unkern remove the last item of a list, if this is a glue or kern respectively. They have no effect in external vertical mode; in that case the best substitute is \vskip-\lastskip and \kern-\lastkern.

In the process of paragraph building TeX itself performs an important \unskip: a paragraph ending with a white line will have a space token inserted by TeX's input processor. This is removed by an \unskip before the \parfillskip glue (see Chapter 17) is inserted.

Glue is treated by TeX as a special case of leaders, which becomes apparent when \unskip is applied to leaders: they are removed.

8.3.8 Examples of backspacing

The plain TeX macro \removelastskip is defined as

```
\ifdim\lastskip=0pt \else \vskip-\lastskip \fi
```

If the last item on the list was a glue, this macro will backspace by its value, provided its natural size was not zero. In all other cases, nothing is added to the list.

Sometimes an intelligent version of commands such as \vskip is necessary, in the sense that two subsequent skip commands should result only in the larger of the two glue amounts. On page 153 such a macro is used:

```
\newskip\tempskipa
\def\vspace#1{\tempskipa=#1\relax
    \ifvmode \ifdim\tempskipa<\lastskip
            \else \vskip-\lastskip \vskip\tempskipa
        \fi
    \else \vskip\tempskipa \fi}
```

First of all, this tests whether the mode is vertical; if not, the argument can safely be placed. Copying the argument into a skip register is necessary because \vspace{2pt plus 3pt} would lead to problems in an \ifdim#1<\lastskip test.

If the surrounding mode was vertical, the argument should only be placed if it is not less than what is already there. The macro would be incorrect if the test read

```
\ifdim\tempskipa>\lastskip
```

```
        \vskip-\lastskip \vskip\tempskipa
     \fi
```

In this case the sequence

```
... last word.\par \vspace{0pt plus 1fil}
```

would not place any glue, because after the \par we are in vertical mode and \lastskip has a value of 0pt.

8.3.9 Glue in trace output

If the workings of TeX are traced by setting \tracingoutput positive, or if TeX writes a box to the log file (because of a \showbox command, or because it is overfull or underfull), glue is denoted by the control sequence \glue. This is not a TeX command; it merely indicates the presence of glue in the current list.

The box representation that TeX generated from, for instance, \showbox inserts a space after every explicit \kern, but no space is inserted after an implicit kern that was inserted by the kerning information in the font tfm file. Thus \kern 2.0pt denotes a kern that was inserted by the user or by a macro, and \kern2.0pt denotes an implicit kern.

Glue that is inserted automatically (\topskip, \baselineskip, et cetera) is denoted by name in TeX's trace output. For example, the box

```
\vbox{\hbox{Vo}\hbox{b}}
```

looks like

```
\vbox(18.83331+0.0)x11.66669
.\hbox(6.83331+0.0)x11.66669
..\tenrm V
..\kern-0.83334
..\tenrm o
.\glue(\baselineskip) 5.05556
.\hbox(6.94444+0.0)x5.55557
..\tenrm b
```

Note the implicit kern inserted between 'V' and 'o'.

CHAPTER 9

Rules and Leaders

Rules and leaders are two ways of getting TeX to draw a line. Leaders are more general than rules: they can also fill available space with copies of a certain box. This chapter explain how rules and leaders work, and how they interact with modes.

\hrule   Rule that spreads in horizontal direction.
\vrule   Rule that spreads in vertical direction.
\leaders   Fill a specified amount of space with a rule or copies of box.
\cleaders   Like \leaders, but with box leaders any excess space is split equally before and after the leaders.
\xleaders   Like \leaders, but with box leaders any excess space is spread equally before, after, and between the boxes.

9.1 RULES

TeX's rule commands give rectangular black patches with horizontal and vertical sides. Most of the times, a rule command will give output that looks like a rule, but ■ can also be produced by a rule.

TeX has both horizontal and vertical rules, but the names do not necessarily imply anything about the shape. They do, however, imply something about modes: an \hrule command can only be used in vertical mode, and a \vrule only in horizontal mode. In fact, an \hrule is a ⟨vertical command⟩, and a \vrule is a ⟨horizontal command⟩, so TeX may change modes when encountering these commands.

Why then is a \vrule called a *vertical* rule? The reason is that a \vrule can expand arbitrarily far in the vertical direction: if its height and depth are not specified explicitly it will take as much room as its surroundings allow.

Example

    \hbox{\vrule\ text \vrule}

looks like

    |text|

and

    \hbox{\vrule\ A gogo! \vrule}

looks like

| A gogo! |

For the `\hrule` command a similar statement is true: a horizontal rule can spread to assume the width of its surroundings. Thus

```
\vbox{\hbox{One line of text}\hrule}
```

looks like

One line of text

9.1.1 Rule dimensions

Horizontal and vertical rules have a default thickness:

`\hrule`   is the same as   `\hrule height.4pt depth0pt`

and

`\vrule`   is the same as   `\vrule width.4pt`

and if the remaining dimension remains unspecified, the rule extends in that direction to fill the enclosing box.

Here is the formal specification of how to indicate rule sizes:

⟨vertical rule⟩ ⟶ `\vrule`⟨rule specification⟩
⟨horizontal rule⟩ ⟶ `\hrule`⟨rule specification⟩
⟨rule specification⟩ ⟶ ⟨optional spaces⟩
   | ⟨rule dimensions⟩⟨rule specification⟩
⟨rule dimension⟩ ⟶ `width`⟨dimen⟩ | `height`⟨dimen⟩ | `depth`⟨dimen⟩

If a rule dimension is specified twice, the second instance takes precedence over the first. This makes it possible to override the default dimensions. For instance, after

`\let\xhrule\hrule   \def\hrule{\xhrule height .8pt}`

the macro `\hrule` gives a horizontal rule of double the original height, and it is still possible with

`\hrule height 2pt`

to specify other heights.

It is possible to specify all three dimensions; then

`\vrule height1ex depth0pt width1ex`

and

`\hrule height1ex depth0pt width1ex`

look the same. Still, each of them can be used only in the appropriate mode.

9.2 LEADERS

Rules are intimately connected to modes, which makes it easy to obtain some effects. For instance, a typical application of a vertical rule looks like

    \hbox{\vrule width1pt\ Important text! \vrule width 1pt}

which gives

    | Important text! |

However, one might want to have a horizontal rule in horizontal mode for effects such as

    ⟵   5cm   ⟶
    from here_____to there

An `\hrule` can not be used in horizontal mode, and a vertical rule will not spread automatically.

However, there is a way to use an `\hrule` command in horizontal mode and a `\vrule` in vertical mode, and that is with 'leaders', so called because they lead your eye across the page. A leader command tells TeX to fill a specified space, in whatever mode it is in, with as many copies of some box or rule specification as are needed. For instance, the above example was given as

    \hbox to 5cm{from here\leaders\hrule\hfil to there}

that is, with an `\hrule` that was allowed to stretch along an `\hfil`. Note that the leader was given a horizontal skip, corresponding to the horizontal mode in which it appeared.

A general leader command looks like

    ⟨leaders⟩⟨box or rule⟩⟨vertical/horizontal/mathematical skip⟩

where ⟨leaders⟩ is `\leaders`, `\cleaders`, or `\xleaders`, a ⟨box or rule⟩ is a ⟨box⟩, `\vrule`, or `\hrule`, and the lists of horizontal and vertical skips appear in Chapter 6; a mathematical skip is either a horizontal skip or an `\mskip` (see page 195). Leaders can thus be used in all three modes. Of course, the appropriate kind of skip must be specified.

A horizontal (vertical) box containing leaders has at least the height and depth (width) of the ⟨box or rule⟩ used in the leaders, even if, as can happen in the case of box leaders, no actual leaders are placed.

9.2.1 Rule leaders

Rule leaders fill the specified amount of space with a rule extending in the direction of the skip specified. The other dimensions of the resulting rule leader are determined by the sort of rule that is used: either dimensions can be specified explicitly, or the default values can be used.

For instance,

    \hbox{g\leaders\hrule\hskip20pt f}

gives

    g———f

because a horizontal rule has a default height of .4pt. On the other hand,

    `\hbox{g\leaders\vrule\hskip20pt f}`

gives

    g▮▮▮▮f

because the height and depth of a vertical rule by default fill the surrounding box.
    Spurious rule dimensions are ignored: in horizontal mode

    `\leaders\hrule width 10pt \hskip 20pt`

is equivalent to

    `\leaders\hrule \hskip 20pt`

If the width or height-plus-depth of either the skip or the box is negative, TeX uses ordinary glue instead of leaders.

9.2.2 Box leaders

Box leaders fill the available spaces with copies of a given box, instead of with a rule.

    For all of the following examples, assume that a box register has been allocated:

    `\newbox\centerdot   \setbox\centerdot=\hbox{\hskip.7em.\hskip.7em}`

Now the output of

    `\hbox to 8cm {here\leaders\copy\centerdot\hfil there}`

is

    here   .   .   .   .   there

That is, copies of the box register fill up the available space.

    Dot leaders, as in the above example, are often used for tables of contents. In such applications it is desirable that dots on subsequent lines are vertically aligned. The `\leaders` command does this automatically:

    `\hbox to 8cm {here\leaders\copy\centerdot\hfil there}`
    `\hbox to 8cm {over here\leaders\copy\centerdot\hfil over there}`

gives

    here   .   .   .   .   there
    over here   .   .   .   .   over there

The mechanism behind this is the following: TeX acts as if an infinite row of boxes starts (invisibly) at the left edge of the surrounding box, and the row of copies actually placed is merely the part of this row that is not obscured by the other contents of the box.

Stated differently, box leaders are a window on an infinite row of boxes, and the row starts at the left edge of the surrounding box. Consider the following example:

```
\hbox to 8cm {\leaders\hfil}
\hbox to 8cm {word\leaders\copy\centerdot\hfil}
```

which gives

>   .   .   .   .
> word   .   .   .   .

The row of leaders boxes becomes visible as soon as it does not coincide with other material.

The above discussion only talked about leaders in horizontal mode. Leaders can equally well be placed in vertical mode; for box leaders the 'infinite row' then starts at the top of the surrounding box.

9.2.3 Evenly spaced leaders

Aligning subsequent box leaders in the way described above means that the white space before and after the leaders will in general be different. If vertical alignment is not an issue it may be aesthetically more pleasing to have the leaders evenly spaced. The `\cleaders` command is like `\leaders`, except that it splits excess space before and after the leaders into two equal parts, centring the row of boxes in the available space.

Example

```
\hbox to 7.8cm {here\cleaders\copy\centerdot\hfil there}
\hbox to 7.8cm {here is\cleaders\copy\centerdot\hfil there}
```

gives

> here   .   .   .   .   there
> here is   .   .   .   .   there

The 'expanding leaders' `\xleaders` spread excess space evenly between the boxes, with equal globs of glue before, after, and in between leader boxes.

Example

```
\hbox to 7.8cm{here\hskip.7em
      \xleaders\copy\centerdot\hfil  \hskip.7em there}
```

gives

> here   .   .   .   .   there

Note that the glue in the leader box is balanced here with explicit glue before and after the leaders; leaving out these glue items, as in

```
\hbox to 7.8cm {here\xleaders\copy\centerdot\hfil there}
```

gives

> here . . . . there

which is clearly not what was intended.

9.3 ASSORTED REMARKS

9.3.1 Rules and modes

Above it was explained how rules can only occur in the appropriate modes. Rules also influence mode-specific quantities: no baselineskip is added before rules in vertical mode. In order to prevent glue after rules, TeX sets \prevdepth to -1000pt (see Chapter 15). Similarly the \spacefactor is set to 1000 after a \vrule in horizontal mode (see Chapter 19).

9.3.2 Ending a paragraph with leaders

An attempt to simulate an \hrule at the end of a paragraph by

```
\nobreak\leaders\hrule\hfill\par
```

does not work. The reason for this is that TeX performs an \unskip at the end of a paragraph, which removes the leaders. Normally this \unskip removes any space token inserted by the input processor after the last line. Remedy: stick an \hbox{} at the end of the leaders.

9.3.3 Leaders and box registers

In the above examples the leader box was inserted with \copy. The output of

```
\hbox to 8cm {here\leaders\box\centerdot\hfil there}
\hbox to 8cm {over here\leaders\box\centerdot\hfil
                    over there}
```

is

> here . . . . there
> over here   over there

The box register is emptied after the first leader command, but more than one copy is placed in that first command.

9.3.4 Output in leader boxes

Any \write, \openout, or \closeout operation appearing in leader boxes is ignored. Otherwise such an operation would be executed once for every copy of the box that would be shipped out.

9.3.5 Box leaders in trace output

The dumped box representation obtained from, for instance, \tracingoutput does not write out box leaders in full: only the total size and one copy of the box used are dumped. In particular, the surrounding white space before and after the leaders is not indicated.

9.3.6 Leaders and shifted margins

If margins have been shifted, leaders may look different depending on how the shift has been realized. For an illustration of how \hangindent and \leftskip influence the look of leaders, consider the following examples, where

```
\setbox0=\hbox{K o }
```

The horizontal boxes above the leaders serve to indicate the starting point of the row of leaders.
First

```
\hbox{\leaders\copy0\hskip5cm}
\noindent\advance\leftskip 1em
      \leaders\copy0\hskip5cm\hbox{}\par
```

gives

K o K o K o K o K o K o K o K o
 K o K o K o K o K o K o K o K o

Then

```
\hbox{\kern1em\hbox{\leaders\copy0\hskip5cm}}
\hangindent=1em \hangafter=-1 \noindent
      \leaders\copy0\hskip5cm\hbox{}\par
```

gives (note the shift with respect to the previous example)

 K o K o K o K o K o K o K o
K o K o K o K o K o K o K o

In the first paragraph the \leftskip glue only obscures the first leader box; in the second paragraph the hanging indentation actually shifts the orientation point for the row of leaders. Hanging indentation is performed in TEX by a \moveright of the boxes containing the lines of the paragraph.

CHAPTER 10

Grouping

TeX has a grouping mechanism that is able to confine most changes to a particular locality. This chapter explains what sort of actions can be local, and how groups are formed.

\bgroup   Implicit beginning of group character.
\egroup   Implicit end of group character.
\begingroup   Open a group that must be closed with \endgroup.
\endgroup   Close a group that was opened with \begingroup.
\aftergroup   Save the next token for insertion after the current group ends.
\global   Make assignments, macro definitions, and arithmetic global.
\globaldefs   Parameter for overriding \global prefixes. IniTeX default: 0.

10.1   THE GROUPING MECHANISM

A group is a sequence of tokens starting with a 'beginning of group' token, and ending with an 'end of group' token, and in which all such tokens are properly balanced.

The grouping mechanism of TeX is not the same as the block structure of ordinary programming languages. Most languages with block structure are only able to have local definitions. TeX's grouping mechanism is stronger: most assignments made inside a group are local to that group unless explicitly indicated otherwise, and outside the group old values are restored.

An example of local definitions

    {\def\a{b}}\a

gives an 'undefined control sequence' message because \a is only defined inside the group. Similarly, the code

    \count0=1 {\count0=2 } \showthe\count0

will display the value 1; the assignment made inside the group is undone at the end of the group.

Bookkeeping of values that are to be restored outside the group is done through the mechanism of the 'save stack'. Overflow of the save stack is treated in Chapter 35. The save stack is also used for a few other purposes: in calls such as

\hbox to 100pt{...} the specification to 100pt is put on the save stack before a new level of grouping is opened.

In order to prevent a lot of trouble with the save stack, IniTeX does not allow dumping a format inside a group. The \end command is allowed to occur inside a group, but TeX will give a diagnostic message about this.

The \aftergroup control sequence saves a token for insertion after the current group. Several tokens can be set aside by this command, and they are inserted in the left-to-right order in which they were stated. This is treated in Chapter 12.

10.2 LOCAL AND GLOBAL ASSIGNMENTS

An assignment or macro definition is usually made global by prefixing it with \global, but non-zero values of the ⟨integer parameter⟩ \globaldefs override \global specifications: if \globaldefs is positive every assignment is implicitly prefixed with \global, and if \globaldefs is negative, \global is ignored. Ordinarily this parameter is zero.

Some assignment are always global: the ⟨global assignment⟩s are

⟨font assignment⟩   assignments involving \fontdimen, \hyphenchar, and \skewchar.
⟨hyphenation assignment⟩   \hyphenation and \patterns commands (see Chapter 19).
⟨box size assignment⟩   altering box dimensions with \ht, \dp, and \wd (see Chapter 5).
⟨interaction mode assignment⟩   run modes for a TeX job (see Chapter 32).
⟨intimate assignment⟩   assignments to a ⟨special integer⟩ or ⟨special dimen⟩; see pages 65 and 72.

10.3 GROUP DELIMITERS

A group can be delimited by character tokens of category code 1 for 'beginning of group' and code 2 for 'end of group', or control sequence tokens that are \let to such characters, the \bgroup and \egroup in plain TeX. Implicit and explicit braces can match to delimit a group.

Groups can also be delimited by \begingroup and \endgroup. These two control sequences must be used together: they cannot be matched with implicit or explicit braces, nor can they function as the braces surrounding, for instance, boxed material.

Delimiting with \begingroup and \endgroup can provide a limited form of run-time error checking. In between these two group delimiters an excess open or close brace would result in

    \begingroup ... } ... \endgroup

or

    \begingroup ... { ... \endgroup

In both cases TeX gives an error message about improper balancing. Using
\bgroup and \egroup here would make an error much harder to find, because
of the incorrect matching that would occur. This idea is used in the environment
macros of several formats.

The choice of the brace characters for the beginning and end of group characters is not hard-wired in TeX. It is arranged like this in the plain format:

```
\catcode'\{=1 % left brace is begin-group character
\catcode'\}=2 % right brace is end-group character
```

Implicit braces have also been defined in the plain format:

```
\let\bgroup={ \let\egroup=}
```

Special cases are the following:

- The replacement text of a macro must be enclosed in explicit beginning and end of group character tokens.
- The open and close braces for boxes, \vadjust, and \insert can be implicit. This makes it possible to define, for instance

   ```
   \def\openbox#1{\setbox#1=\hbox\bgroup}
   \def\closebox#1{\egroup\box#1}
   \openbox{15}Foo bar\closebox{15}
   ```

- The right-hand side of a token list assignment and the argument of the commands \write, \message, \errmessage, \uppercase, \lowercase, \special, and \mark is a ⟨general text⟩, defined as

   ⟨general text⟩ ⟶ ⟨filler⟩{⟨balanced text⟩⟨right brace⟩

   meaning that the left brace can be implicit, but the closing right brace must be an explicit character token with category code 2.

In cases where an implicit left brace suffices, and where expansion is not explicitly inhibited, TeX will expand tokens until a left brace is encountered. This is the basis for such constructs as \uppercase\expandafter{\romannumeral80}, which in this unexpanded form do not adhere to the syntax. If the first unexpandable token is not a left brace TeX gives an error message.

The grammar of TeX (see Chapter 36) uses ⟨left brace⟩ and ⟨right brace⟩ for explicit characters, that is, character tokens, and { and } for possibly implicit characters, that is, control sequences that have been \let to such explicit characters.

10.4 MORE ABOUT BRACES

10.4.1 Brace counters

TeX has two counters for keeping track of grouping levels: the *master counter* and the *balance counter*. Both of these counters are syntactic counters: they count the explicit brace character tokens, but are not affected by implicit braces (such as \bgroup) that are semantically equivalent to an explicit brace.

The balance counter handles braces in all cases except in alignment. Its workings are intuitively clear: it goes up by one for every opening and down for every closing brace that is not being skipped. Thus

```
\iffalse{\fi
```

increases the balance counter if this statement is merely scanned (for instance if it appears in a macro definition text); if this statement is executed the brace is skipped, so there is no effect on the balance counter.

The master counter is more tricky; it is used in alignments instead of the balance counter. This counter records all braces, even when they are skipped such as in \iffalse{\fi. For this counter uncounted skipped braces are still possible: the alphabetic constants '{ and '} have no effect on this counter when they are use by the execution processor as a ⟨number⟩; they do affect this counter when they are seen by the input processor (which merely sees characters, and not the context).

10.4.2 The brace as a token

Explicit braces are character tokens, and as such they are unexpandable. This implies that they survive until the last stages of TeX processing. For example,

```
\count255=1{2}
```

will assign 1 to \count255, and print '2', because the opening brace functions as a delimiter for the number 1. Similarly

```
f{f}
```

will prevent TeX from forming an 'ff' ligature.

From the fact that braces are unexpandable, it follows that their nesting is independent of the nesting of conditionals. For instance

```
\iftrue{\else}\fi
```

will give an open brace, as conditionals are handled by expansion. The closing brace is simply skipped as part of the ⟨false text⟩; any consequences it has for grouping only come into play in a later stage of TeX processing.

Undelimited macro arguments are either single tokens or groups of tokens enclosed in explicit braces. Thus it is not possible for an explicit open or close brace to be a macro argument. However, braces can be assigned with \let, for instance as in

```
\let\bgroup={
```

This is used in the plain \footnote macro (see page 115).

10.4.3 \{ and \}

The control sequences \{ and \} do not really belong in this chapter, not being concerned with grouping. They have been defined with \let as synonyms of \lbrace and \rbrace respectively, and these control sequences are \delimiter instructions (see Chapter 21).

The Computer Modern Roman font has no braces, but there are braces in the typewriter font, and for mathematics there are braces of different sizes – and extendable ones – in the extension font.

CHAPTER 11

Macros

Macros are TeX's abbreviation mechanism for sequences of commands that are needed more than once, somewhat like procedures in ordinary programming languages. TeX's parameter mechanism, however, is quite unusual. This chapter explains how TeX macros work. It also treats the commands \let and \futurelet.

\def   Start a macro definition.
\gdef   Synonym for \global\def.
\edef   Start a macro definition; the replacement text is expanded at definition time. This command is treated also in the next chapter.
\xdef   Synonym for \global\edef.
\csname   Start forming the name of a control sequence.
\endcsname   Stop forming the name of a control sequence.
\global   Make the next definition, arithmetic statement, or assignment global.
\outer   Prefix indicating that the macro being defined can be used on the 'outer' level only.
\long   Prefix indicating that the arguments of the macro being defined may contain \par tokens.
\let   Define a control sequence to be equivalent to the next token.
\futurelet   Define a control sequence to be equivalent to the token after the next token.

11.1 INTRODUCTION

A macro is basically a sequence of tokens that has been abbreviated into a control sequence. Statements starting with (among others) \def are called *macro definitions*, and writing

```
\def\abc{\de f\g}
```

defines the macro \abc, with the *replacement text* \de f\g. Macros can be used in this way to abbreviate pieces of text or sequences of commands that have to be given more than once. Any time that TeX's expansion processor encounters the control sequence \abc, it replaces it by the replacement text.

If a macro should be sensitive to the context where it is used, it can be defined with parameters:

```
\def\PickTwo#1#2{(#1,#2)}
```

takes two arguments and reproduces them in parentheses. The call \PickTwo 12 gives '(1,2)'.

The activity of substituting the replacement text for a macro is called *macro expansion*.

11.2 LAYOUT OF A MACRO DEFINITION

A macro definition consists of, in sequence,

1. any number of \global, \long, and \outer prefixes,
2. a ⟨def⟩ control sequence, or anything that has been \let to one,
3. a control sequence or active character to be defined,
4. possibly a ⟨parameter text⟩ specifying among other things how many parameters the macro has, and
5. a replacement text enclosed in explicit character tokens with category codes 1 and 2, by default { and } in plain TeX.

The 'expanding' definitions \edef and \xdef are treated in Chapter 12.

11.3 PREFIXES

There are three prefixes that alter the status of the macro definition:

\global   If the definition occurs inside a group, this prefix makes the definition global. This prefix can also be used for assignments other than macro definitions; in fact, for macro definitions abbreviations exist obviating the use of \global:

> \gdef\foo...   is equivalent to   \global\def\foo...

and

> \xdef\foo...   is equivalent to   \global\edef\foo...

If the parameter \globaldefs is positive, all assignments are implicitly global; if \globaldefs is negative any \global prefixes are ignored, and \gdef and \xdef make local definitions (see Chapter 10).

\outer   The mechanism of 'outer' macros is supposed to facilitate locating (among other errors) unbalanced braces: an \outer macro is supposed to appear only in non-embedded contexts. To be precise, it is not allowed to occur

- in macro replacement texts (but it can appear in for instance \edef after \noexpand, and after \meaning),
- in parameter texts,
- in skipped conditional text,
- in alignment preambles, and

- in the ⟨balanced text⟩ of a \message, \write, et cetera.

For certain applications, however, it is inconvenient that some of the plain macros are outer, in particular macros such as \newskip. One remedy is to redefine them, without the 'outer' option, which is done for instance in L^AT_EX, but cleverer tricks are possible.

\long   Ordinarily, macro parameters are not supposed to contain \par tokens. This restriction is useful (much more so than the \outer definitions) in locating forgotten closing braces. For example, T_EX will complain about a 'runaway argument' in the following sequence:

```
\def\a#1{ ... #1 ... }
\a {This sentence should be in braces.

And this is not supposed to be part of the argument
```

The empty line generates a \par, which most of the times means that a closing brace has been forgotten.

If arguments to a particular macro should be allowed to contain \par tokens, then the macro must be declared to be \long.

The \ifx test for equality of tokens (see Chapter 13) takes prefixes into account when testing whether two tokens have the same definition.

11.4   THE DEFINITION TYPE

There are four ⟨def⟩ control sequences in T_EX: \def, \gdef, \edef, and \xdef. The control sequence \gdef is a synonym for \global\def and \xdef is a synonym for \global\edef. The 'expanding definition' \edef is treated in Chapter 12.

The difference between the various types of macro definitions is only relevant at the time of the definition. When a macro is called there is no way of telling how it was defined.

11.5   THE PARAMETER TEXT

Between the control sequence or active character to be defined and the opening brace of the replacement text, a ⟨parameter text⟩ can occur. This specifies whether the macro has parameters, how many, and how they are delimited. The ⟨parameter text⟩ cannot contain explicit braces.

A macro can have at most nine parameters. A parameter is indicated by a parameter token, consisting of a macro parameter character (that is, a character of category code 6, in plain T_EX #) followed by a digit 1–9. For instance, #6 denotes the sixth parameter of a macro. Parameter tokens cannot appear outside the context of a macro definition.

In the parameter text, parameters must be numbered consecutively, starting at 1. A space after a parameter token is significant, both in the parameter text and the replacement text.

Parameters can be delimited or undelimited. A parameter is called undelimited if it is followed immediately by another parameter in the ⟨parameter text⟩ or by the opening brace of the replacement text; it is called delimited if it is followed by any other token.

The tokens (zero or more) that are substituted for a parameter when a macro is expanded (or 'called') are called the 'argument' corresponding to that parameter.

11.5.1 Undelimited parameters

When a macro with an undelimited parameter, for instance a macro \foo with one parameter

    \def\foo#1{ ... #1 ...}

is expanded, TeX scans ahead (without expanding) until a non-blank token is found. If this token is not an explicit ⟨left brace⟩, it is taken to be the argument corresponding to the parameter. Otherwise a ⟨balanced text⟩ is absorbed by scanning until the matching explicit ⟨right brace⟩ has been found. This balanced text then constitutes the argument.

An example with three undelimited parameters follows: with

    \def\foo#1#2#3{#1(#2)#3}

the macro call \foo123 gives '1(2)3'; but \foo 1 2 3 also gives the same result. In the call

    \foo␣1␣2␣3

the first space is skipped in the input processor of TeX. The argument corresponding to the first parameter is then the 1. In order to find the second parameter TeX then skips all blanks, in this case exactly one. As second parameter TeX finds then the 2. Similarly the third parameter is 3.

In order to pass several tokens as one undelimited argument one can use braces. With the above definition of \foo the call \foo a{bc}d gives 'a(bc)d'. When the argument of a macro is a balanced text instead of a single token, the delimiting braces are not inserted when the argument is inserted in the replacement text. For example:

    \def\foo#1{\count0=1#1\relax}
    \foo{23}

will expand to \count0=123\relax, which assigns the value of 123 to the counter. On the other hand, the statement

    \count0=1{23}

would assign 1 and print 23.

11.5.2 Delimited parameters

Apart from enclosing it in braces there is another way to pass a sequence of tokens as a single argument to a macro, namely by using delimited parameters.

Any non-parameter tokens in the ⟨parameter text⟩ occurring after a macro parameter (that is, after the parameter number following the parameter character) act as a delimiter for that parameter. This includes space tokens: a space after a parameter number is significant. Delimiting tokens can also occur between the control sequence being defined and the first parameter token #1.

Character tokens acting as delimiters in the parameter text have both their character code and category code stored; the delimiting character tokens of the actual arguments have to match both. Category codes of such characters may include some that can normally only appear in special contexts; for instance, after the definition

```
\def\foo#1_#2^{...}
```

the macro \foo can be used outside math mode.

When looking for the argument corresponding to a delimited parameter, TeX absorbs all tokens without expansion (but balancing braces) until the (exact sequence of) delimiting tokens is encountered. The delimiting tokens are not part of the argument; they are removed from the input stream during the macro call.

11.5.3 Examples with delimited arguments

As a simple example,

```
\def\DoASentence#1#2.{{#1#2.}}
```

defines a macro with an undelimited first parameter, and a second parameter delimited by a period. In the call

```
\DoASentence \bf This sentence is the argument.
```

the arguments are:

```
#1<-\bf
#2<-This sentence is the argument
```

Note that the closing period is not in the argument, but it has been absorbed; it is no longer in the input stream.

A commonly used delimiter is \par:

```
\def\section#1. #2\par{\medskip\noindent {\bf#1. #2\par}}
```

This macro has a first parameter that is delimited by '.␣', and a second parameter that is delimited by \par. The call

```
\section 2.5. Some title

The text of the section...
```

will give

```
#1<-2.5
#2<-Some title␣
```

Note that there is a space at the end of the second argument generated by the line end. If this space is unwanted one might define

```
\def\section#1. #2 \par{...}
```

with ␣\par delimiting the second argument. This approach, however, precludes the user's writing the \par explicitly:

```
\section 2.5 Some title\par
```

One way out of this dilemma is to write #2\unskip on all places in the definition text where the trailing space would be unwanted.

Control sequences acting as delimiters need not be defined, as they are absorbed without expansion. Thus

```
\def\control#1\sequence{...}
```

is a useful definition, even if \sequence is undefined.

The importance of category codes in delimited arguments is shown by the following example:

```
\def\a#1 #2.{ ... }
\catcode'\ =12
\a b c
d.
```

which gives

```
\a #1 #2.-> ...
#1<- b c
#2<-d
```

Explanation: the delimiter between parameters 1 and 2 is a space of category 10. In between a and b there is a space of category 12; the first space of category 10 is the space that is generated by the line end.

For a 'real-life' application of matching of category codes, see the explanation of \newif in Chapter 13, and the example on page 15.

11.5.4 Empty arguments

If the user specifies a ⟨balanced text⟩ in braces when T_EX expects a macro argument, that text is used as the argument. Thus, specifying {} will give an argument that is an empty list of tokens; this is called an 'empty argument'.

Empty arguments can also arise from the use of delimited parameters. For example, after the definition

```
\def\mac#1\ro{ ... }
```

the call

```
\mac\ro
```

will give an empty argument.

11.5.5 The macro parameter character

When TeX's input processor scans a macro definition text, it inserts a parameter token for any occurrence of a macro parameter character followed by a digit. In effect, a parameter token in the replacement text states 'insert parameter number such and such here'. Two parameter characters in a row are replaced by a single one.
The latter fact can be used for nested macro definitions. Thus

```
\def\a{\def\b#1{...}}
```

gives an error message because \a was defined without parameters, and yet there is a parameter token in its replacement text.
The following

```
\def\a#1{\def\b#1{...}}
```

defines a macro \a that defines a macro \b. However, \b still does not have any parameters: the call

```
\a z
```

defines a macro \b without parameters, that has to be followed by a z. Note that this does not attempt to define a macro \bz, because the control sequence \b has already been formed in TeX's input processor when that input line was read.
Finally,

```
\def\a{\def\b##1{...}}
```

defines a macro \b with one parameter.
Let us examine the handling of the parameter character in some detail. Consider

```
\def\a#1{ .. #1 .. \def\b##1{ ... }}
```

When this is read as input, the input processor

- replaces the characters #1 by $\langle\text{parameter token}_1\rangle$, and
- replaces the characters ## by #

A macro call of \a will then let the input processor scan

```
\def\b#1{ ... }
```

in which the two characters #1 are replaced by a parameter token.

11.5.6 Brace delimiting

Ordinarily, it is not possible to have left or right braces in the ⟨parameter text⟩ of a definition. There is a special mechanism, however, that can make the last parameter of a macro act as if it is delimited by an opening brace.
If the last parameter token is followed by a parameter character (#), which in turn is followed by the opening brace of the replacement text, TeX makes the last

parameter be delimited by a beginning-of-group character. Furthermore, unlike other delimiting tokens in parameter texts, this opening brace is not removed from the input stream.

Consider an example. Suppose we want to have a macro `\every` that can fill token lists as follows:

```
\every par{abc} \every display{def}
```

This macro can be defined as

```
\def\every#1#{\csname every#1\endcsname}
```

In the first call above, the argument corresponding to the parameter is abc, so the call expands to

```
\csname everypar\endcsname{abc}
```

which gives the desired result.

11.6 CONSTRUCTION OF CONTROL SEQUENCES

The commands `\csname` and `\endcsname` can be used to construct a control sequence. For instance

```
\csname hskip\endcsname 5pt
```

is equivalent to `\hskip5pt`.

During this construction process all macros and other expandable control sequences between `\csname` and `\endcsname` are expanded as usual, until only unexpandable character tokens remain. A variation of the above example,

```
\csname \ifhmode h\else v\fi skip\endcsname 5pt
```

performs an `\hskip` or `\vskip` depending on the mode. The final result of the expansion should consist of only character tokens, but their category codes do not matter. An unexpandable control sequence gives an error here: TeX will insert an `\endcsname` right before it as an attempt at error recovery.

With `\csname` it is possible to construct control sequences that cannot ordinarily be written, because the constituent character tokens may have another category than 11, letter. This principle can be used to hide inner control sequences of a macro package from the user.

Example

```
\def\newcounter#1{\expandafter\newcount
    \csname #1:counter\endcsname}
\def\stepcounter#1{\expandafter\advance
    \csname #1:counter\endcsname 1\relax}
```

In the second definition the `\expandafter` is superfluous, but it does no harm, and it is conceptually clearer.

The name of the actual counter created by \newcounter contains a colon, so that it takes some effort to write this control sequence. In effect, the counter is now hidden from the user, who can only access it through control sequences such as \stepcounter. By the way, the macro \newcount is defined \outer in the plain format, so the above definition of \newcounter can only be written after \newcount has been redefined.

If a control sequence formed with \csname...\endcsname has not been defined before, its meaning is set to \relax. Thus if \xx is an undefined control sequence, the command

```
\csname xx\endcsname
```

will *not* give an error message, as it is equivalent to \relax. Moreover, after this execution of the \csname...\endcsname statement, the control sequence \xx is itself equivalent to \relax, so it will no longer give an 'undefined control sequence' error (see also page 118).

11.7 TOKEN ASSIGNMENTS BY \let AND \futurelet

There are two ⟨let assignment⟩s in TeX. Their syntax is

\let⟨control sequence⟩⟨equals⟩⟨one optional space⟩⟨token⟩
\futurelet⟨control sequence⟩⟨token⟩⟨token⟩

In the syntax of a \futurelet assignment no optional equals sign appears.

11.7.1 \let

The primitive command \let assigns the current meaning of a token to a control sequence or active character.

For instance, in the plain format \endgraf is defined as

```
\let\endgraf=\par
```

This enables macro writers to redefine \par, while still having the functionality of the primitive \par command available. For example,

```
\everypar={\bgroup\it\def\par{\endgraf\egroup}}
```

The case where the ⟨token⟩ to be assigned is not a control sequence but a character token instead has been treated in Chapter 3.

11.7.2 \futurelet

As was explained above, the sequence with \let

\let⟨control sequence⟩⟨token$_1$⟩⟨token$_2$⟩⟨token$_3$⟩⟨token···⟩

assigns (the meaning of) ⟨token$_1$⟩ to the control sequence, and the remaining input stream looks like

⟨token$_2$⟩⟨token$_3$⟩⟨token···⟩

That is, the ⟨token₁⟩ has disappeared from the stream.

The command `\futurelet` works slightly differently: given the input stream

`\futurelet`⟨control sequence⟩⟨token₁⟩⟨token₂⟩⟨token₃⟩⟨token···⟩

it assigns (the meaning of) ⟨token₂⟩ to the control sequence, and the remaining stream looks like

⟨token₁⟩⟨token₂⟩⟨token₃⟩⟨token···⟩

That is, neither ⟨token₁⟩ nor ⟨token₂⟩ has been lifted from the stream. However, now ⟨token₁⟩ 'knows' what ⟨token₂⟩ is, without having had to absorb it as a macro parameter. See an example below.

If a character token has been `\futurelet` to a control sequence, its category code is fixed. The subsequent ⟨token₁⟩ cannot change it anymore.

11.8 ASSORTED REMARKS

11.8.1 Active characters

Character tokens of category 13, 'active characters', can be defined just like control sequences. If the definition of the character appears inside a macro, the character has to be active at the time of the definition of that macro.

Consider for example the following definition (taken from Chapter 2):

```
{\catcode`\^^M=13 %
 \gdef\obeylines{\catcode`\^^M=13 \def^^M{\par}}%
}
```

The unusual category of the `^^M` character has to be set during the definition of `\obeylines`, otherwise TEX would think that the line ended after `\def`.

11.8.2 Macros versus primitives

The distinction between primitive commands and user macros is not nearly as important in TEX as it is in other programming languages.

- The user can use primitive commands under different names:

    `\let\StopThisParagraph=\par`

- Names of primitive commands can be used for user macros:

    `\def\par{\hfill$\bullet$\endgraf}`

- Both user macros and a number of TEX primitives are subject to expansion, for instance all conditionals, and commands such as `\number` and `\jobname`.

11.8.3 Tail recursion

Macros in TEX, like procedures in most modern programming languages, are allowed to be recursive: that is, the definition of a macro can contain a call to this same macro, or to another macro that will call this macro. Recursive macros tend to clutter up TeX's memory if too many 'incarnations' of such a macro are active at the same time. However, TeX is able to prevent this in one frequently occurring case of recursion: tail recursion.

In order to appreciate what goes on here, some background knowledge is needed. When TeX starts executing a macro it absorbs the parameters, and places an item pointing to the replacement text on the input stack, so that the scanner will next be directed to this replacement. Once it has been processed, the item on the input stack can be removed. However, if the definition text of a macro contains further macros, this process will be repeated for them: new items may be placed on the input stack directing the scanner to other macros even before the first one has been completed.

In general this 'stack build-up' is a necessary evil, but it can be prevented if the nested macro call is the *last* token in the replacement text of the original macro. After the last token no further tokens need to be considered, so one might as well clear the the top item from the input stack before a new one is put there. This is what TeX does.

The \loop macro of plain TeX provides a good illustration of this principle. The definition is

```
\def\loop#1\repeat{\def\body{#1}\iterate}
\def\iterate{\body \let\next=\iterate
    \else \let\next=\relax\fi \next}
```

and this macro can be called for example as follows:

```
\loop \message{\number\MyCount}
    \advance\MyCount by 1
    \ifnum\MyCount<100 \repeat
```

The macro \iterate can call itself and, when it does so, the recursive call is performed by the last token in the list. It would have been possible to define \iterate as

```
\def\iterate{\body \iterate\fi}
```

but then TeX would not have been able to resolve the recursion as the call \iterate is not the last token in the replacement text of \iterate. Assigning \let\next=\iterate is here a way to let the recursive call be the last token in the list.

Another way of resolving tail recursion is to use \expandafter (see page 134): in

```
\def\iterate{\body \expandafter\iterate\fi}
```

it removes the \fi token. Tail recursion would also be resolved if the last tokens in the list were arguments for the recursive macro.

An aside: by defining \iterate as

```
\def\iterate{\let\next\relax
    \body \let\next\iterate \fi \next}
```

it becomes possible to write

```
\loop ... \if... ... \else ... \repeat
```

11.9 MACRO TECHNIQUES

11.9.1 Unknown number of arguments

In some applications, a macro is needed that can have a number of arguments that is not specified in advance.

Consider the problem of translating a position on a chess board (for full macros and fonts, see Rubinstein (1989) and Tutelaers (1991)), given like

```
\White(Ke1,Qd1,Na1,e2,f4)
```

to a sequence of typesetting instructions

```
\WhitePiece{K}{e1} \WhitePiece{Q}{d1} \WhitePiece{N}{a1}
\WhitePiece{P}{e2} \WhitePiece{P}{f4}
```

Note that for pawns the 'P' is omitted in the list of positions.

The first problem is that the list of pieces is of variable length, so we append a terminator piece:

```
\def\White(#1){\xWhite#1,xxx,}
\def\endpiece{xxx}
```

for which we can test. Next, the macro \xWhite takes one position from the list, tests whether it is the terminator, and if not, subjects it to a test to see whether it is a pawn.

```
\def\xWhite#1,{\def\temp{#1}%
    \ifx\temp\endpiece
    \else \WhitePieceOrPawn#1XY%
         \expandafter\xWhite
    \fi}
```

An \expandafter command is necessary to remove the \fi (see page 134), so that \xWhite will get the next position as argument instead of \fi.

Positions are either two or three characters long. The call to \WhitePieceOrPawn, a four-parameter macro, appended a terminator string XY. In the case of a pawn, therefore, argument 3 is the character X and argument 4 is empty; for all other pieces argument 1 is the piece, 2 and 3 are the position, and argument 4 is X.

```
\def\WhitePieceOrPawn#1#2#3#4Y{
    \if#3X \WhitePiece{P}{#1#2}%
    \else  \WhitePiece{#1}{#2#3}\fi}
```

11.9.2 Examining the argument

It may be necessary in some cases to test whether a macro argument contains some element. For a real-life example, consider the following (see also the \DisplayEquation example on page 204).

Suppose the title and author of an article are given as

```
\title{An angle trisector}
\author{A.B. Cee\footnote*{Research supported by the
Very Big Company of America}}
```

with multiple authors given as

```
\author{A.B. Cee\footnote*{Supported by NSF grant 1}
     \and
     X.Y. Zee\footnote{**}{Supported by NATO grant 2}}
```

Suppose further that the \title and \author macros are defined as

```
\def\title#1{\def\TheTitle{#1}}   \def\author#1{\def\TheAuthor{#1}}
```

which will be used as

```
\def\ArticleHeading{ ... \TheTitle ... \TheAuthor ... }
```

For some journals it is required to have the authorship and the title of the article in all capitals. The implementation of this could be

```
\def\ArticleCapitalHeading
   { ...
    \uppercase\expandafter{\TheTitle}
     ...
    \uppercase\expandafter{\TheAuthor}
     ...
   }
```

Now the \expandafter commands will expand the title and author into the actual texts, and the \uppercase commands will capitalize them. However, for the authors this is wrong, since the \uppercase command will also capitalize the footnote texts. The problem is then to uppercase only the parts of the title in between the footnotes.

As a first attempt, let us take the case of one author, and let the basic call be

```
\expandafter\UCnoFootnote\TheAuthor
```

This expands into

```
\UCnoFootnote A.B. Cee\footnote*{Supported ... }
```

The macro

```
\def\UCnoFootnote#1\footnote#2#3{\uppercase{#1}\footnote{#2}{#3}}
```

will analyse this correctly:

```
#1<-A.B. Cee
```

```
#2<-*
#3<-Supported ...
```

However, if there is no footnote, this macro is completely wrong.

As a first refinement we add a footnote ourselves, just to make sure that one is present:

```
\expandafter\UCnoFootnote\TheAuthor\footnote 00
```

Now we have to test what kind of footnote we find:

```
\def\stopper{0}
\def\UCnoFootnote#1\footnote#2#3{\uppercase{#1}\def\tester{#2}%
    \ifx\stopper\tester
    \else\footnote{#2}{#3}\fi}
```

With \ifx we test the delimiter footnote sign against the actual sign encountered. Note that a solution with

```
\ifx0#2
```

would be wrong if the footnote sign consists of more than one token, for instance {**}.

The macro so far is correct if there was no footnote, but if there was one it is wrong: the terminating tokens remain to be disposed of. They are taken care of in the following version:

```
\def\stopper{0}
\def\UCnoFootnote#1\footnote#2#3{\uppercase{#1}\def\tester{#2}%
    \ifx\stopper\tester
    \else\footnote{#2}{#3}\expandafter\UCnoFootnote
    \fi}
```

A repeated call to \UCnoFootnote removes the delimiter tokens (the \expandafter first removes the \fi), and as an added bonus, this macro is also correct for multiple authors.

11.9.3 Optional macro parameters with \futurelet

One standard application of \futurelet is implementing optional parameters of macros. The general course of action is as follows:

```
\def\Com{\futurelet\testchar\MaybeOptArgCom}
\def\MaybeOptArgCom{\ifx[\testchar \let\next\OptArgCom
              \else \let\next\NoOptArgCom \fi \next}
\def\OptArgCom[#1]#2{ ... }\def\NoOptArgCom#1{ ... }
```

Note that \ifx is used even though it tests for a character. The reason is of course that, if the optional argument is omitted, there might be an expandable control sequence behind the \Com.

The macro \Com now has one optional and one regular argument; it can be called as

\Com{argument}

or as

\Com[optional]{argument}

Often the call without the optional argument will insert some default value:

\def\NoOptArgCom#1{\OptArgCom[*default*]{#1}}

This mechanism is widely used in formats such as LaTeX and LAMS-TeX; see also von Bechtolsheim (1988).

11.9.4 Two-step macros

Often what looks to the user like one macro is in reality a two-step process, where one macro will set up conditions, and a second macro will do the work.

As an example, here is a macro \PickToEol with an argument that is delimited by the line end. First we write a macro without arguments, that changes the category code of the line end, and then calls the second macro.

\def\PickToEol{\begingroup\catcode`\^^M=12 \xPickToEol}

The second macro can then take as an argument everything up to the end of the line:

\def\xPickToEol#1^^M{ ... #1 ... \endgroup}

There is one problem with this definition: the ^^M character should have category 12. We arrive at the following:

```
\def\PickToEol{\begingroup\catcode`\^^M=12 \xPickToEol}
{\catcode`\^^M=12 %
 \gdef\xPickToEol#1^^M{ ... #1 ... \endgroup}%
}
```

where the category code of ^^M is changed for the sake of the definition of \xPickToEol. Note that the ^^M in \PickToEol occurs in a control symbol, so there the category code is irrelevant. Therefore that definition can be outside the group where the category code of ^^M is redefined.

11.9.5 A comment environment

As an application of the above idea of two-step macros, and in order to illustrate tail recursion, here are macros for a 'comment' environment.

Often it is necessary to remove a part of TeX input temporarily. For this one would like to write

\comment

```
...
\endcomment
```

The simplest implementation of this,

```
\def\comment#1\endcomment{}
```

has a number of weaknesses. For instance, it cannot cope with outer macros or input that does not have balanced braces. Its worst shortcoming, however, is that it reads the complete comment text as a macro argument. This limits the size of the comment to that of TeX's input buffer.

It would be a better idea to take on the out-commented text one line at a time. For this we want to write a recursive macro with a basic structure

```
\def\comment#1^^M{ ... \comment }
```

In order to be able to write this definition at all, the category code of the line end must be changed; as above we will have

```
\def\comment{\begingroup \catcode`\^^M=12 \xcomment}
{\catcode`\^^M=12 \endlinechar=-1 %
 \gdef\xcomment#1^^M{ ... \xcomment}
}
```

Changing the \endlinechar is merely to prevent having to put comment characters at the end of every line of the definition.

Of course, the process must stop at a certain time. To this purpose we investigate the line that was scooped up as macro argument:

```
{\catcode`\^^M=12 \endlinechar=-1 %
 \gdef\xcomment#1^^M{\def\test{#1}
    \ifx\test\endcomment \let\next=\endgroup
    \else \let\next=\xcomment \fi
    \next}
}
```

and we have to define \endcomment:

```
\def\endcomment{\endcomment}
```

This command will never be executed: it is merely for purposes of testing whether the end of the environment has been reached.

We may want to comment out text that is not syntactically correct. Therefore we switch to a verbatim mode when commenting. The following macro is given in plain TeX:

```
\def\dospecials{\do\ \do\\\do\{\do\}\do\$\do\&%
   \do\#\do\^\do\^^K\do\_\do\^^A\do\%\do\~}
```

We use it to define \comment as follows:

```
\def\makeinnocent#1{\catcode`#1=12 }
\def\comment{\begingroup
```

```
\let\do=\makeinnocent \dospecials
\endlinechar`\^^M \catcode`\^^M=12 \xcomment}
```

Apart from the possibility mentioned above of commenting out text that is not syntactically correct, for instance because of unmatched braces, this solution can handle outer macros. The former implementation of \xcomment would cause a TeX error if one occurred in the comment text.

However, using verbatim mode poses the problem of concluding the environment. The final line of the comment is now not the control sequence \endcomment, but the characters constituting it. We have to test for these then:

```
{\escapechar=-1
 \xdef\endcomment{\string\\endcomment}
}
```

The sequence \string\\ gives a backslash. We could not have used

```
\edef\endcomment{\string\endcomment}
```

because the letters of the word endcomment would then have category code 12, instead of the 11 that the ones on the last line of the comment will have.

CHAPTER 12

Expansion

Expansion in TeX is rather different from procedure calls in most programming languages. This chapter treats the commands connected with expansion, and gives a number of (non-trivial) examples.

\relax   Do nothing.
\expandafter   Take the next two tokens and place the expansion of the second after the first.
\noexpand   Do not expand the next token.
\edef   Start a macro definition; the replacement text is expanded at definition time.
\aftergroup   Save the next token for insertion after the current group.
\afterassignment   Save the next token for execution after the next assignment.
\the   Expand the value of various quantities in TeX into a string of character tokens.

12.1 INTRODUCTION

TeX's expansion processor accepts a stream of tokens coming out of the input processor, and its result is again a stream of tokens, which it feeds to the execution processor. For the input processor there are two kinds of tokens: expandable and unexpandable ones. The latter category is passed untouched, and it contains largely assignments and typesettable material; the former category is expanded, and the result of that expansion is examined anew.

12.2 ORDINARY EXPANSION

The following list gives those constructs that are expanded, unless expansion is inhibited:

- macros
- conditionals
- \number, \romannumeral
- \string, \fontname, \jobname, \meaning, \the

- \csname ... \endcsname
- \expandafter, \noexpand
- \topmark, \botmark, \firstmark, \splitfirstmark, \splitbotmark
- \input, \endinput

This is the list of all instances where expansion is inhibited:

- when TeX is reading a token to be defined by
  - a ⟨let assignment⟩, that is, by \let or \futurelet,
  - a ⟨shorthand definition⟩, that is, by \chardef or \mathchardef, or a ⟨register def⟩, that is, \countdef, \dimendef, \skipdef, \muskipdef, or \toksdef,
  - a ⟨definition⟩, that is a macro definition with \def, \gdef, \edef, or \xdef,
  - the ⟨simple assignment⟩s \read and \font;
- when a ⟨parameter text⟩ or macro arguments are being read; also when the replacement text of a control sequence being defined by \def, \gdef, or \read is being read;
- when the token list for a ⟨token variable⟩ or \uppercase, \lowercase, or \write is being read; however, the token list for \write will be expanded later when it is shipped out;
- when tokens are being deleted during error recovery;
- when part of a conditional is being skipped;
- in two instances when TeX has to know what follows
  - after a left quote in a context where that is used to denote an integer (thus in \catcode`\a the \a is not expanded), or
  - after a math shift character that begins math mode to see whether another math shift character follows (in which case a display opens);
- when an alignment preamble is being scanned; however, in this case a token preceded by \span and the tokens in a \tabskip assignment are still expanded.

12.3   REVERSING EXPANSION ORDER

Every once in a while you need to change the normal order of expansion of tokens. TeX provides several mechanisms for this. Some of the control sequences in this section are not strictly concerned with expansion.

12.3.1   One step expansion: \expandafter

The most obvious tool for reversed expansion order is \expandafter. The sequence

   \expandafter⟨token$_1$⟩⟨token$_2$⟩

expands to

⟨token₁⟩⟨*the expansion of token₂*⟩

Note the following.

- If ⟨token₂⟩ is a macro, it is replaced by its replacement text, not by its final expansion. Thus, if

    ```
    \def\tokentwo{\ifsomecondition this \else that \fi}
    \def\tokenone#1{ ... }
    ```

    the call

    ```
    \expandafter\tokenone\tokentwo
    ```

    will give \ifsomecondition as the parameter to \tokenone:

    ```
    \tokenone #1-> ...
    #1<-\ifsomecondition
    ```

- If the \tokentwo is a macro with one or more parameters, sufficiently many subsequent tokens will be absorbed to form the replacement text.

12.3.2 Total expansion: \edef

Macros are usually defined by \def, but for the cases where one wants the replacement text to reflect current conditions (as opposed to conditions at the time of the call), there is an 'expanding define', \edef, which expands everything in the replacement text, before assigning it to the control sequence.

Example

```
\edef\modedef{This macro was defined in
    '\ifhmode vertical\else \ifmmode math
    \else horizontal\fi' mode}
```

The mode tests will be executed at definition time, so the replacement text will be a single string.

As a more useful example, suppose that in a file that will be \input the category code of the @ will be changed. One could then write

```
\edef\restorecat{\catcode'@=\the\catcode'@}
```

at the start, and

```
\restorecat
```

at the end. See page 124 for a fully worked-out version of this.

Contrary to the 'one step expansion' of \expandafter, the expansion inside an \edef is complete: it goes on until only unexpandable character and control sequence tokens remain. There are two exceptions to this total expansion:

- any control sequence preceded by \noexpand is not expanded, and,

- if \sometokenlist is a token list, the expression

    \the\sometokenlist

is expanded to the contents of the list, but the contents are not expanded any further (see Chapter 14 for examples).

On certain occasions the \edef can conveniently be abused, in the sense that one is not interested in defining a control sequence, but only in the result of the expansion. For example, with the definitions

```
\def\othermacro{\ifnum1>0 {this}\else {that}\fi}
\def\somemacro#1{ ... }
```

the call

```
\expandafter\somemacro\othermacro
```

gives the parameter assignment

```
#1<-\ifnum
```

This can be repaired by calling

```
\edef\next{\noexpand\somemacro\othermacro}\next
```

Conditionals are completely expanded inside an \edef, so the replacement text of \next will consist of the sequence

```
\somemacro{this}
```

and a subsequent call to \next executes this statement.

12.3.3 \afterassignment

The \afterassignment command takes one token and sets it aside for insertion in the token stream after the next assignment or macro definition. If the first assignment is of a box to a box register, the token will be inserted right after the opening brace of the box (see page 48).

Only one token can be saved this way; a subsequent token saved by \afterassignment will override the first.

Let us consider an example of the use of \afterassignment. It is often desirable to have a macro that will

- assign the argument to some variable, and then
- do a little calculation, based on the new value of the variable.

The following example illustrates the straightforward approach:

```
\def\setfontsize#1{\thefontsize=#1pt\relax
    \baselineskip=1.2\thefontsize\relax}
\setfontsize{10}
```

A more elegant solution is possible using \afterassignment:

```
\def\setbaselineskip
```

```
        {\baselineskip=1.2\thefontsize\relax}
\def\fontsize{\afterassignment\setbaselineskip
    \thefontsize}
\fontsize=10pt
```

Now the macro looks like an assignment: the equals sign is even optional. In reality its expansion ends with a variable to be assigned to. The control sequence `\setbaselineskip` is saved for execution after the assignment to `\thefontsize`.

Examples of `\afterassignment` in plain TeX are the `\magnification` and `\hglue` macros. See Maus (1990) for another creative application of this command.

12.3.4 \aftergroup

Several tokens can be saved for insertion after the current group with an

> `\aftergroup`⟨token⟩

command. The tokens are inserted after the group in the sequence the `\aftergroup` commands were given in. The group can be delimited either by implicit or explicit braces, or by `\begingroup` and `\endgroup`.

Example

```
    {\aftergroup\a \aftergroup\b}
```

is equivalent to

```
    \a \b
```

This command has many applications. One can be found in the `\textvcenter` macro on page 126; another one is provided by the footnote mechanism of plain TeX.

The footnote command of plain TeX has the layout

> `\footnote`⟨footnote symbol⟩`{`⟨footnote text⟩`}`

which looks like a macro with two arguments. However, it is undesirable to scoop up the footnote text, since this precludes for instance category code changes in the footnote.

What happens in the plain footnote macro is (globally) the following.

- The `\footnote` command opens an insert,

  ```
  \def\footnote#1{ ...#1... %treat the footnote sign
      \insert\footins\bgroup
  ```

- In the insert box a group is opened, and an `\aftergroup` command is given to close off the insert properly:

  ```
  \bgroup\aftergroup\@foot
  ```

  This command is meant to wind up after the closing brace of the text that the user typed to end the footnote text; the opening brace of the user's footnote text must be removed by

  ```
  \let\next=}%end of definition \footnote
  ```

which assigns the next token, the brace, to \next.
- The footnote text is set as ordinary text in this insert box.
- After the footnote the command \@foot defined by

    \def\@foot{\strut\egroup}

will be executed.

12.4 PREVENTING EXPANSION

Sometimes it is necessary to prevent expansion in a place where it normally occurs. For this purpose the control sequences \string and \noexpand are available.

The use of \string is rather limited, since it converts a control sequence token into a string of characters, with the value of \escapechar used for the character of category code 0. It is eminently suitable for use in a \write, in order to output a control sequence name (see also Chapter 30); for another application see the explanation of \newif in Chapter 13.

All characters resulting from \string have category code 12, 'other', except for space characters; they receive code 10. See also Chapter 3.

12.4.1 \noexpand

The \noexpand command is expandable, and its expansion is the following token. The meaning of that token is made temporarily equal to \relax, so that it cannot be expanded further.

For \noexpand the most important application is probably in \edef commands (but in write statements it can often replace \string). Consider as an example

    \edef\one{\def\noexpand\two{\the\prevdepth}}

Without the \noexpand, TeX would try to expand \two, thus giving an 'undefined control sequence' error.

A (rather pointless) illustration of the fact that \noexpand makes the following token effectively into a \relax is

    \def\a{b}
    \noexpand\a

This will not produce any output, because the effect of the \noexpand is to make the control sequence \a temporarily equal to \relax.

12.4.2 \noexpand and active characters

The combination \noexpand⟨token⟩ is equivalent to \relax, even if the token is an active character. Thus,

    \csname\noexpand~\endcsname

will not be the same as \char'\~. Instead it will give an error message, because unexpandable commands – such as \relax – are not allowed to appear in between \csname and \endcsname. The solution is to use \string instead; see page 124 for an example.

In another context, however, the sequence \noexpand⟨active character⟩ is equivalent to the character, but in unexpandable form. This is when the conditionals \if and \ifcat are used (for an explanation of these, see Chapter 13). Compare

```
\if\noexpand~\relax % is false
```

where the character code of the tilde is tested, with

```
\def\a{ ... } \if\noexpand\a\relax % is true
```

where two control sequences are tested.

12.5 \relax

The control sequence \relax cannot be expanded, but when it is executed nothing happens.

This statement sounds a bit paradoxical, so consider an example. Let counters

```
\newcount\MyCount
\newcount\MyOtherCount  \MyOtherCount=2
```

be given. In the assignment

```
\MyCount=1\number\MyOtherCount3\relax4
```

the command \number is expandable, and \relax is not. When TeX constructs the number that is to be assigned it will expand all commands, either until a non-digit is found, or until an unexpandable command is encountered. Thus it reads the 1; it expands the sequence \number\MyOtherCount, which gives 2; it reads the 3; it sees the \relax, and as this is unexpandable it halts. The number to be assigned is then 123, and the whole call has been expanded into

```
\MyCount=123\relax4
```

Since the \relax token has no effect when it is executed, the result of this line is that 123 is assigned to \MyCount, and the digit 4 is printed.

Another example of how \relax can be used to indicate the end of a command is

```
\everypar{\hskip 0cm plus 1fil }
\indent Later that day, ...
```

This will be misunderstood: TeX will see

```
\hskip 0cm plus 1fil L
```

and fil L is a valid, if bizarre, way of writing fill (see Chapter 36). One remedy is to write

```
\everypar{\hskip 0cm plus 1fil\relax}
```

12.5.1 \relax and \csname

If a \csname ... \endcsname command forms the name of a previously undefined control sequence, that control sequence is made equal to \relax, and the whole statement is also equivalent to \relax (see also page 101).

However, this assignment of \relax is only local:

```
{\xdef\test{\expandafter\noexpand\csname xx\endcsname}}
\test
```

gives an error message for an undefined control sequence \xx.

Consider as an example the LaTeX environments, which are delimited by

```
\begin{...} ... \end{...}
```

The begin and end commands are (in essence) defined as follows:

```
\def\begin#1{\begingroup\csname#1\endcsname}
\def\end#1{\csname end#1\endcsname \endgroup}
```

Thus, for the list environment the commands \list and \endlist are defined, but any command can be used as an environment name, even if no corresponding \end... has been defined. For instance,

```
\begin{it} ... \end{it}
```

is equivalent to

```
\begingroup\it ... \relax\endgroup
```

See page 90 for the rationale behind using \begingroup and \endgroup instead of \bgroup and \egroup.

12.5.2 Preventing expansion with \relax

Because \relax cannot be expanded, a control sequence can be prevented from being expanded (for instance in an \edef or a \write) by making it temporarily equal to \relax:

```
{\let\somemacro=\relax \write\outfile{\somemacro}}
```

will write the string '\somemacro' to an output file. It would write the expansion of the macro \somemacro (or give an error message if the macro is undefined) if the \let statement had been omitted.

12.5.3 TeX inserts a \relax

TeX itself inserts \relax on some occasions. For instance, \relax is inserted if TeX encounters an \or, \else, or \fi while still determining the extent of the test.

Example

```
\ifvoid1\else ... \fi
```

is changed into

>   \ifvoid1\relax \else ...\fi

internally.

Similarly, if one of the tests \if, \ifcat is given only one comparand, as in

>   \if1\else ...

a \relax token is inserted. Thus this test is equivalent to

>   \if1\relax\else ...

Another place where \relax is used is the following. While a control sequence is being defined in a ⟨shorthand definition⟩ – that is, a ⟨registerdef⟩ or \chardef or \mathchardef – its meaning is temporarily made equal to \relax. This makes it possible to write \chardef\foo=123\foo.

12.5.4 The value of non-macros; \the

Expansion is a precisely defined activity in TeX. The full list of tokens that can be expanded was given above. Other tokens than those in the above list may have an 'expansion' in an informal sense. For instance one may wish to 'expand' the \parindent into its value, say 20pt.

Converting the value of (among others) an ⟨integer parameter⟩, a ⟨glue parameter⟩, ⟨dimen parameter⟩ or a ⟨token parameter⟩ into a string of character tokens is done by the expansion processor. The command \the is expanded whenever expansion is not inhibited, and it takes the value of various sorts of parameters. Its result (in most cases) is a string of tokens of category 12, except that spaces have category code 10.

Here is the list of everything that can be prefixed with \the.

⟨parameter⟩ *or* ⟨register⟩   If the parameter or register is of type integer, glue, dimen or muglue, its value is given as a string of character tokens; if it is of type token list (for instance \everypar or \toks5), the result is a string of tokens. Box registers are excluded here.

⟨codename⟩⟨8-bit number⟩   See page 31.

⟨special register⟩   The integer registers \prevgraf, \deadcycles, \insertpenalties \inputlineno, \badness, \parshape, \spacefactor (only in horizontal mode), or \prevdepth (only in vertical mode). The dimension registers \pagetotal, \pagegoal, \pagestretch, \pagefilstretch, \pagefillstretch, \pagefilllstretch, \pageshrink, or \pagedepth.

Font properties: \fontdimen⟨parameter number⟩⟨font⟩, \skewchar⟨font⟩, \hyphenchar⟨font⟩.

Last quantities: \lastpenalty, \lastkern, \lastskip.

⟨defined character⟩   Any control sequence defined by \chardef or \mathchardef; the result is the decimal value.

In some cases \the can give a control sequence token or list of such tokens.

⟨font⟩   The result is the control sequence that stands for the font.

⟨token variable⟩   Token list registers and ⟨token parameter⟩s can be prefixed with \the; the result is their contents.

Let us consider an example of the use of \the. If in a file that is to be \input the category code of a character, say the at sign, is changed, one could write

```
\edef\restorecat{\catcode`@=\the\catcode`@}
```

and call \restorecat at the end of the file. If the category code was 11, \restorecat is defined equivalent to

```
\catcode`@=11
```

See page 124 for more elaborate macros for saving and restoring catcodes.

12.6 EXAMPLES

12.6.1 Expanding after

The most obvious use of \expandafter is to reach over a control sequence:

```
\def\stepcounter
    #1{\expandafter\advance\csname
            #1:counter\endcsname 1\relax}
\stepcounter{foo}
```

Here the \expandafter lets the \csname command form the control sequence \foo:counter; after \expandafter is finished the statement has reduced to

```
\advance\foo:counter 1\relax
```

It is possible to reach over tokens other than control sequences: in

```
\uppercase\expandafter{\romannumeral \year}
```

it expands \romannumeral on the other side of the opening brace.

You can expand after two control sequences:

```
\def\globalstepcounter
    #1{\expandafter\global\expandafter\advance
            \csname #1:counter\endcsname 1\relax}
```

If you think of \expandafter as reversing the evaluation order of *two* control sequences, you can reverse *three* by

```
\expandafter\expandafter\expandafter\a\expandafter\b\c
```

which reaches across the three control sequences

$$\texttt{\textbackslash expandafter} \qquad \texttt{\textbackslash a} \qquad \texttt{\textbackslash b}$$

to expand \c first.

There is even an unexpected use for \expandafter in conditionals; with

```
\def\bold#1{{\bf #1}}
```

the sequence

```
\ifnum1>0 \bold \fi {word}
```

will not give a boldface 'word', but

```
\ifnum1>0 \expandafter\bold \fi {word}
```

will. The \expandafter lets TeX see the \fi and remove it before it tackles the macro \bold (see also page 134).

12.6.2 Defining inside an \edef

There is one TeX command that is executed instead of expanded that is worth pointing out explicitly: the primitive command \def (and all other ⟨def⟩ commands) is not expanded.
    Thus the call

```
\edef\next{\def\thing{text}}
```

will give an 'undefined control sequence' for \thing, even though after \def expansion is ordinarily inhibited (see page 112). After

```
\edef\next{\def\noexpand\thing{text}}
```

the 'meaning' of \next will be

```
macro: \def \thing {text}
```

The definition

```
\edef\next{\def\noexpand\thing{text}\thing}
```

will again give an 'undefined control sequence' for \thing (this time on its second occurrence), as it will only be defined when \next is called, not when \next is defined.

12.6.3 Expansion and \write

The argument token list of \write is treated in much the same way as the replacement text of an \edef; that is, expandable control sequences and active characters are completely expanded. Unexpandable control sequences are treated by \write as if they are prefixed by \string.
    Because of the expansion performed by \write, some care has to be taken when outputting control sequences with \write. Even more complications arise from the fact that the expansion of the argument of \write is only performed when it is shipped out. Here follows a worked-out example.
    Suppose \somecs is a macro, and you want to write the string

```
\def\othercs{the expansion of \somecs}
```

to a file.

The first attempt is

```
\write\myfile{\def\othercs{\somecs}}
```

This gives an error 'undefined control sequence' for \othercs, because the \write will try to expand that token. Note that the \somecs is also expanded, so that part is right.

The next attempt is

```
\write\myfile{\def\noexpand\othercs{\somecs}}
```

This is almost right, but not quite. The statement written is

\def\othercs{*expansion of* \somecs}

which looks right.

However, writes – and the expansion of their argument – are not executed on the spot, but saved until the part of the page on which they occur is shipped out (see Chapter 30). So, in the meantime, the value of \somecs may have changed. In other words, the value written may not be the value at the time the \write command was given. Somehow, therefore, the current expansion must be inserted in the write command.

The following is an attempt at repair:

```
\edef\act{\write\myfile{\def\noexpand\othercs{\somecs}}}
\act
```

Now the write command will be

\write\myfile{\def\othercs{*value of* \somecs}}

The \noexpand prevented the \edef from expanding the \othercs, but after the definition it has disappeared, so that execution of the write will again give an undefined control sequence. The final solution is

```
\edef\act{\write\myfile
          {\def \noexpand\noexpand \noexpand\othercs{\somecs}}}
\act
```

In this case the write command caused by the expansion of \act will be

\write\myfile{\def\noexpand\othercs{*current value of* \somecs}}

and the string actually written is

\def\othercs{*current value of* \somecs}

This mechanism is the basis for cross-referencing macros in several macro packages.

12.6.4 Controlled expansion inside an \edef

Sometimes you may need an \edef to evaluate current conditions, but you want to expand something in the replacement text only to a certain level. Suppose that

```
\def\a{\b} \def\b{c} \def\d{\e} \def\e{f}
```

is given, and you want to define \g as \a expanded one step, followed by \d fully expanded. The following works:

    \edef\g{\expandafter\noexpand\a \d}

Explanation: the \expandafter reaches over the \noexpand to expand \a one step, after which the sequence \noexpand\b is left.

This trick comes in handy when you need to construct a control sequence with \csname inside an \edef. The following sequence inside an \edef

    \expandafter\noexpand\csname name\endcsname

will expand exactly to \name, but not further. As an example, suppose

    \def\condition{true}

has been given, then

    \edef\setmycondition{\expandafter\noexpand
            \csname mytest\condition\endcsname}

will let \setmycondition expand to \mytesttrue.

12.6.5 Multiple prevention of expansion

As was pointed out above, prefixing a command with \noexpand prevents its expansion in commands such as \edef and \write. However, if a sequence of tokens passes through more than one expanding command stronger measures are needed.

The following trick can be used: in order to protect a command against expansion it can be prefixed with \protect. During the stages of processing where expansion is not desired the definition of \protect is

    \def\protect{\noexpand\protect\noexpand}

Later on, when the command is actually needed, \protect is defined as

    \def\protect{}

Why does this work? The expansion of

    \protect\somecs

is at first

    \noexpand\protect\noexpand\somecs

Inside an \edef this sequence is expanded further, and the subsequent expansion is

    \protect\somecs

That is, the expansion is equal to the original sequence.

12.6.6 More examples with \relax

Above, a first example was given in which \relax served to prevent TEX from scanning too far. Here are some more examples, using \relax to bound numbers.
After

```
\countdef\pageno=0 \pageno=1
\def\Par{\par\penalty200}
```

the sequence

```
\Par\number\pageno
```

is misunderstood as

```
\par\penalty2001
```

In this case it is sufficient to define

```
\def\Par{\par\penalty200 }
```

as an ⟨optional space⟩ is allowed to follow a number.
Sometimes, however, such a simple escape is not possible. Consider the definition

```
\def\ifequal#1#2{\ifnum#1=#2 1\else 0\fi}
```

The question is whether the space after #2 is necessary, superfluous, or simply wrong. Calls such as \ifequal{27}{28} that compare two numbers (denotations) will correctly give 1 or 0, and the space is necessary to prevent misinterpretation.
However, \ifequal\somecounter\othercounter will give ␣1 if the counters are equal; in this case the space could have been dispensed with. The solution that works in both cases is

```
\def\ifequal#1#2{\ifnum#1=#2\relax 1\else 0\fi}
```

Note that \relax is not expanded, so

```
\edef\foo{1\ifequal\counta\countb}
```

will define \foo as either 1\relax1 or 10.

12.6.7 Example: category code saving and restoring

In many applications it is necessary to change the category code of a certain character during the execution of some piece of code. If the writer of that code is also the writer of the surrounding code, s/he can simply change the category code back and forth. However, if the surrounding code is by another author, the value of the category code will have to be stored and restored.
Thus one would like to write

```
\storecat@
... some code ...
```

```
    \restorecat@
```
or maybe
```
    \storecat\%
```
for characters that are possibly a comment character (or ignored or invalid). The basic idea is to define
```
    \def\storecat#1{%
        \expandafter\edef\csname restorecat#1\endcsname
            {\catcode`#1=\the\catcode`#1}}
```
so that, for instance, `\storecat$` will define the single control sequence '`\restorecat$`' (one control sequence) as
```
    \catcode`$=3
```
The macro `\restorecat` can then be implemented as
```
    \def\restorecat#1{%
        \csname restorecat#1\endcsname}
```
Unfortunately, things are not so simple.

The problems occur with active characters, because these are expanded inside the `\csname` ... `\endcsname` pairs. One might be tempted to write `\noexpand#1` everywhere, but this is wrong. As was explained above, this is essentially equal to `\relax`, which is unexpandable, and will therefore lead to an error message when it appears between `\csname` and `\endcsname`. The proper solution is then to use `\string#1`. For the case where the argument was given as a control symbol (for example `\%`), the escape character has to be switched off for a while.

Here are the complete macros. The `\storecat` macro gives its argument a default category code of 12.
```
    \newcount\tempcounta % just a temporary
    \def\csarg#1#2{\expandafter#1\csname#2\endcsname}
    \def\storecat#1%
       {\tempcounta\escapechar \escapechar=-1
        \csarg\edef{restorecat\string#1}%
            {\catcode`\string#1=
                \the\catcode\expandafter`\string#1}%
        \catcode\expandafter`\string#1=12\relax
        \escapechar\tempcounta}
    \def\restorecat#1%
       {\tempcounta\escapechar \escapechar=-1
        \csname restorecat\string#1\endcsname
        \escapechar\tempcounta}
```

12.6.8 Combining \aftergroup and boxes

At times, one wants to construct a box and immediately after it has been constructed to do something with it. The `\aftergroup` command can be used to put both the commands creating the box, and the ones handling it, in one macro.

As an example, here is a macro \textvcenter whichdefines a variant of the \vcenter box (see page 195) that can be used outside math mode.

```
\def\textvcenter
    {\hbox \bgroup$\everyvbox{\everyvbox{}%
        \aftergroup$\aftergroup\egroup}\vcenter}
```

The idea is that the macro inserts \hbox {$, and that the matching $} gets inserted by the \aftergroup commands. In order to get the \aftergroup commands inside the box, an \everyvbox command is used.

This macro can even be used with a ⟨box specification⟩ (see page 39), for example

```
\textvcenter spread 8pt{\hbox{a}\vfil\hbox{b}}
```

and because it is really just an \hbox, it can also be used in a \setbox assignment.

12.6.9 More expansion

There is a particular charm to macros that work purely by expansion. See the articles by Eijkhout (1991), Jeffrey (1990), and Maus (1991).

CHAPTER 13

Conditionals

Conditionals are an indispensible tool for powerful macros. TeX has a large repertoire of conditionals for querying such things as category codes or processing modes. This chapter gives an inventory of the various conditionals, and it treats the evaluation of conditionals in detail.

\if   Test equality of character codes.
\ifcat   Test equality of category codes.
\ifx   Test equality of macro expansion, or equality of character code and category code.
\ifcase   Enumerated case statement.
\ifnum   Test relations between numbers.
\ifodd   Test whether a number is odd.
\ifhmode   Test whether the current mode is (possibly restricted) horizontal mode.
\ifvmode   Test whether the current mode is (possibly internal) vertical mode.
\ifmmode   Test whether the current mode is (possibly display) math mode.
\ifinner   Test whether the current mode is an internal mode.
\ifdim   Compare two dimensions.
\ifvoid   Test whether a box register is empty.
\ifhbox   Test whether a box register contains a horizontal box.
\ifvbox   Test whether a box register contains a vertical box.
\ifeof   Test for end of input stream or non-existence of file.
\iftrue   A test that is always true.
\iffalse   A test that is always false.
\fi   Closing delimiter for all conditionals.
\else   Select ⟨false text⟩ of a conditional or default case of \ifcase.
\or   Separator for entries of an \ifcase.
\newif   Create a new test.

13.1   THE SHAPE OF CONDITIONALS

Conditionals in TeX have one of the following two forms

```
\if...⟨test tokens⟩⟨true text⟩\fi
\if...⟨test tokens⟩⟨true text⟩\else⟨false text⟩\fi
```

where the ⟨test tokens⟩ are zero or more tokens, depending on the particular conditional; the ⟨true text⟩ is a series of tokens to be processed if the test turns out true, and the ⟨false text⟩ is a series of tokens to be processed if the test turns out false. Both the ⟨true text⟩ and the ⟨false text⟩ can be empty.

The exact process of how TeX expands conditionals is treated below.

13.2 CHARACTER AND CONTROL SEQUENCE TESTS

Three tests exist for testing character tokens and control sequence tokens.

13.2.1 \if

Equality of character codes can be tested by

\if⟨token$_1$⟩⟨token$_2$⟩

In order to allow the tokens to be control sequences, TeX assigns character code 256 to control sequences, the lowest positive number that is not the character code of a character token (remember that the legal character codes are 0–255).

Thus all control sequences are equal as far as \if is concerned, and they are unequal to all character tokens. As an example, this fact can be used to define

\def\ifIsControlSequence#1{\if\noexpand#1\relax}

which tests whether a token is a control sequence token instead of a character token (its result is unpredictable if the argument is a {...} group).

After \if TeX will expand until two unexpandable tokens are obtained, so it is necessary to prefix expandable control sequences and active characters with \noexpand when testing them with \if.

Examples
After

\catcode`\b=13 \catcode`\c=13 \def b{a} \def c{a} \let\d=a

we find that

\if bc is true, because both b and c expand to a,
\if\noexpand b\noexpand c is false, and
\if b\d is true because b expands to the character a, and \d is an implicit character token a.

13.2.2 \ifcat

The \if test ignores category codes; these can be tested by

\ifcat⟨token$_1$⟩⟨token$_2$⟩

This test is a lot like \if: TeX expands after it until unexpandable tokens remain. For this test control sequences are considered to have category code 16 (ordinarily, category codes are in the range 0–15), which makes them all equal to each other, and different from all character tokens.

13.2.3 \ifx

Equality of tokens is tested in a stronger sense than the above by

\ifx⟨token$_1$⟩⟨token$_2$⟩

- Character tokens are equal for \ifx if they have the same character code and category code.
- Control sequence tokens are equal if they represent the same TEX primitive, or have been similarly defined by \font, \countdef, or some such. For example,

```
\let\boxhor=\hbox \ifx\boxhor\hbox %is true
\font\a=cmr10 \font\b=cmr10 \ifx\a\b %is true
```

- Control sequences are also equal if they are macros with the same parameter text and replacement text, and the same status with respect to \outer and \long. For example,

```
\def\a{z} \def\b{z} \def\c1{z} \def\d{\a}
\ifx\a\b %is true
\ifx\a\c %is false
\ifx\a\d %is false
```

Tokens following this test are not expanded.

By way of example of the use of \ifx consider string testing. A simple implementation of string testing in TEX is as follows:

```
\def\ifEqString#1#2{\def\testa{#1}\def\testb{#2}%
    \ifx\testa\testb}
```

The two strings are used as the replacement text of two macros, and equality of these macros is tested. This is about as efficient as string testing can get: TEX will traverse the definition texts of the macros \testa and \testb, which has precisely the right effect.

As another example, one can test whether a control sequence is defined by

```
\def\ifDefinedCs#1{\expandafter
    \ifx\csname#1\endcsname\relax}
\ifDefinedCs{parindent} %is true
\ifDefinedCs{undefined} %is (one hopes) not true
```

This uses the fact that a \csname...\endcsname command is equivalent to \relax if the control sequence has not been defined before. Unfortunately, this test also turns out true if a control sequence has been \let to \relax.

13.3 MODE TESTS

In order to determine in which of the six modes (see Chapter 6) TeX is currently operating, the tests \ifhmode, \ifvmode, \ifmmode, and \ifinner are available.

- \ifhmode is true if TeX is in horizontal mode or restricted horizontal mode.
- \ifvmode is true if TeX is in vertical mode or internal vertical mode.
- \ifmmode is true if TeX is in math mode or display math mode.

The \ifinner test is true if TeX is in any of the three internal modes: restricted horizontal mode, internal vertical mode, and non-display math mode.

13.4 NUMERICAL TESTS

Numerical relations between ⟨number⟩s can be tested with

\ifnum⟨number$_1$⟩⟨relation⟩⟨number$_2$⟩

where the relation is a character <, =, or >, of category 12.
Quantities such as glue can be used as a number here through the conversion to scaled points, and TeX will expand in order to arrive at the two ⟨number⟩s.
Testing for odd or even numbers can be done with \ifodd: the test

\ifodd⟨number⟩

is true if the ⟨number⟩ is odd.

13.5 OTHER TESTS

13.5.1 Dimension testing

Relations between ⟨dimen⟩ values (Chapter 8) can be tested with \ifdim using the same three relations as in \ifnum.

13.5.2 Box tests

Contents of box registers (Chapter 5) can be tested with

\ifvoid⟨8-bit number⟩

which is true if the register contains no box,

\ifhbox⟨8-bit number⟩

which is true if the register contains a horizontal box, and

\ifvbox⟨8-bit number⟩

which is true if the register contains a vertical box.

13.5.3 I/O tests

The status of input streams (Chapter 30) can be tested with the end-of-file test `\ifeof`⟨number⟩, which is only true if the number is in the range 0–15, and the corresponding stream is open and not fully read. In particular, this test is false if the file name connected to this stream (through `\openin`) does not correspond to an existing file. See the example on page 239.

13.5.4 Case statement

The TeX case statement is called `\ifcase`; its syntax is

  `\ifcase`⟨number⟩⟨case$_0$⟩`\or`...`\or`⟨case$_n$⟩`\else`⟨other cases⟩`\fi`

where for n cases there are $n-1$ `\or` control sequences. Each of the ⟨case$_i$⟩ parts can be empty, and the `\else`⟨other cases⟩ part is optional.

13.5.5 Special tests

The tests `\iftrue` and `\iffalse` are always true and false respectively. They are mainly useful as tools in macros.

For instance, the sequences

  `\iftrue{\else}\fi`

and

  `\iffalse{\else}\fi`

yield a left and right brace respectively, but they have balanced braces, so they can be used inside a macro replacement text.

The `\newif` macro, treated below, provides another use of `\iftrue` and `\iffalse`. On page 260 of *The TeXbook* these control sequences are also used in an interesting manner.

13.6 THE `\newif` MACRO

The plain format defines an (outer) macro `\newif` by which the user can define new conditionals. If the user defines

  `\newif\iffoo`

TeX defines three new control sequences, `\footrue` and `\foofalse` with which the user can set the condition, and `\iffoo` which tests the 'foo' condition.

The macro call `\newif\iffoo` expands to

  `\def\footrue{\let\iffoo=\iftrue} \def\foofalse{\let\iffoo=\iffalse}`
  `\foofalse`

The actual definition, especially the part that ensures that the `\iffoo` indeed starts with `\if`, is a pretty hack. An explanation follows here. This uses concepts from Chapters 11 and 12.

The macro `\newif` starts as follows:

`\outer\def\newif#1{\count@\escapechar \escapechar\m@ne`

This saves the current escape character in `\count@`, and sets the value of `\escapechar` to -1. The latter action has the effect that no escape character is used in the output of `\string`⟨control sequence⟩.

An auxiliary macro `\if@` is defined by

`{\uccode`1=`i \uccode`2=`f \uppercase{\gdef\if@12{}}}`

Since the uppercase command changes only character codes, and not category codes, the macro `\if@` now has to be followed by the characters if of category 12. Ordinarily, these characters have category code 11. In effect this macro then eats these two characters, and TeX complains if they are not present.

Next there is a macro `\@if` defined by

`\def\@if#1#2{\csname\expandafter\if@\string#1#2\endcsname}`

which will be called like `\@if\iffoo{true}` and `\@if\iffoo{false}`.

Let us examine the call `\@if\iffoo{true}`.

- The `\expandafter` reaches over the `\if@` to expand `\string` first. The part `\string\iffoo` expands to `iffoo` because the escape character is not printed, and all characters have category 12.
- The `\if@` eats the first two characters $i_{12}f_{12}$ of this.
- As a result, the final expansion of `\@if\iffoo{true}` is then

  `\csname footrue\endcsname`

Now we can treat the relevant parts of `\newif` itself:

`\expandafter\expandafter\expandafter`
`   \edef\@if#1{true}{\let\noexpand#1=\noexpand\iftrue}%`

The three `\expandafter` commands may look intimidating, so let us take one step at a time.

- One `\expandafter` is necessary to reach over the `\edef`, such that `\@if` will expand:

  `\expandafter\edef\@if\iffoo{true}`

  gives

  `\edef\csname footrue\endcsname`

- Then another `\expandafter` is necessary to activate the `\csname`:

  `\expandafter \expandafter \expandafter \edef \@if ...`
  `%   new             old             new`

- This makes the final expansion

    `\edef\footrue{\let\noexpand\iffoo=\noexpand\iftrue}`

After this follows a similar statement for the `false` case:

`\expandafter\expandafter\expandafter`
`\edef\@if#1{false}{\let\noexpand#1=\noexpand\iffalse}%`

The conditional starts out false, and the escape character has to be reset:

`\@if#1{false}\escapechar\count@`

13.7 EVALUATION OF CONDITIONALS

TeX's conditionals behave differently from those in ordinary programming languages. In many instances one may not notice the difference, but in certain contexts it is important to know precisely what happens.

When TeX evaluates a conditional, it first determines what is to be tested. This in itself may involve some expansion; as we saw in the previous chapter, only after an `\ifx` test does TeX not expand. After all other tests TeX will expand tokens until the extent of the test and the tokens to be tested have been determined. On the basis of the outcome of this test the ⟨true text⟩ and the ⟨false text⟩ are either expanded or skipped.

For the processing of the parts of the conditional let us consider some cases separately.

- `\if... ... \fi` and the result of the test is false. After the test TeX will start skipping material without expansion, without counting braces, but balancing nested conditionals, until a `\fi` token is encountered. If the `\fi` is not found an error message results at the end of the file:

    `Incomplete \if...; all text was ignored after line ...`

    where the line number indicated is that of the line where TeX started skipping, that is, where the conditional occurred.

- `\if... \else ... \fi` and the result of the test is false. Any material in between the condition and the `\else` is skipped without expansion, without counting braces, but balancing nested conditionals.

    The `\fi` token can be the result of expansion; if it never turns up TeX will give a diagnostic message

    `\end occurred when \if... on line ... was incomplete`

    This sort of error is not visible in the output.

    This point plus the previous may jointly be described as follows: after a false condition TeX skips until an `\else` or `\fi` is found; any material in between `\else` and `\fi` is processed.

- `\if... ... \fi` and the result of the test is true. TeX will start processing the material following the condition. As above, the `\fi` token may be inserted by expansion of a macro.

- \if... \else ... \fi and the result of the test is true. Any material following the condition is processed until the \else is found; then TeX skips everything until the matching \fi is found.

This point plus the previous may be described as follows: after a true test TeX starts processing material until an \else or \fi is found; if an \else is found TeX skips until it finds the matching \fi.

13.8 ASSORTED REMARKS

13.8.1 The test gobbles up tokens

A common mistake is to write the following:

```
\ifnum\x>0\someaction \else\anotheraction \fi
```

which has the effect that the \someaction is expanded, regardless of whether the test succeeds or not. The reason for this is that TeX evaluates the input stream until it is certain that it has found the arguments to be tested. In this case it is perfectly possible for the \someaction to yield a digit, so it is expanded. The remedy is to insert a space or a \relax control sequence after the last digit of the number to be tested.

13.8.2 The test wants to gobble up the \else or \fi

The same mechanism that underlies the phenomenon in the previous point can lead to even more surprising effects if TeX bumps into an \else, \or, or \fi while still busy determining the extent of the test itself.

Recall that \pageno is a synonym for \count0, and consider the following examples:

```
\newcount\nct \nct=1\ifodd\pageno\else 2\fi 1
```

and

```
\newcount\nct \nct=1\ifodd\count0\else 2\fi 1
```

The first example will assign either 11 or 121 to \nct, but the second one will assign 1 or 121. The explanation is that in cases like the second, where an \else is encountered while the test still has not been delimited, a \relax is inserted. In the case that \count0 is odd the result will thus be \relax, and the example will yield

```
\nct=1\relax2
```

which will assign 1 to \nct, and print 2.

13.8.3 Macros and conditionals; the use of \expandafter

Consider the following example:

```
\def\bold#1{{\bf #1}} \def\slant#1{{\sl #1}}
```

```
\ifnum1>0 \bold \else \slant \fi {some text} ...
```

This will make not only 'some text', but *all* subsequent text bold. Also, at the end of the job there will be a notice that 'end occurred inside a group at level 1'. Switching on `\tracingmacros` reveals that the argument of `\bold` was `\else`. This means that, after expansion of `\bold`, the input stream looked like

```
\ifnum1>0 {\bf \else }\fi {some text} rest of the text
```

so the closing brace was skipped as part of the ⟨false text⟩. Effectively, then, the resulting stream is

```
{\bf {some text} rest of the text
```

which is unbalanced.

One solution to this sort of problem would be to write

```
\ifnum1>0 \let\next=\bold \else \let\next=\slant \fi \next
```

but a solution using `\expandafter` is also possible:

```
\ifnum1>0 \expandafter \bold \else \expandafter \slant \fi
```

This works, because the `\expandafter` commands let TeX determine the boundaries of the ⟨true text⟩ and the ⟨false text⟩.

In fact, the second solution may be preferred over the first, since conditionals are handled by the expansion processor, and the `\let` statements are tackled only by the execution processor; that is, they are not expandable. Thus the second solution will (and the first will not) work, for instance, inside an `\edef`.

Another example with `\expandafter` is the sequence

```
\def\get#1\get{ ... }
\expandafter \get \ifodd1 \ifodd3 5\fi \fi \get
```

This gives

```
#1<- \ifodd3 5\fi \fi
```

and

```
\expandafter \get \ifodd2 \ifodd3 5\fi\fi \get
```

gives

```
#1<-
```

This illustrates again that the result of evaluating a conditional is not the final expansion, but the start of the expansion of the ⟨true text⟩ or ⟨false text⟩, depending on the outcome of the test.

A detail should be noted: with `\expandafter` it is possible that the `\else` is encountered before the ⟨true text⟩ has been expanded completely. This raises the question as to the exact timing of expansion and skipping. In the example

```
\def\hello{\message{Hello!}}
\ifnum1>0 \expandafter \hello \else \message{goodbye} \bye
```

the error message caused by the missing `\fi` is given without `\hello` ever having been expanded. The conclusion must be that the ⟨false text⟩ is skipped as soon as it has been located, even if this is at a time when the ⟨true text⟩ has not been expanded completely.

13.8.4 Incorrect matching

TeX's matching of `\if`, `\else`, and `\fi` is easily upset. For instance, *The TeXbook* warns you that you should not say

```
\let\ifabc=\iftrue
```

inside a conditional, because if this text is skipped TeX sees at least one `\if` to be matched.

The reason for this is that when TeX is skipping it recognizes all `\if...`, `\or`, `\else`, and `\fi` tokens, and everything that has been declared a synonym of such a token by `\let`. In `\let\ifabc=\iftrue` TeX will therefore at least see the `\iftrue` as the opening of a conditional, and, if the current meaning of `\ifabc` was for instance `\iffalse`, it will also be considered as the opening of a conditional statement.

As another example, if

```
\csname if\sometest\endcsname \someaction \fi
```

is skipped as part of conditional text, the `\fi` will unintentionally close the outer conditional.

It does not help to enclose such potentially dangerous constructs inside a group, because grouping is independent of conditional structure. Burying such commands inside macros is the safest approach.

Sometimes another solution is possible, however. The `\loop` macro of plain TeX (see page 104) is used as

```
\loop ... \if ... \repeat
```

where the `\repeat` is not an actually executable command, but is merely a delimiter:

```
\def\loop#1\repeat{ ... }
```

Therefore, by declaring

```
\let\repeat\fi
```

the `\repeat` balances the `\if...` that terminates the loop, and it becomes possible to have loops in skipped conditional text.

13.8.5 Conditionals and grouping

It has already been mentioned above that group nesting in TeX is independent of conditional nesting. The reason for this is that conditionals are handled by the expansion part of TeX; in that stage braces are just unexpandable tokens that require no special treatment. Grouping is only performed in the later stage of execution processing.

An example of this independence is now given. One may write a macro that yields part of a conditional:

```
\def\elsepart{\else \dosomething \fi}
```

The other way around, the following macros yield a left brace and a right brace respectively:

```
\def\leftbrace{\iftrue{\else}\fi}
\def\rightbrace{\iffalse{\else}\fi}
```

Note that braces in these definitions are properly nested.

13.8.6 A trick

In some contexts it may be hard to get rid of \else or \fi tokens in a proper manner. The above approach with \expandafter works only if there is a limited number of tokens involved. In other cases the following trick may provide a way out:

```
\def\hop#1\fi{\fi #1}
```

Using this as

```
\if... \hop ⟨lots of tokens⟩\fi
```

will place the tokens outside the conditional. This is for instance used in Eijkhout (1991).

As a further example of this sort of trick, consider the problem (suggested to me and solved by Alan Jeffrey) of implementing a conditional \ifLessThan#1#2#3#4 such that the arguments corresponding to #3 or #4 result, depending on whether #1 is less than #2 or not.

The problem here is how to get rid of the \else and the \fi. The – or at least, one – solution is to scoop them up as delimiters for macros:

```
\def\ifLessThan#1#2{\ifnum#1<#2\relax\taketrue \else \takefalse \fi}
\def\takefalse\fi#1#2{\fi#2}
\def\taketrue\else\takefalse\fi#1#2{\fi#1}
```

Note that \ifLessThan has only two parameters (the things to be tested); however, its result is a macro that chooses between the next two arguments.

13.8.7 More examples of expansion in conditionals

Above, the macro \ifEqString was given that compares two strings:

```
\def\ifEqString#1#2%
    {\def\csa{#1}\def\csb{#2}\ifx\csa\csb }
```

However, this macro relies on \def, which is not an expandable command. If we need a string tester that will work, for instance, inside an \edef, we need some more ingenuity (this solution was taken from Eijkhout (1991)). The basic principle of this solution is to compare the strings one character at a time. Macro delimiting by \fi is used; this was explained above.

First of all, the \ifEqString call is replaced by a sequence \ifAllChars ...\Are ...\TheSame, and both strings are delimited by a dollar sign, which is not supposed to appear in the strings themselves.

```
\def\ifEqString
    #1#2{\ifAllChars#1$\Are#2$\TheSame}
```

The test for equality of characters first determines whether either string has ended. If both have ended, the original strings were equal; if only one has ended, they were of unequal length, hence unequal. If neither string has ended, we test whether the first characters are equal, and if so, we make a recursive call to test the remainder of the string.

```
\def\ifAllChars#1#2\Are#3#4\TheSame
   {\if#1$\if#3$\say{true}%
            \else \say{false}\fi
     \else \if#1#3\ifRest#2\TheSame#4\else
               \say{false}\fi\fi}
\def\ifRest#1\TheSame#2\else#3\fi\fi
    {\fi\fi \ifAllChars#1\Are#2\TheSame}
```

The \say macro is supposed to give \iftrue for \say{true} and \iffalse for \say{false}. Observing that all calls to this macro occur two conditionals deep, we use the 'hop' trick explained above as follows.

```
\def\say#1#2\fi\fi
    {\fi\fi\csname if#1\endcsname}
```

Similar to the above example, let us write a macro that will test lexicographic ('dictionary') precedence of two strings:

```
\let\ex=\expandafter
\def\ifbefore
    #1#2{\ifallchars#1$\are#2$\before}
\def\ifallchars#1#2\are#3#4\before
   {\if#1$\say{true\ex}\else
      \if#3$\say{false\ex\ex\ex}\else
       \ifnum`#1>`#3 \say{false%
          \ex\ex\ex\ex\ex\ex\ex}\else
        \ifnum`#1<`#3 \say{true%
          \ex\ex\ex\ex\ex\ex\ex
          \ex\ex\ex\ex\ex\ex\ex}\else
         \ifrest#2\before#4\fi\fi\fi\fi}
\def\ifrest#1\before#2\fi\fi\fi\fi
    {\fi\fi\fi\fi
```

```
    \ifallchars#1\are#2\before}
\def\say#1{\csname if#1\endcsname}
```

In this macro a slightly different implementation of \say is used.

Simplified, a call to \ifbefore will eventually lead to a situation that looks (in the 'true' case) like

```
\ifbefore{...}{...}
        \if... %% some comparison that turns out true
            \csname iftrue\expandafter\endcsname
        \else .... \fi
    ... %% commands for the 'before' case
\else
    ... %% commands for the 'not-before' case
\fi
```

When the comparison has turned out true, TeX will start processing the ⟨true text⟩, and make a mental note to remove any \else ... \fi part once an \else token is seen. Thus, the sequence

```
\csname iftrue\expandafter\endcsname \else ... \fi
```

is replaced by

```
\csname iftrue\endcsname
```

as the \else is seen while TeX is still processing \csname...\endcsname.

Calls to \say occur inside nested conditionals, so the number of \expandafter commands necessary may be larger than 1: for level two it is 3, for level three it is 7, and for level 4 it is 15. Slightly more compact implementations of this macro do exist.

CHAPTER 14

Token Lists

TeX has only one type of data structure: the token list. There are token list registers that are available to the user, and TeX has some special token lists: the \every... variables, \errhelp, and \output.

\toks   Prefix for a token list register.
\toksdef   Define a control sequence to be a synonym for a \toks register.
\newtoks   Macro that allocates a token list register.

14.1   TOKEN LISTS

Token lists are the only type of data structure that TeX knows. They can contain character tokens and control sequence tokens. Spaces in a token list are significant. The only operations on token lists are assignment and unpacking.

TeX has 256 token list registers \toks*nnn* that can be allocated using the macro \newtoks, or explicitly assigned by \toksdef; see below.

14.2   USE OF TOKEN LISTS

Token lists are assigned by a ⟨variable assignment⟩, which is in this case takes one of the forms

⟨token variable⟩⟨equals⟩⟨general text⟩
⟨token variable⟩⟨equals⟩⟨filler⟩⟨token variable⟩

Here a ⟨token variable⟩ is an explicit \toks*nnn* register, something that has been defined to such a register by \toksdef (probably hidden in \newtoks), or one of the special ⟨token parameter⟩ lists below. A ⟨general text⟩ has an explicit closing brace, but the open brace can be implicit.

Examples of token lists are (the first two lines are equivalent):

\toks0=\bgroup \a \b cd}
\toks0={\a \b cd}
\toks1=\toks2

Unpacking a token list is done by the command \the: the expansion of \the⟨token variable⟩ is the sequence of tokens that was in the token list.

Token lists have a special behaviour in \edef: when prefixed by \the they are unpacked, but the resulting tokens are not evaluated further. Thus

\toks0={\a \b} \edef\SomeCs{\the\toks0}

gives

\SomeCs: macro:-> \a \b

This is in contrast to what happens ordinarily in an \edef; see page 113.

14.3 ⟨token parameter⟩

There are in TeX a number of token lists that are automatically inserted at certain points. These ⟨token parameter⟩s are the following:

\output   this token list is inserted whenever TeX decides it has sufficient material for a page, or when the user forces activation by a penalty $\leq -10\,000$ in vertical mode (see Chapter 28);
\everypar   is inserted when TeX switches from external or internal vertical mode to unrestricted horizontal mode (see Chapter 16);
\everymath   is inserted after a single math-shift character that starts a formula;
\everydisplay   is inserted after a double math-shift character that starts a display formula;
\everyhbox   is inserted when an \hbox begins (see Chapter 5);
\everyvbox   is inserted when a vertical box begins (see Chapter 5);
\everyjob   is inserted when a job begins (see Chapter 32);
\everycr   is inserted in alignments after \cr or a non-redundant \crcr (see Chapter 25);
\errhelp   contains tokens to supplement an \errmessage (see Chapter 35).

A ⟨token parameter⟩ behaves the same as an explicit \toks*nnn* list, or a quantity defined by \toksdef.

14.4 TOKEN LIST REGISTERS

Token lists can be stored in \toks registers:

\toks⟨8-bit number⟩

which is a ⟨token variable⟩. Synonyms for token list registers can be made by the ⟨registerdef⟩ command \toksdef in a ⟨shorthand definition⟩:

\toksdef⟨control sequence⟩⟨equals⟩⟨8-bit number⟩

A control sequence defined this way is called a ⟨toksdef token⟩, and this is also a token variable (the remaining third kind of token variable is the ⟨token parameter⟩).

The plain TeX macro `\newtoks` uses `\toksdef` to allocate unused token list registers. This macro is `\outer`.

14.5 EXAMPLES

Token lists are probably among the least obvious components of TeX: most TeX users will never find occasion for their use, but format designers and other macro writers can find interesting applications. Following are some examples of the sorts of things that can be done with token lists.

14.5.1 Operations on token lists: stack macros

The number of primitive operations available for token lists is rather limited: assignment and unpacking. However, these are sufficient to implement other operations such as appending.

Let us say we have allocated a token register

```
\newtoks\list \list={\c}
```

and we want to add tokens to it, using the syntax

```
\Prepend \a \b (to:)\list
```

such that

```
\showthe\list
```

gives

```
> \a \b \c .
```

For this the original list has to be unpacked, and the new tokens followed by the old contents have to assigned again to the register. Unpacking can be done with `\the` inside an `\edef`, so we arrive at the following macro:

```
\def\Prepend#1(to:)#2{\toks0={#1}%
    \edef\act{\noexpand#2={\the\toks0 \the#2}}%
    \act}
```

Note that the tokens that are to be added are first packed into a temporary token list, which is then again unpacked inside the `\edef`. Including them directly would have led to their expansion.

Next we want to use token lists as a sort of stack: we want a 'pop' operation that removes the first element from the list. Specifically,

```
\Pop\list(into:)\first
\show\first \showthe\list
```

should give

```
> \first=macro:
```

```
->\a  .
```

and for the remaining list

```
>  \b \c  .
```

Here we make creative use of delimited and undelimited parameters. With an `\edef` we unpack the list, and the auxiliary macro `\SplitOff` scoops up the elements as one undelimited argument, the first element, and one delimited argument, the rest of the elements.

```
\def\Pop#1(into:)#2{%
    \edef\act{\noexpand\SplitOff\the#1%
             (head:)\noexpand#2(tail:)\noexpand#1}%
    \act}
\def\SplitOff#1#2(head:)#3(tail:)#4{\def#3{#1}#4={#2}}
```

14.5.2 Executing token lists

The `\the` operation for unpacking token lists was used above only inside an `\edef`. Used on its own it has the effect of feeding the tokens of the list to TeX's expansion mechanism. If the tokens have been added to the list in a uniform syntax, this gives rise to some interesting possibilities.

Imagine that we are implementing the bookkeeping of external files for a format. Such external files can be used for table of contents, list of figures, et cetera. If the presence of such objects is under the control of the user, we need some general routines for opening and closing files, and keeping track of what files we have opened at the user's request.

Here only some routines for bookkeeping will be described. Let us say there is a list of auxiliary files, and an auxiliary counter:

```
\newtoks\auxlist  \newcount\auxcount
```

First of all there must be an operation to add auxiliary files:

```
\def\NewAuxFile#1{\addtoauxlist{#1}%
    % plus other actions
    }
\def\AddToAuxList#1{\let\\=\relax
    \edef\act{\noexpand\auxlist={\the\auxlist \\{#1}}}%
    \act}
```

This adds the name to the list in a uniform format:

```
\NewAuxFile{toc} \NewAuxFile{lof}
\showthe\auxlist
> \\{toc}\\{lof}.
```

using the control sequence `\\` which is left undefined.

Now this control sequence can be used for instance to count the number of elements in the list:

```
\def\ComputeLengthOfAuxList{\auxcount=0
```

```
    \def\\##1{\advance\auxcount1\relax}%
    \the\auxlist}
\ComputeLengthOfAuxList \showthe\auxcount
> 2.
```

Another use of this structure is the following: at the end of the job we can now close all auxiliary files at once, by

```
\def\CloseAuxFiles{\def\\##1{\CloseAuxFile{##1}}%
    \the\auxlist}
\def\CloseAuxFile#1{\message{closing file: #1. }%
    % plus other actions
    }
\CloseAuxFiles
```

which gives the output

```
closing file: toc.  closing file: lof.
```

CHAPTER 15

Baseline Distances

Lines of text are in most cases not of equal height or depth. Therefore TeX adds interline glue to keep baselines at a uniform distance from one another. This chapter treats the computation of such interline glue.

\baselineskip   The 'ideal' baseline distance between neighbouring boxes on a vertical list. Plain TeX default: 12pt.
\lineskiplimit   Distance to be maintained between the bottom and top of neighbouring boxes on a vertical list. Plain TeX default: 0pt.
\lineskip   Glue added if the distance between bottom and top of neighbouring boxes is less than \lineskiplimit. Plain TeX default: 1pt.
\prevdepth   Depth of the last box added to a vertical list as it is perceived by TeX.
\nointerlineskip   Macro to prevent interline glue insertion once.
\offinterlineskip   Macro to prevent interline glue globally henceforth.
\openup   Increase \baselineskip, \lineskip, and \lineskiplimit by specified amount.

15.1 INTERLINE GLUE

TeX tries to keep a certain distance between the reference points of boxes that are added to a vertical list; in particular it tries to keep the baselines of ordinary text at a constant distance, the \baselineskip. Actually, the \baselineskip is a ⟨glue⟩, so line distances can stretch or shrink. However, the natural sizes, as well as the stretch and the shrink, are the same between all lines.

When boxes, whether they are lines of a paragraph or explicit boxes, are appended to a vertical list, glue is added usually so that the depth of the preceding box and the height of the current one add up to the \baselineskip. This has the effect of keeping the reference points of subsequent lines at regular intervals.

[figure: diagram showing height of the first line, depth of the first line, interline glue, lineskip limit, height of the second line, depth of the second line, Baselineskip]

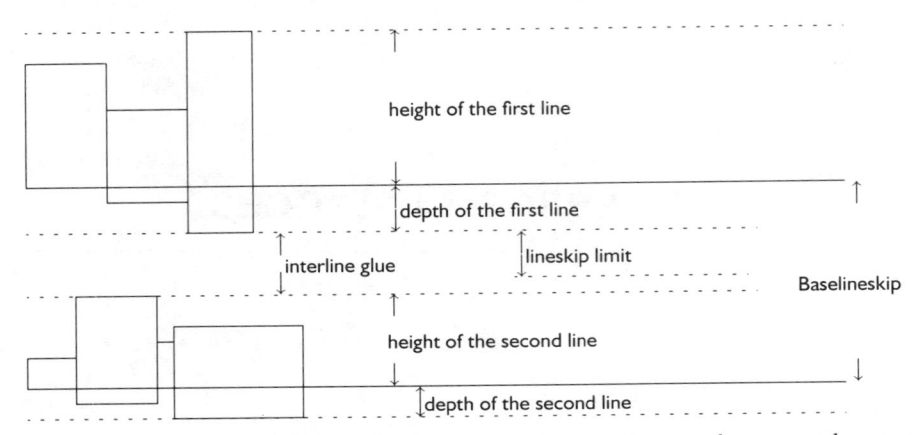

However, this process can bring the bottom and top of two subsequent boxes to be less than \lineskiplimit apart:

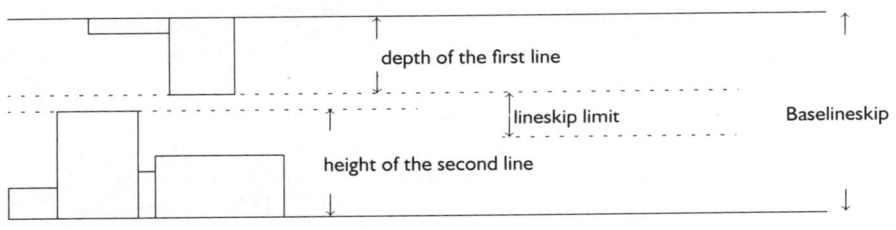

[figure: diagram showing depth of the first line, lineskip limit, height of the second line, Baselineskip]

In that case, \lineskip glue is added:

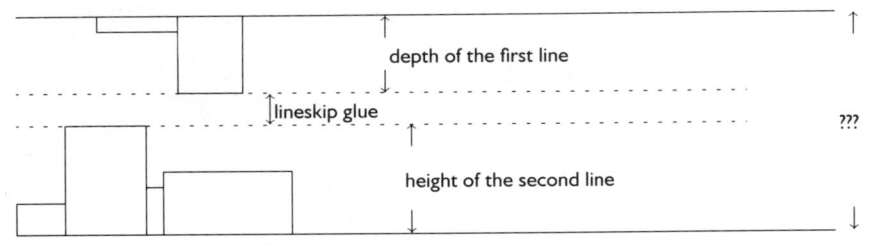

[figure: diagram showing depth of the first line, lineskip glue, height of the second line, ???]

Note that this will usually increase the distance between the baselines of the boxes to more than the \baselineskip.

The exact process is this:

- if \prevdepth is -1000pt or less, no glue is added, otherwise
- TeX calculates the distance between the bottom of the previous box and the top of the current one as the natural width of the \baselineskip minus \prevdepth (the depth of the last box) and minus the height of the current box;
- if this distance is at least \lineskiplimit, glue is added with the calculated distance as natural size, and with the stretch and shrink of the \baselineskip,
- otherwise \lineskip glue is added.

- \prevdepth is set to the depth of the current item.

There are two exceptional situations: no interline glue is added before and after a rule, and the \prevdepth is not updated by an \unvbox or \unvcopy command. After a rule interline glue is prevented by a value of -1000pt of the \prevdepth.

The above process is carried out, irrespective of what extra glue may have been inserted in between the boxes. Thus a skip in between boxes in vertical mode will not affect the distance calculated from the baseline distances, and therefore also not the amount of baselineskip glue. The same holds for glue added with \vadjust inside a paragraph.

Examples

```
\baselineskip=10pt \lineskiplimit=2pt \lineskip=2pt
\setbox0=\vbox{\hbox{\vrule depth4pt}
               \hbox{\vrule height 3pt}}
\showbox0
```

gives

```
\box0=
\vbox(10.0+0.0)x0.4
.\hbox(0.0+4.0)x0.4
..\rule(*+4.0)x0.4
.\glue(\baselineskip) 3.0
.\hbox(3.0+0.0)x0.4
..\rule(3.0+*)x0
```

Bringing the boxes to within \lineskiplimit of each other, that is

```
\setbox0\vbox{\hbox{\vrule depth4pt}
              \hbox{\vrule height 5pt}}
\showbox0
```

gives

```
\box0=
\vbox(11.0+0.0)x0.4
.\hbox(0.0+4.0)x0.4
..\rule(*+4.0)x0.4
.\glue(\lineskip) 2.0
.\hbox(5.0+0.0)x0.4
..\rule(5.0+*)x0.4
```

where \lineskip glue has been inserted instead of the usual \baselineskip glue.

The plain TeX default values are

```
\lineskiplimit=0pt lineskip=1pt
```

so, when boxes start to touch each other, they are moved one point apart.

15.2 THE PERCEIVED DEPTH OF BOXES

The decision process for interline glue uses \prevdepth as the perceived depth of the preceding box on the vertical list. The \prevdepth parameter can be used only in vertical mode.

The \prevdepth is set to the depth of boxes added to the vertical list, but it is not affected by \unvbox or \unvcopy. After an \hrule it is set to -1000pt to prevent interline glue before the next box.

At the beginning of a vertical list \prevdepth is set to -1000pt, except in an \halign and \noalign code contained therein, where it is carried over from the surrounding list. At the end of the alignment the value of \prevdepth set by the last alignment row is carried to the outer list.

In order to prevent interline glue just once, all that is needed is to alter the \prevdepth. This is done in the macro \nointerlineskip:

```
\def\nointerlineskip{\prevdepth=-1000pt}
```

The \offinterlineskip macro is much more drastic: it prevents *all* interline glue from the moment of its call onwards, or, if it is used inside a paragraph, from the start of that paragraph. Its definition is

```
\baselineskip=-1000pt  \lineskip=0pt
\lineskiplimit\maxdimen
```

where the second line is the essential one: it causes TeX to add \lineskip glue (which is zero) always. Settings for \baselineskip do not matter any more then.

The \offinterlineskip macro has an important application in alignments (see Chapter 25).

By setting

```
\lineskiplimit=-\maxdimen
```

you can force TeX to apply the \baselineskip always, regardless of whether this would bring boxes too close together or, indeed, if this would make them overlap.

15.3 TERMINOLOGY

In hot metal typesetting, all letters of a particular font were on a 'body' of the same size. Thus every line of type had the same height and depth, and the resulting distance between the baselines would be some suitable value for that type. If for some reason this distance should be larger (see White (1988) for a discussion of this), strips of lead would be inserted. The extra distance was called the 'leading' (pronounced 'ledding').

With phototypesetting, when the baseline distance was sometimes called the 'film transport', this terminology blurred, and the term 'leading' was also used for the baseline distance. Some of this confusion is also present in TeX: the parameter \baselineskip specifies the baseline distance, but in the trace output (see the examples above) the glue inserted to make the baseline distance equal to \baselineskip is called \baselineskip.

15.4 ADDITIONAL REMARKS

In general, for documents longer than one page it is desirable to have the same baseline distance throughout. However, for one-page documents you may add stretchability to the baselineskip, for instance if the text has to be flush bottom.

Increasing the distance between just one pair of lines can be done with \vadjust. The argument of this command is vertical material that will be inserted in the vertical list right after the line where this command was given. The second line of this paragraph, for instance, contains the command \vadjust{\kern2pt}.

The amount of leading cannot be changed in the middle of a paragraph, because the value for \baselineskip that is used is the one that is current when the paragraph is finally broken and added to the main vertical list. The same holds for the \lineskip and \lineskiplimit.

The plain TeX macro \openup increases the \baselineskip, \lineskip, and \lineskiplimit by the amount of the argument to the macro. In effect, this increases line distances by this amount regardless of whether they are governed by \baselineskip or \lineskip.

CHAPTER 16

Paragraph Start

At the start of a paragraph TeX inserts a vertical skip as a separation from the preceding paragraph, and a horizontal skip as an indentation for the current paragraph. This chapter explains the exact sequence of actions, and it discusses how TeX's decisions can be altered.

`\indent`   Switch to horizontal mode and insert a box of width `\parindent`.
`\noindent`   Switch to horizontal mode with an empty horizontal list.
`\parskip`   Amount of glue added to the surrounding vertical list when a paragraph starts. Plain TeX default: `0pt plus 1pt`.
`\parindent`   Size of the indentation box added in front of a paragraph. Plain TeX default: `20pt`.
`\everypar`   Token list inserted in front of paragraph text;
`\leavevmode`   Macro to switch to horizontal mode if necessary.

16.1   WHEN DOES A PARAGRAPH START

TeX starts a paragraph whenever it switches from vertical mode to (unrestricted) horizontal mode. This switch can be effected by one of the commands `\indent` and `\noindent`, for example

```
{\bf And now~\dots}
\vskip3pt
\noindent It's~\dots
```

or by any ⟨horizontal command⟩. Horizontal commands include characters, inline formulas, and horizontal skips, but not boxes. Consider the following examples. The character 'I' is a horizontal command:

```
\vskip3pt
It's~\dots
```

A single `$` is a horizontal command:

```
$x$ is supposed~\dots
```

The control sequence `\hskip` is a horizontal command:

```
\hskip .5\hsize Long indentation~\dots
```

The full list of horizontal commands is given on page 57.

Upon recognizing a horizontal command in vertical mode, TeX will perform an \indent command (and all the actions associated with it; see below), and after that it will reexamine the horizontal command, this time executing it.

16.2   WHAT HAPPENS WHEN A PARAGRAPH STARTS

The \indent and \noindent commands cause a paragraph to be started. An \indent command can either be placed explicitly by the user or a macro, or it can be inserted by TeX when a ⟨horizontal command⟩ occurs in vertical mode; a \noindent command can only be placed explicitly.

After either command is encountered, \parskip glue is appended to the surrounding vertical list, unless TeX is in internal vertical mode and that list is empty (for example, at the start of a \vbox or \vtop). TeX then switches to unrestricted horizontal mode with an empty horizontal list. In the case of \indent (which may be inserted implicitly) an empty \hbox of width \parindent is placed at the start of the horizontal list; after \noindent no indentation box is inserted.

The contents of the \everypar ⟨token parameter⟩ are then inserted into the input (see some applications below). After that, the page builder is exercised (see Chapter 27). Note that this happens in horizontal mode: this is to move the \parskip glue to the current page.

If an \indent command is given while TeX is already in horizontal mode, the indentation box is inserted just the same. This is not very useful.

16.3   ASSORTED REMARKS

16.3.1   Starting a paragraph with a box

An \hbox does not imply horizontal mode, so an attempt to start a paragraph with a box, for instance

```
\hbox to 0cm{\hss$\bullet$\hskip1em}Text ....
```

will make the text following the box wind up one line below the box. It is necessary to switch to horizontal mode explicitly, using for instance \noindent or \leavevmode. The latter is defined using \unhbox, which is a horizontal command.

16.3.2   Starting a paragraph with a group

If the first ⟨horizontal command⟩ of a paragraph is enclosed in braces, the \everypar is evaluated inside the group. This may give unexpected results. Consider this example:

```
\everypar={\setbox0=\vbox\bgroup\def\par{\egroup}}
```

```
{\bf Start} a paragraph ... \par
```

The ⟨horizontal command⟩ starting the paragraph is the character 'S', so when \everypar has been inserted the input is essentially

```
{\bf \indent\setbox0=\vbox\bgroup
    \def\par{\egroup}Start} a paragraph ... \par
```

which is equivalent to

```
{\bf \setbox0=\vbox{Start} a paragraph ... \par
```

The effect of this is rather different from what was intended. Also, TeX will probably end the job inside a group.

16.4 EXAMPLES

16.4.1 Stretchable indentation

Considering that \parindent is a ⟨dimen⟩, not a ⟨glue⟩, it is not possible to declare

```
\parindent=1cm plus 1fil
```

in order to get a variable indentation at the start of a paragraph. This problem may be solved by putting

```
\everypar={\nobreak\hskip 1cm plus 1fil\relax}
```

The \nobreak serves to prevent (in rare cases) a line break at the stretchable glue.

16.4.2 Suppressing indentation

Inserting {\setbox0=\lastbox} in the horizontal list at the beginning of the paragraph removes the indentation: indentation consists of a box, which is available through \lastbox. Assigning it effectively removes it from the list.

However, this command sequence has to be inserted at a moment when TeX has already switched to horizontal mode, so explicit insertion of these commands in front of the first ⟨horizontal command⟩ of the paragraph does not work. The moment of insertion of the \everypar tokens is a better candidate: specifying

```
\everypar={{\setbox0=\lastbox}}
```

leads to unindented paragraphs, even if \parindent is not zero.

16.4.3 An indentation scheme

The above idea of letting the indentation box be removed by \everypar can be put to use in a systematic approach to indentation, where two conditionals

```
\newif\ifNeedIndent %as a rule
```

```
\newif\ifneedindent   %special cases
```

control whether paragraphs should indent as a rule, and whether in special cases indentation is needed. This section is taken from Eijkhout (1990b).

We take a fixed `\everypar`:

```
\everypar={\ControlledIndentation}
```

which executes in some cases the macro `\RemoveIndentation`

```
\def\RemoveIndentation{{\setbox0=\lastbox}}
```

The implementation of `\ControlledIndentation` is:

```
\def\ControlledIndentation
   {\ifNeedIndent \ifneedindent
                  \else \RemoveIndentation\needindenttrue \fi
    \else \ifneedindent \needindentfalse
          \else         \RemoveIndentation
    \fi   \fi}
```

In order to regulate indentation for a whole document, the user now once specifies, for instance,

```
\NeedIndenttrue
```

to indicate that, in principle, all paragraphs should indent. Macros such as `\section` can then prevent indentation in individual cases:

```
\def\section#1{ ... \needindentfalse}
```

16.4.4 A paragraph skip scheme

The use of `\everypar` to control indentation, as was sketched above, can be extended to the paragraph skip.

A visible white space between paragraphs can be created by the `\parskip` parameter, but, once this parameter has been set to some value, it is difficult to prevent paragraph skip in certain places elegantly. Usually, white space above and below environments and section headings should be specifiable independently of the paragraph skip. This section sketches an approach where `\parskip` is set to zero directly above and below certain constructs, while the `\everypar` is used to restore former values. This section is taken from Eijkhout (1990c).

First of all, here are two tools. The control sequence `\csarg` will be used only inside other macros; a typical call will look like

```
\csarg\vskip{#1Parskip}
```

Here is the definition:

```
\def\csarg#1#2{\expandafter#1\csname#2\endcsname}
```

Next follows a generalization of `\vskip`: the macro `\vspace` will not place its argument if the previous glue item is larger; otherwise it will eliminate the preceding glue, and place its argument.

```
\newskip\tempskipa
```

```
\def\vspace#1{\tempskipa=#1\relax
    \ifvmode \ifdim\tempskipa<\lastskip
             \else \vskip-\lastskip \vskip\tempskipa \fi
    \else    \vskip\tempskipa \fi}
```

Now assume that any construct foo with surrounding white space starts and ends with macro calls \StartEnvironment{foo} and \EndEnvironment{foo} respectively. Furthermore, assume that to this environment there correspond three glue registers: the \fooStartskip (glue above the environment), \fooParskip (the paragraph skip inside the environment), and the \fooEndskip (glue below the environment).

For restoring the value of the paragraph skip a conditional and a glue register are needed:

```
\newskip\TempParskip \newif\ifParskipNeedsRestoring
```

The basic sequence for the starting and ending macros for the environments is then

```
\TempParskip=\parskip\parskip=0cm\relax
\ParskipNeedsRestoringtrue
```

The implementations can now be given as:

```
\def\StartEnvironment#1{\csarg\vspace{#1Startskip}
    \begingroup % make changes local
    \csarg\TempParskip{#1Parskip} \parskip=0cm\relax
    \ParskipNeedsRestoringtrue}
\def\EndEnvironment#1{\csarg\vspace{#1Endskip}
    \endgroup % restore global values
    \ifParskipNeedsRestoring
    \else \TempParskip=\parskip \parskip=0cm\relax
          \ParskipNeedsRestoringtrue
    \fi}
```

The \EndEnvironment macro needs a little comment: if an environment is used inside another one, and it occurs before the first paragraph in that environment, the value of the paragraph skip for the outer environment has already been saved. Therefore no further actions are required in that case.

Note that both macros start with a vertical skip. This prevents the \begingroup and \endgroup statements from occurring in a paragraph.

We now come to the main point: if necessary, the \everypar will restore the value of the paragraph skip.

```
\everypar={\ControlledIndentation\ControlledParskip}
\def\ControlledParskip
   {\ifParskipNeedsRestoring
       \parskip=\TempParskip \ParskipNeedsRestoringfalse
    \fi}
```

CHAPTER

17

Paragraph End

TeX's mechanism for ending a paragraph is ingenious and effective. This chapter explains the mechanism, the role of \par in it, and it gives a number of practical remarks.

\par   Finish off a paragraph and go into vertical mode.
\endgraf   Synonym for \par: \let\endgraf=\par
\parfillskip   Glue that is placed between the last element of the paragraph and the line end. Plain TeX default: `0pt plus 1fil`.

17.1 THE WAY PARAGRAPHS END

A paragraph is terminated by the primitive \par command, which can be explicitly typed by the user (or inserted by a macro expansion):

```
... last words.\par
A new paragraphs ...
```

It can be implicitly generated in the input processor of TeX by an empty line (see Chapter 2):

```
... last words.

A new paragraphs ...
```

The \par can be inserted because a ⟨vertical command⟩ occurred in unrestricted horizontal mode:

```
... last words.\vskip6pt
A new paragraphs ...
```

Also, a paragraph ends if a closing brace is found in horizontal mode inside \vbox, \insert, or \output.

After the \par command TeX goes into vertical mode and exercises the page builder (see page 224). If the \par was inserted because a vertical command occurred in horizontal mode, the vertical command is then examined anew. The \par does not insert any vertical glue or penalties itself. A \par command also clears the paragraph shape parameters (see Chapter 18).

17.1.1 The \par command and the \par token

It is important to distinguish between the \par token and the primitive \par command that is the initial meaning of that token. The \par token is inserted when the input processor sees an empty line, or when the execution processor finds a ⟨vertical command⟩ in horizontal mode; the \par command is what actually closes off a paragraph. Decoupling the token and the command is an important tool for special effects in paragraphs (see some examples in Chapters 5 and 9).

17.1.2 Paragraph filling: \parfillskip

After the last element of the paragraph TEX implicitly inserts the equivalent of

```
\unskip \penalty10000 \hskip\parfillskip
```

The \unskip serves to remove any spurious glue at the paragraph end, such as the space generated by the line end if the \par was inserted by the input processor. For example:

```
end.

\noindent Begin
```

results in the tokens

```
end.␣\par Begin
```

With the sequence inserted by the \par this becomes

```
end.␣\unskip\penalty10000\hskip ...
```

which in turn gives

```
end.\penalty ...
```

The \parfillskip is in plain TEX first-order infinite (0pt plus 1fil), so ending a paragraph with \hfil$\bullet$\par will give a bullet halfway between the last word and the line end; with \hfill$\bullet$\par it will be flush right.

17.2 ASSORTED REMARKS

17.2.1 Ending a paragraph and a group at the same time

If a paragraph is set in a group, it may be necessary to ensure that the \par ending the paragraph occurs inside the group. The parameters influencing the typesetting of the paragraph, such as the \leftskip and the \baselineskip, are only looked at when the paragraph is finished. Thus finishing off a paragraph with

```
... last words.}\par
```

causes the values to be used that prevail outside the group, instead of those inside.
Better ways to end the paragraph are

    ... last words.\par}

or

    ... last words.\medskip}

In the second example the vertical command \medskip causes the \par token to be inserted.

17.2.2 Ending a paragraph with \hfill\break

The sequence \hfill\break is a way to force a 'newline' inside a paragraph. If you end a paragraph with this, however, you will probably get an Underfull \hbox error. Surprisingly, the underfull box is not the broken line – after all, that one was filled – but a completely empty box following it (actually, it does contain the \leftskip and \rightskip).

What happens? The paragraph ends with

    \hfill\break\par

which turns into

    \hfill\break\unskip\nobreak\hskip\parfillskip

The \unskip finds no preceding glue, so the \break is followed by a penalty item and a glue item, both of which disappear after the line break has been chosen at the \break. However, TeX has already decided that there should be an extra line, that is, an \hbox to \hsize. And there is nothing to fill it with, so an underfull box results.

17.2.3 Ending a paragraph with a rule

See page 87 for paragraphs ending with rule leaders instead of the default \parfillskip white space.

17.2.4 No page breaks in between paragraphs

The \par command does not insert any glue in the vertical list, so in the sequence

    ... last words.\par \nobreak \medskip
    \noindent First words ...

no page breaks will occur between the paragraphs. The vertical list generated is

    \hbox(6.94444+0.0)x ...   % last line of paragraph
    \penalty 10000   % \nobreak
    \glue 6.0 plus 2.0 minus 2.0   % \medskip

```
\glue(\parskip) 0.0 plus 1.0     % \parskip
\glue(\baselineskip) 5.05556     % interline glue
\hbox(6.94444+0.0)x ...          % first line of paragraph
```

TeX will not break this vertical list above the \medskip, because the penalty value prohibits it; it will not break at any other place, because it can only break at glue if that glue is preceded by a non-discardable item.

17.2.5 Finite \parfillskip

In plain TeX, \parfillskip has a (first-order) infinite stretch component. All other glue in the last line of a paragraph will then be set at natural width. If the \parfillskip has only finite (or possibly zero) stretch, other glue will be stretched or shrunk. A display formula in a paragraph with such a last line will be surrounded by \abovedisplayskip and \belowdisplayskip, even if \abovedisplayshortskip glue would be in order.

The reason for this is that glue setting is slightly machine-dependent, and any such processes should be kept out of TeX's global decisions.

17.2.6 A precaution for paragraphs that do not indent

If you are setting a text with both the paragraph indentation and the white space between paragraphs zero, you run the risk that the start of a new paragraph may be indiscernible when the last line of the previous paragraph ends almost or completely flush right. A sensible precaution for this is to set the \parfillskip to, for instance

```
\parfillskip=1cm plus 1fil
```

instead of the usual 0cm plus 1fil.

On the other hand, you may let yourself be convinced by Tschichold (1975) that paragraphs should always indent.

CHAPTER 18

Paragraph Shape

This chapter treats the parameters and commands that influence the shape of a paragraph.

\parindent   Width of the indentation box added in front of a paragraph. Plain TeX default: 20pt.
\hsize   Line width used for typesetting a paragraph. Plain TeX default: 6.5in.
\leftskip   Glue that is placed to the left of all lines of a paragraph.
\rightskip   Glue that is placed to the right of all lines of a paragraph.
\hangindent   If positive, this indicates indentation from the left margin; if negative, this is the negative of the indentation from the right margin.
\hangafter   If positive, this denotes the number of lines before indenting starts; if negative, the absolute value of this is the number of indented lines starting with the first line of the paragraph. Default: 1.
\parshape   Command for general paragraph shapes.

18.1   THE WIDTH OF TEXT LINES

When TeX has finished absorbing a paragraph, it has formed a horizontal list, starting with an indentation box, and ending with \parfillskip glue. This list is then broken into lines of length \hsize. Each line of a paragraph is padded left and right with certain amounts of glue, the \leftskip and \rightskip, which are taken into account in reaching \hsize.

The values of \leftskip and \rightskip are taken into account in the line-breaking algorithm. Thus the main point about the \raggedright macro in plain TeX and the LaTeX 'flushleft' environment is that they set the \rightskip to zero plus some stretch.

The commands \parshape and \hangindent also affect line width. They work by altering the \hsize and afterwards shifting the boxes containing the lines.

18.2   SHAPE PARAMETERS

18.2.1   Hanging indentation

A simple, and frequently occurring, paragraph shape is that with a number of starting or trailing lines indented. TeX can realize such shapes using two parameters: \hangafter and \hangindent. Both can assume positive and negative values. The \hangindent controls the amount of indentation:

- \hangindent > 0: the paragraph is indented at the left margin by this amount.
- \hangindent < 0: the paragraph is indented at the right margin by the absolute value of this amount.

For example (assume \parindent=0pt),

```
                                         a a a a a
                                         a a a a a
    a a a a a a a a a a a ...            a a ...
                                         a a a a a
    \hangindent=10pt                     a a a
    a a a a a a a a a a a ...   gives    a a a
                                         a ...
    \hangindent=-10pt                    a a a a a
    a a a a a a a a a a a ...            a a a
                                         a a a
                                         a ...
```

The default value of \hangindent is 0pt.

The \hangafter parameter determines the number of lines that is indented:

- \hangafter ≥ 0: after this number of lines the rest of the lines will be indented; in other words, this many lines from the start of the paragraph will not be indented.
- \hangafter < 0: the absolute value of this is the number of lines that will be indented starting at the beginning of the paragraph.

For example,

```
                                             a a a a a
                                             a a a a a
    a a a a a a a a a a a ...                a a ...
                                             a a a a a
    \hangindent=10pt  \hangafter=2           a a a a
    a a a a a a a a a a a ...   looks like   a a a
                                             ...
    \hangindent=10pt  \hangafter=-2          a a a
    a a a a a a a a a a a ...                a a a
                                             a a a a a
                                             a ...
```

The default value for \hangafter is 1.

With both parameters having the possibility to be positive and negative, four ways of hanging indentation result. See below for hanging indentation into the margin ('outdent').

Hanging indentation is implemented as follows. The amount of hanging indentation is subtracted from the \hsize for the lines that indent; after the paragraph has been broken into horizontal boxes, the lines that should indent on the left are shifted right.

Regular indentation of size \parindent is not influenced by hanging indentation. Thus you should start a paragraph with hanging indentation explicitly by \noindent if the extra indentation is unwanted.

The default values of \hangindent and \hangafter are restored after every \par command.

18.2.2 General paragraph shapes: \parshape

Quite general paragraph shapes can be implemented using \parshape. With this command line lengths and indentation for the first n lines of a paragraph can be specified. Thus this command takes $2n + 1$ parameters: the number of lines n, followed by n pairs of an indentation and a line length.

\parshape⟨equals⟩ $n\ i_1\ \ell_1\ \ldots\ i_n\ \ell_n$

The specification for the last line is repeated if the paragraph following has more than n lines. If there are fewer than n lines the remaining specifications are ignored. The default value is (naturally) \parshape = 0.

A \parshape command takes precedence over a \hangindent if both have been specified. Regular \parindent indentation is suppressed if \parshape is in effect.

The \parshape parameter is, like \hangindent, \hangafter, and \looseness (see Chapter 19), cleared after a \par command. Since every empty line generates a \par token, one should not leave an empty line between a paragraph shape (or hanging indentation) declaration and the following paragraph.

The control sequence \parshape is an ⟨internal integer⟩: its value is the number of lines n with which it was set.

18.3 ASSORTED REMARKS

18.3.1 Centred last lines

Equal stretch and shrink amounts for the \leftskip and \rightskip give centred texts, in the sense that each line is centred. For proper centring of the first and last lines of a paragraph the \parindent and \parfillskip have to be made zero. However, the margins are ragged.

A surprising application of \leftskip and \rightskip leads to paragraphs with flush margins and a centred last line.

```
\leftskip=0cm plus 0.5fil \rightskip=0cm plus -0.5fil
\parfillskip=0cm plus 1fil
```

For all lines of a paragraph but the last one the stretch components add up to zero so the \leftskip and \rightskip inserted are zero. On the last line the

`\parfillskip` adds `plus 1fil` of stretch; therefore there is a total of `plus 0.5fil` of stretch at both the left and right end of the line.

It would have been incorrect to specify

```
\leftskip=0cm plus 0.5fil \rightskip=0cm minus 0.5fil
```

TeX gives an error about this: it complains about 'infinite shrinkage'.

Centring not only the last line, but also the first line of a paragraph can be done by the parameter settings

```
\parindent=0pt \everypar{\hskip 0pt plus -1fil}
\leftskip=0pt plus .5fil
\rightskip=0pt plus -.5fil
```

This time a horizontal skip inserted by `\everypar` combines with the `\leftskip` to give the same amount of stretchability on both sides of the first line of the paragraph.

18.3.2 Indenting into the margin

Suppose you want a hanging indent of 1cm *into* the left margin after the first two lines of a paragraph. Specifying `\hangindent=-1cm` will give a hanging indentation of one centimetre from the *right* margin, so another approach is necessary. The following does the job:

```
\leftskip=-1cm \hangindent=1cm \hangafter=-2
```

The only problem with this is that the leftskip needs to be reset after the paragraph. Suitable redefinition of `\par` removes this objection:

```
\def\hangintomargin{\bgroup
    \leftskip=-1cm \hangindent=1cm \hangafter=-2
    \def\par{\endgraf\egroup}}
```

The redefinition of `\par` is here local to the paragraph that should be outdented.

Another, elegant, solution uses `\parshape`:

```
\dimen0=\hsize \advance\dimen0 by 1cm
\parshape=3         % three lines:
   0cm\hsize        % first  line specification
   0cm\hsize        % second line specification
   -1cm\dimen0      % third  line specification
```

18.3.3 Hang a paragraph from an object

The LaTeX format has a macro, `\@hangfrom`, to have one paragraph of text hanging from some object, usually a box or a short line of text.

Example This paragraph is an example of the `\hangfrom` macro defined below. In the LaTeX document styles, the `\@hangfrom` macro (which is similar to this) is used for multi-line section headings.

Consider then the macro `\hangfrom`:

```
\def\hangfrom#1{\def\hangobject{#1}\setbox0=\hbox{\hangobject}%
    \hangindent \wd0 \noindent \hangobject \ignorespaces}
```

Because of the default `\hangafter=1`, this will produce one line of width `\hsize`, after which the rest of the paragraph will be left indented by the width of the `\hangobject`.

18.3.4 Another approach to hanging indentation

Hanging indentation can also be attained by a combination of shifting the left margin and outdenting. Itemized lists can for instance be implemented in this manner:

```
\newdimen\listindent
\def\itemlist{\begingroup
    \advance\leftskip by \listindent
    \parindent=-\listindent}
\def\stopitemlist{\par\endgroup}
\def\item#1{\par\leavevmode
    \hbox to \listindent{#1\hfil}\ignorespaces
    }
```

If an item should encompass more than one paragraph, the implementation could be

```
\newdimen\listindent \newdimen\listparindent
\def\itemlist{\begingroup
    \advance\leftskip by \listindent
    \parindent=\listparindent}
\def\stopitemlist{\par\endgroup}
\def\item#1{\par\noindent
    \hbox to 0cm{\kern-\listindent #1\hfil}\ignorespaces
    }
```

Example

```
\itemlist\item{1.}First item\par
Is two paragraphs long.
\item{2.}Second item.\stopitemlist
```

gives

> 1. First item
>   Is two paragraphs long.
> 2. Second item.

18.3.5 Hanging indentation versus `\leftskip` shifting

From the above examples it would seem that hanging indentation and modifying the \leftskip and \rightskip are interchangeable. They are, but only to a certain extent.

Setting \leftskip to some positive value for a paragraph means that the \hsize stays the same, but every line starts with a glue item. Hanging indentation, on the other hand, is implemented by decreasing the \hsize value for the lines that hang, and shifting the finished horizontal boxes horizontally in the surrounding vertical list.

The difference between the two approaches becomes visible mainly in the fact that display formulas are not shifted when the \leftskip is altered. See Chapter 9 for an example showing how leaders are affected by margin shifting.

18.3.6 More examples

Some more examples of paragraph shapes (effected by various means) can be found in Eijkhout (1990a). One example from that article appears on page 53.

CHAPTER 19

Line Breaking

This chapter treats line breaking and the concept of 'badness' that TEX uses to decide how to break a paragraph into lines, or where to break a page. The various penalties contributing to the cost of line breaking are treated here, as is hyphenation. Page breaking is treated in Chapter 27.

\penalty   Specify desirability of not breaking at this point.

\linepenalty   Penalty value associated with each line break. Plain TEX default: 10.

\hyphenpenalty   Penalty associated with break at a discretionary item in the general case. Plain TEX default: 50.

\exhyphenpenalty   Penalty for breaking a horizontal line at a discretionary item in the special case where the prebreak text is empty. Plain TEX default: 50.

\adjdemerits   Penalty for adjacent visually incompatible lines. Plain TEX default: 10 000.

\doublehyphendemerits   Penalty for consecutive lines ending with a hyphen. Plain TEX default: 10 000.

\finalhyphendemerits   Penalty added when the penultimate line of a paragraph ends with a hyphen. Plain TEX default: 5000.

\allowbreak   Macro for creating a breakpoint by inserting a \penalty0.

\pretolerance   Tolerance value for a paragraph without hyphenation. Plain TEX default: 100.

\tolerance   Tolerance value for lines in a paragraph with hyphenation. Plain TEX default: 200.

\emergencystretch   (TEX3 only) Assumed extra stretchability in lines of a paragraph.

\looseness   Number of lines by which this paragraph has to be made longer than it would be ideally.

\prevgraf   The number of lines in the paragraph last added to the vertical list.

\discretionary   Specify the way a character sequence is split up at a line break.

\-   Discretionary hyphen; this is equivalent to \discretionary{-}{}{}.

\hyphenchar   Number of the hyphen character of a font.

\defaulthyphenchar   Value of \hyphenchar when a font is loaded. Plain TEX default: `\-.

\uchyph   Positive to allow hyphenation of words starting with a capital letter. Plain TeX default: 1.
\lefthyphenmin   (TeX3 only) Minimal number of characters before a hyphenation. Plain TeX default: 2.
\righthyphenmin   (TeX3 only) Minimum number of characters after a hyphenation. Plain TeX default: 3.
\patterns   Define a list of hyphenation patterns for the current value of \language; allowed only in IniTeX.
\hyphenation   Define hyphenation exceptions for the current value of \language.
\language   Choose a set of hyphenation patterns and exceptions.
\setlanguage   Reset the current language.

19.1 PARAGRAPH BREAK COST CALCULATION

A paragraph is broken such that the amount d of *demerits* associated with breaking it is minimized. The total amount of demerits for a paragraph is the sum of those for the individual lines, plus possibly some extra penalties. Considering a paragraph as a whole instead of breaking it on a line-by-line basis can lead to better line breaking: TeX can choose to take a slightly less beautiful line in the beginning of the paragraph in order to avoid bigger trouble later on.

For each line demerits are calculated from the *badness* b of stretching or shrinking the line to the break, and the *penalty* p associated with the break. The badness is not allowed to exceed a certain prescribed tolerance.

In addition to the demerits for breaking individual lines, TeX assigns demerits for the way lines combine; see below.

The implementation of TeX's paragraph-breaking algorithm is explained in Knuth and Plass (1981).

19.1.1 Badness

From the ratio between the stretch or shrink present in a line, and the actual stretch or shrink taken, the 'badness' of breaking a line at a certain point is calculated. This badness is an important factor in the process of line breaking. See page 78 for the formula for badness.

In this chapter badness will only be discussed in the context of line breaking. Badness is also computed when a vertical list is stretched or shrunk (see Chapter 27).

The following terminology is used to describe badness:

tight (3)   is any line that has shrunk with a badness $b \geq 13$, that is, by using at least one-half of its amount of shrink (see page 78 for the computation).
decent (2)   is any line with a badness $b \leq 12$.
loose (1)   is any line that has stretched with a badness $b \geq 13$, that is, by using at least one-half of its amount of stretch.

very loose (0)   is any line that has stretched with a badness $b \geq 100$, that is, by using its full amount of stretch or more. Recall that glue can stretch, but not shrink more than its allowed amount.

The numbering is used in trace output (Chapter 34), and it is also used in the following definition: if the classifications of two adjacent lines differ by more than 1, the lines are said to be *visually incompatible*. See below for the \adjdemerits parameter associated with this.

Overfull horizontal and vertical boxes are passed unnoticed if their excess width or height is less than \hfuzz or \vfuzz respectively; they are not reported if the badness is less than \hbadness or \vbadness (see Chapter 5).

19.1.2 Penalties and other break locations

Line breaks can occur at the following places in horizontal lists:

1. At a penalty. The penalty value is the 'aesthetic cost' of breaking the line at that place. Negative penalties are considered as bonuses. A penalty of 10 000 or more inhibits, and a penalty of −10 000 or less forces, a break.

    Putting more than one penalty in a row is equivalent to putting just the one with the minimal value, because that one is the best candidate for line breaking.

    Penalties in horizontal mode are inserted by the user (or a user macro). The only exception is the \nobreak inserted before the \parfillskip glue.

2. At a glue, if it is not part of a math formula, and if it is preceded by a non-discardable item (see Chapter 6). There is no penalty associated with breaking at glue.

    The condition about the non-discardable precursor is necessary, because otherwise breaking in between two pieces of glue would be possible, which would cause ragged edges to the paragraph.

3. At a kern, if it is not part of a math formula and if it is followed by glue. There is no penalty associated with breaking at a kern.

4. At a math-off, if that is followed by glue. Since math-off (and math-on) act as kerns (see Chapter 23), this is very much like the previous case. There is no penalty associated with breaking at a math-off.

5. At a discretionary break. The penalty is the \hyphenpenalty or the \exhyphenpenalty. This is treated below.

Any discardable material following the break – glue, kerns, math-on/off and penalties – is discarded. If one considers a line break at glue (kern, math-on/off) to occur at the front end of the glue item, this implies that that piece of glue disappears in the break.

19.1.3 Demerits

From the badness of a line and the penalty, if any, the demerits of the line are calculated. Let l be the value of \linepenalty, b the badness of the line, p the penalty at the break; then the demerits d are given by

$$d = \begin{cases} (l+b)^2 + p^2 & \text{if } 0 \leq p < 10\,000 \\ (l+b)^2 - p^2 & \text{if } -10\,000 < p < 0 \\ (l+b)^2 & \text{if } p \leq -10\,000 \end{cases}$$

Both this formula and the one for the badness are described in Knuth and Plass (1981) as 'quite arbitrary', but they have been shown to lead to good results in practice.

The demerits for a paragraph are the sum of the demerits for the lines, plus

- the \adjdemerits for any two adjacent lines that are not visually compatible (see above),
- \doublehyphendemerits for any two consecutive lines ending with a hyphen, and the
- \finalhyphendemerits if the penultimate line of a paragraph ends with a hyphen.

At the start of a paragraph TeX acts as if there was a preceding line which was 'decent'. Therefore \adjdemerits will be added if the first line is 'very loose'. Also, the last line of a paragraph is ordinarily also 'decent' – all spaces are set at natural width owing to the infinite stretch in the \parfillskip – so \adjdemerits are added if the preceding line is 'very loose'.

Note that the penalties at which a line break is chosen weigh about as heavily as the badness of the line, so they can be relatively small. However, the three extra demerit parameters have to be of the order of the square of penalties and badnesses to weigh equally heavily.

19.1.4 The number of lines of a paragraph

After a paragraph has been completed (or partially completed prior to a display), the variable \prevgraf records the number of lines in the paragraph. By assigning to this variable – and because this is a ⟨special integer⟩ such an assignment is automatically global – TeX's decision processes can be influenced. This may be useful in combination with hanging indentation or \parshape specifications (see Chapter 18).

Some direct influence of the line-breaking process on the resulting number of lines exists. One factor is the \linepenalty which is included in the demerits of each line. By increasing the line penalty TeX can be made to minimize the number of lines in a paragraph.

Deviations from the optimal number of lines, that is, the number of lines stemming from the optimal way of breaking a paragraph into lines, can be forced by the user by means of the \looseness parameter. This parameter, which is reset every time the shape parameters are cleared (see Chapter 18), indicates by how many lines the current paragraph should be made longer than is optimal. A negative value of \looseness will attempt to make the paragraph shorter by a number of lines that is the absolute value of the parameter.

TeX will still observe the values of \pretolerance and \tolerance (see below) when lengthening or shortening a paragraph under influence of \looseness. Therefore, TeX will only lengthen or shorten a paragraph for as far as is possible without exceeding these parameters.

19.1.5 Between the lines

TeX's paragraph mechanism packages lines into horizontal boxes that are appended to the surrounding vertical list. The resulting sequence of vertical items is then a repeating sequence of

- a box containing a line of text,
- possibly migrated vertical material (see page 59),
- a penalty item reflecting the cost of a page break at that point, which is normally the \interlinepenalty (see Chapter 27), and
- interline glue, which is calculated automatically on basis of the \prevdepth (see Chapter 15).

19.2 THE PROCESS OF BREAKING

TeX tries to break paragraphs in such a way that the badness of each line does not exceed a certain tolerance. If there exists more than one solution to this, the one with the fewest demerits is taken.

By setting \tracingparagraphs to a positive value, TeX can be made to report the calculations of the paragraph mechanism in the log file. Some implementations of TeX may have this option disabled to make TeX run faster.

19.2.1 Three passes

First an attempt is made to split the paragraph into lines without hyphenating, that is, without inserting discretionary hyphens. This attempt succeeds if none of the lines has a badness exceeding \pretolerance.

Otherwise, a second pass is made, inserting discretionaries and using \tolerance. If \pretolerance is negative, the first pass is omitted.

TeX can be made to make a third pass if the first and second pass fail. If \emergencystretch is a positive dimension, TeX will assume this much extra stretchability in each line when badness and demerits are calculated. Thus solutions that only slightly exceeded the given tolerances will now become feasible. However, no glue of size \emergencystretch is actually present, so underfull box messages may still occur.

19.2.2 Tolerance values

How much trouble TeX will have typesetting a piece of text depends partly on the tolerance value. Therefore it is sensible to have some idea of what badness values mean in visual terms.

For lines that are stretched, the badness is 100 times the cube of the stretch ratio. A badness of 800 thus means that the stretch ratio is 2. If the space is, as in the ten-point Computer Modern Font,

```
3.33pt plus 1.67pt minus 1.11pt
```

a badness of 800 means that spaces have been stretched to

$$3.33\text{pt} + 2 \times 1.67\text{pt} = 6.66\text{pt}$$

that is, to exactly double their natural size. It is up to you to decide whether this is too large.

19.3 DISCRETIONARIES

A discretionary item `\discretionary{..}{..}{..}` marks a place where a word can be broken. Each of the three arguments is a ⟨general text⟩ (see Chapter 36): they are, in sequence,

- the *pre-break* text, which is appended to the part of the word before the break,
- the *post-break* text, which is prepended to the part of the word after the break, and
- the *no-break* text, which is used if the word is not broken at the discretionary item.

For example: `ab\discretionary{g}{h}{cd}ef` is the word `abcdef`, but it can be hyphenated with `abg` before the break and `hef` after. Note that there is no automatic hyphen character.

All three texts may contain any sorts of tokens, but any primitive commands and macros should expand to boxes, kerns, and characters.

19.3.1 Hyphens and discretionaries

Internally, TeX inserts the equivalent of

```
\discretionary{\char\hyphenchar\font}{}{}
```

at every place where a word can be broken. No such discretionary is inserted if `\hyphenchar\font` is not in the range 0–255, or if its position in the font is not filled. When a font is loaded, its `\hyphenchar` value is set to `\defaulthyphenchar`. The `\hyphenchar` value can be changed after this.

In plain TeX the `\defaulthyphenchar` has the value '`\-`, so for all fonts character 45 (the ASCII hyphen character) is the hyphen sign, unless it is specified otherwise.

The primitive command `\-` (called a 'discretionary hyphen') is equivalent to the above `\discretionary{\char\hyphenchar\font}{}{}`. Breaking at such a discretionary, whether inserted implicitly by TeX or explicitly by the user, has a cost of `\hyphenpenalty`.

In unrestricted horizontal mode an empty discretionary \discretionary{}{}{} is automatically inserted after characters whose character code is the \hyphenchar value of the font, thus enabling hyphenation at that point. The penalty for breaking a line at such a discretionary with an empty pre-break text is \exhyphenpenalty, that is, the 'explicit hyphen' penalty.

If a word contains discretionary breaks, for instance because of explicit hyphen characters, TeX will not consider it for further hyphenation. People have solved the ensuing problems by tricks such as

```
\def\={\penalty10000 \hskip0pt -\penalty0 \hskip0pt\relax}
... integro\=differential equations...
```

The skips before and after the hyphen lead TeX into treating the first and second half of the compound expression as separate words; the penalty before the first skip inhibits breaking before the hyphen.

19.3.2 Examples of discretionaries

Languages such as German or Dutch have words that change spelling when hyphenated (German: 'backen' becomes 'bak-ken'; Dutch: 'autootje' becomes 'auto-tje'). This problem can be solved with TeX's discretionaries.

For instance, for German (this is inspired by Partl (1988)):

```
\catcode'\"=\active
\def"#1{\ifx#1k\discretionary{k-}{k}{ck}\fi}
```

which enables the user to write ba"ken.

In Dutch there is a further problem which allows a nice systematic solution. Umlaut characters ('trema' is the Dutch term) should often disappear in a break, for instance 'naäpen' hyphenates as 'na-apen', and 'onbeïnvloedbaar' hyphenates as 'onbe-invloedbaar'. A solution (inspired by Braams (1991)) is

```
\catcode'\"=\active
\def"#1{\ifx#1i\discretionary{-}{i}{\"i}%
        \else   \discretionary{-}{#1}{\"#1}\fi}
```

which enables the user to type na"apen and onbe"invloedbaar.

19.4 HYPHENATION

TeX's hyphenation algorithm uses a list of patterns to determine at what places a word that is a candidate for hyphenation can be broken. Those aspects of hyphenation connected with these patterns are treated in appendix H of *The TeXbook*; the method of generating hyphenation patterns automatically is described in Liang (1983). People have been known to generate lists of patterns by hand; see for instance Kuiken (1990). Such hand-generated lists may be superior to automatically generated lists.

Here it will mainly be described how TeX declares a word to be a candidate for hyphenation. The problem here is how to cope with punctuation and things such as quotation marks that can be attached to a word. Also, *implicit kerns*, that is, kerns inserted because of font information, must be handled properly.

19.4.1 Start of a word

TeX starts at glue items (if they are not in math mode) looking for a *starting letter* of a word: a character with non-zero \lccode, or a ligature starting with such a character (upper/lowercase codes are explained on page 29). Looking for this starting letter, TeX bypasses any implicit kerns, and characters with zero \lccode (this includes, for instance, punctuation and quotation marks), or ligatures starting with such a character.

If no suitable starting letter turns up, that is, if something is found that is not a character or ligature, TeX skips to the next glue, and starts this algorithm anew. Otherwise a trial word is collected consisting of all following characters with non-zero \lccode from the same font as the starting letter, or ligatures consisting completely of such characters. Implicit kerns are allowed between the characters and ligatures.

If the starting letter is from a font for which the value of \hyphenchar is invalid, or for which this character does not exist, hyphenation is abandoned for this word. If the starting letter is an uppercase letter (that is, it is not equal to its own \lccode), TeX will abandon hyphenation unless \uchyph is positive. The default value for this parameter is 1 in plain TeX, implying that capitalized words are subject to hyphenation.

19.4.2 End of a word

Following the trial word can be characters (from another font, or with zero \lccode), ligatures or implicit kerns. After these items, if any, must follow

- glue or an explicit kern,
- a penalty,
- a whatsit, or
- a \mark, \insert, or \vadjust item.

In particular, the word will not be hyphenated if it is followed by a

- box,
- rule,
- math formula, or
- discretionary item.

Since discretionaries are inserted after the \hyphenchar of the font, occurrence of this character inhibits further hyphenation. Also, placement of accents is implemented using explicit kerns (see Chapter 3), so any \accent command is considered to be the end of a word, and inhibits hyphenation of the word.

19.4.3 TeX2 versus TeX3

There is a noticeable difference in the treatment of hyphenated fragments between TeX2 and TeX3. TeX2 insists that the part before the break should be at least two characters, and the part after the break three characters, long. Typographically this is a sound decision: this way there are no two-character pieces of a word stranded at the end or beginning of the line. Both before and after the break there are at least three characters.

In TeX3 two integer parameters have been introduced to control the length of these fragments: \lefthyphenmin and \righthyphenmin. These are set to 2 and 3 respectively in the plain format for TeX3. If the sum of these two is 63 or more, all hyphenation is suppressed.

Another addition in TeX3, the possibility to have several sets of hyphenation patterns, is treated below.

19.4.4 Patterns and exceptions

The statements

> \patterns⟨general text⟩
> \hyphenation⟨general text⟩

are ⟨hyphenation assignment⟩s, which are ⟨global assignment⟩s. The \patterns command, which specifies a list of hyphenation patterns, is allowed only in IniTeX (see Chapter 33), and all patterns must be specified before the first paragraph is typeset.

Hyphenation exceptions can be specified at any time with statements such as

> \hyphenation{oxy-mo-ron gar-goyle}

which specify locations where a word may be hyphenated. Subsequent \hyphenation statements are cumulative.

In TeX3 these statements are taken to hold for the language that is the current value of the \language parameter.

19.5 SWITCHING HYPHENATION PATTERNS

When typesetting paragraphs, TeX (version 3) can use several sets of patterns and hyphenation exceptions, for at most 256 languages.

If a \patterns or \hyphenation command is given (see above), TeX stores the patterns or exceptions under the current value of the \language parameter. The \patterns command is only allowed in IniTeX, and patterns must be specified before any typesetting is done. Hyphenation exceptions, however, can be specified cumulatively, and not only in IniTeX.

In addition to the \language parameter, which can be set by the user, TeX has internally a 'current language'. This is set to zero at the start of every paragraph.

For every character that is added to a paragraph the current language is compared with the value of \language, and if they differ a whatsit element is added to the horizontal list, resetting the current language to the value of \language.

At the start of a paragraph, this whatsit is inserted after the \everypar tokens, but \lastbox can still access the indentation box.

As an example, suppose that a format has been created such that language 0 is English, and language 1 is Dutch. English hyphenations will then be used if the user does not specify otherwise; if a job starts with

```
\language=1
```

the whole document will be set using Dutch hyphenations, because TeX will insert a command changing the current language at the start of every paragraph. For example:

```
\language=1
T...
```

gives

```
.\hbox(0.0+0.0)x20.0          % indentation
.\setlanguage1 (hyphenmin 2,3) % language whatsit
.\tenrm T                     % start of text
```

The whatsit can be inserted explicitly, without changing the value of \language, by specifying

```
\setlanguage⟨number⟩
```

However, this will hardly ever be needed. One case where it may be necessary is when the contents of a horizontal box are unboxed to a paragraph: inside the box no whatsits are added automatically, since inside such a box no hyphenation can take place. See page 50 for another problem with text in horizontal boxes.

CHAPTER 20

Spacing

The usual interword space in TeX is specified in the font information, but the user can override this. This chapter explains the rules by which TeX calculates interword space.

\␣ Control space. Insert the same amount of space as a space token would if \spacefactor = 1000.
\spaceskip   Interword glue if non-zero.
\xspaceskip   Interword glue if non-zero and \spacefactor $\geq$ 2000.
\spacefactor   1000 times the ratio by which the stretch (shrink) component of the interword glue should be multiplied (divided).
\sfcode   Value for \spacefactor associated with a character.
\frenchspacing   Macro to switch off extra space after punctuation.
\nonfrenchspacing   Macro to switch on extra space after punctuation.

20.1 AUTOMATIC INTERWORD SPACE

For every space token in horizontal mode the interword glue of the current font is inserted, with stretch and shrink components. This allows, for instance, lines to be right justified. The size of the interword space is determined by \fontdimen parameters. To be specific, font dimension 2 is the normal interword space, dimension 3 is the amount of stretch of the interword space, and 4 is the amount of shrink. Font dimension 7 is called the 'extra space'; see below (the list of all the font dimensions appears on page 35).

Ordinarily all spaces between words (in one font) would be of equal size. To allow for differently sized spaces – for instance a typeset equivalent of the double spacing after punctuation in typewritten documents – TeX associates with each character a so-called 'space factor'.

When a character is added to the current horizontal list, the current value of the space factor (\spacefactor) becomes the space factor code (\sfcode) of that character, except that when that code is zero, the space factor does not change. Also, when the space factor code of the last character is >1000 and the current space factor is <1000, the space factor becomes 1000. The maximum space factor is 32 767.

The stretch component of the interword space is multiplied by the space factor divided by 1000; the shrink component is divided by this factor. The extra space (font dimension 7) is added to the natural component of the interword space when the space factor is ≥ 2000.

20.2 USER INTERWORD SPACE

The user can override the interword space contained in the \fontdimen parameters by setting the \spaceskip and the \xspaceskip to non-zero values. If \spaceskip is non-zero, it is taken instead of the normal interword space (\fontdimen2 plus \fontdimen3 minus \fontdimen4), but a non-zero \xspaceskip is used as interword space if the space factor is ≥ 2000.

If the \spaceskip is used, its stretch and shrink components are multiplied and divided respectively by \spacefactor/1000.

Note that, if \spaceskip and \xspaceskip are defined in terms of em, they change with the font.

Example
Let the following macros be given:

```
\def\a.{\vrule height10pt width4pt\spacefactor=1000\relax}
\def\b.{\vrule height10pt width4pt\spacefactor=3000\relax}
\def\c{\vrule height10pt width4pt\relax}
```

then

```
\vbox{
\fontdimen2\font=4pt % normal space
\fontdimen7\font=3pt % extra space
\a. \b. \c\par
% zero extra space
\fontdimen7\font=0pt
\a. \b. \c\par
% set \spaceskip for normal space
\spaceskip=2\fontdimen2\font
\a. \b. \c\par
% set \xspaceskip
\xspaceskip=2pt
\a. \b. \c\par
}
```

gives

In all of these lines the glue is set at natural width. In the first line the high space factor value after \b causes the extra space \fontdimen7 to be added. If this is zero (second line), the only difference between space factor values is the stretch/shrink ratio. In the third line the \spaceskip is taken for all space factor values. If the \xspaceskip is nonzero, it is taken (fourth line) instead of the \spaceskip for the high value of the space factor.

20.3 CONTROL SPACE AND TIE

Control space, `\ `, is a horizontal command which inserts a space, acting as if the current space factor is 1000. It can therefore be used after abbreviations when `\nonfrenchspacing` (see below) is in effect. For example:

```
\hbox spread 9pt{\nonfrenchspacing
        The reverend dr. Drofnats}
```

gives

> The reverend dr.   Drofnats

while

```
\hbox spread 9pt{\nonfrenchspacing
        The reverend dr.\ Drofnats}
```

gives

> The reverend dr. Drofnats

The `spread 9pt` is used to make the effect more visible.

The active character (in the plain format) tilde, ~, uses control space: it is defined as

```
\catcode`\~=\active
\def~{\penalty10000\ }
```

Such an active tilde is called a 'tie'; it inserts an ordinary amount of space, and prohibits breaking at this space.

20.4 MORE ON THE SPACE FACTOR

20.4.1 Space factor assignments

The space factor of a particular character can be assigned as

> `\sfcode`⟨8-bit number⟩⟨equals⟩⟨number⟩

IniTeX assigns a space factor code of 1000 to all characters except uppercase characters; they get a space factor code of 999. The plain format then assigns space factor codes greater than 1000 to various punctuation symbols, for instance `\sfcode`\`\.=3000`, which triples the stretch and shrink after a full stop. Also, for all space factor values ≥ 2000 the extra space is added; see above.

20.4.2 Punctuation

Because the space factor cannot jump from a value below 1000 to one above, a punctuation symbol after an uppercase character will not have the effect on the interword space that punctuation after a lowercase character has.

Example

```
a% \sfcode`a=1000, space factor becomes 1000
.% \sfcode`.=3000, spacefactor becomes 3000
% subsequent spaces will be increased.

A% \sfcode`A=999,  space factor becomes 999
.% \sfcode`.=3000, space factor becomes 1000
% subsequent spaces will not be increased.
```

Thus, initials are not mistaken for sentence ends. If an uppercase character does end a sentence, for instance

    `... and NASA.`

there are several solutions:

    `... NASA\spacefactor=1000.`

or

    `... NASA\hbox{}.`

which abuses the fact that after a box the space factor is set to 1000. The L^AT_EX macro `\@` is equivalent to the first possibility.

In the plain format two macros are defined that switch between uniform interword spacing and extra space after punctuation. The macro `\frenchspacing` sets the space factor code of all punctuation to 1000; the macro `\nonfrenchspacing` sets it to values greater than 1000.

Here are the actual definitions from `plain.tex`:

```
\def\frenchspacing{\sfcode`\.\@m \sfcode`\?\@m
   \sfcode`\!\@m \sfcode`\:\@m
   \sfcode`\;\@m \sfcode`\,\@m}
\def\nonfrenchspacing{\sfcode`\.3000 \sfcode`\?3000
   \sfcode`\!3000 \sfcode`\:2000
   \sfcode`\;1500 \sfcode`\,1250 }
```

where

    `\mathchardef\@m=1000`

is given in the plain format.

French spacing is a somewhat controversial issue: *The T_EXbook* acts as if non-French spacing is standard practice in printing, but for instance in Oxford University Press (1983) one finds 'The space of the line should be used after all points in normal text'. Extra space after punctuation may be considered a 'typewriter habit', but this is not entirely true. It used to be a lot more common than it is nowadays, and there are rational arguments against it: the full stop (point, period) at the end of a sentence, where extra punctuation is most visible, is rather small, so it carries some extra visual space of its own above it. This book does not use extra space after punctuation.

20.4.3 Other non-letters

The zero value of the space factor code makes characters that are not a letter and not punctuation 'transparent' for the space factor.

Example

```
a% \sfcode`a=1000, space factor becomes 1000
.% \sfcode`.=3000, spacefactor becomes 3000
 % subsequent spaces will be increased.

a% \sfcode`a=1000, space factor becomes 1000
.% \sfcode`.=3000, space factor becomes 3000
)% \sfcode`)=0,    space factor stays 3000
 % subsequent spaces will be increased.
```

20.4.4 Other influences on the space factor

The space factor is 1000 when TeX starts forming a horizontal list, in particular after \indent, \noindent, and directly after a display. It is also 1000 after a \vrule, an accent, or a ⟨box⟩ (in horizontal mode), but it is not influenced by \unhbox or \unhcopy commands.

In the first column of a \valign the space factor of the surrounding horizontal list is carried over; similarly, after a vertical alignment the space factor is set to the value reached in the last column.

CHAPTER 21

Characters in Math Mode

In math mode every character specifies by its \mathcode what position of a font to access, among other things. For delimiters this story is a bit more complicated. This chapter explains the concept of math codes, and shows how TeX implements variable size delimiters.

\mathcode   Code of a character determining its treatment in math mode.
\mathchar   Explicit denotation of a mathematical character.
\mathchardef   Define a control sequence to be a synonym for a math character code.
\delcode   Code specifying how a character should be used as delimiter.
\delimiter   Explicit denotation of a delimiter.
\delimiterfactor   1000 times the fraction of a delimited formula that should be covered by a delimiter. Plain TeX default: 901
\delimitershortfall   Size of the part of a delimited formula that is allowed to go uncovered by a delimiter. Plain TeX default: 5pt
\nulldelimiterspace   Width taken for empty delimiters. Plain TeX default: 1.2pt
\left   Use the following character as an open delimiter.
\right   Use the following character as a closing delimiter.
\big   One line high delimiter.
\Big   One and a half line high delimiter.
\bigg   Two lines high delimiter.
\Bigg   Two and a half lines high delimiter.
\bigl etc.   Left delimiters.
\bigm etc.   Delimiters used as binary relations.
\bigr etc.   Right delimiters.
\radical   Command for setting things such as root signs.
\mathaccent   Place an accent in math mode.
\skewchar   Font position of an after-placed accent.
\defaultskewchar   Value of \skewchar when a font is loaded.
\skew   Macro to shift accents on top of characters explicitly.
\widehat   Hat accent that can accommodate wide expressions.
\widetilde   Tilde accent that can accommodate wide expressions.

21.1 MATHEMATICAL CHARACTERS

Each of the 256 permissible character codes has an associated \mathcode, which can be assigned by

\mathcode⟨8-bit number⟩⟨equals⟩⟨15-bit number⟩

When processing in math mode, TeX replaces all characters of categories 11 and 12, and \char and \chardef characters, by their associated mathcode.

The 15-bit math code is most conveniently denoted hexadecimally as "xyzz, where

x ≤ 7 is the class (see page 193),
y is the font family number (see Chapter 22), and
zz is the position of the character in the font.

Math codes can also be specified directly by a ⟨math character⟩, which can be

- \mathchar⟨15-bit number⟩;
- ⟨mathchardef token⟩, a control sequence that was defined by

    \mathchardef⟨control sequence⟩⟨equals⟩⟨15-bit number⟩

  or
- a delimiter command

    \delimiter⟨27-bit number⟩

  where the last 12 bits are discarded.

The commands \mathchar and \mathchardef are analogous to \char and \chardef in text mode. Delimiters are treated below. A ⟨mathchardef token⟩ can be used as a ⟨number⟩, even outside math mode.

In IniTeX all letters receive \mathcode "71zz and all digits receive "70zz, where "zz is the hexadecimal position of the character in the font. Thus, letters are initially from family 1 (math italic in plain TeX), and digits are from family 0 (roman). For all other characters, IniTeX assigns

\mathcode $x = x$,

thereby placing them also in family 0.

If the mathcode is "8000, the smallest integer that is not a ⟨15-bit number⟩, the character is treated as an active character with the original character code. Plain TeX assigns a \mathcode of "8000 to the space, underscore and prime.

21.2 DELIMITERS

After \left and \right commands TeX looks for a delimiter. A delimiter is either an explicit \delimiter command (or a macro abbreviation for it), or a character with a non-zero delimiter code.

The \left and \right commands implicitly delimit a group, which is considered as a subformula. Since the enclosed formula can be arbitrarily large, the quest for the proper delimiter is a complicated story of looking at variants in two different fonts, linked chains of variants in a font, and building extendable delimiters from repeatable pieces.

The fact that a group enclosed in \left...\right is treated as an independent subformula implies that a sub- or superscript at the start of this formula is not considered to belong to the delimiter. For example, TeX acts as if \left(_2 is equivalent to \left({}_2. (A subscript after a \right delimiter is positioned with respect to that delimiter.)

21.2.1 Delimiter codes

To each character code there corresponds a delimiter code, assigned by

\delcode⟨8-bit number⟩⟨equals⟩⟨24-bit number⟩

A delimiter code thus consists of six hexadecimal digits "uvvxyy, where

uvv is the small variant of the delimiter, and
xyy is the large variant;
u, x are the font families of the variants, and
vv, yy are the locations in those fonts.

Delimiter codes are used after \left and \right commands. IniTeX sets all delimiter codes to -1, except \delcode`.=0, which makes the period an empty delimiter. In plain TeX delimiters have typically $u = 2$ and $x = 3$, that is, first family 2 is tried, and if no big enough delimiter turns up family 3 is tried.

21.2.2 Explicit \delimiter commands

Delimiters can also be denoted explicitly by a ⟨27-bit number⟩,

\delimiter"tuvvxyy

where uvvxyy are the small and large variant of the delimiter as above; the extra digit t (which is < 8) denotes the class (see page 193). For instance, the \langle macro is defined as

\def\langle{\delimiter "426830A }

which means it belongs to class 4, opening. Similarly, \rangle is of class 5, closing; and \uparrow is of class 3, relation.

After \left and \right – that is, when TeX is looking for a delimiter – the class digit is ignored; otherwise – when TeX is not looking for a delimiter – the rightmost three digits are ignored, and the four remaining digits are treated as a \mathchar; see above.

21.2.3 Finding a delimiter; successors

Typesetting a delimiter is a somewhat involved affair. First TeX determines the size y of the formula to be covered, which is twice the maximum of the height and depth of the formula. Thus the formula may not look optimal if it is not centred itself.

The size of the delimiter should be at least `\delimiterfactor` $\times\, y/1000$ and at least $y -$ `\delimitershortfall`. TeX then tries first the small variant, and if that one is not satisfactory (or if the uvv part of the delimiter is 000) it tries the large variant. If trying the large variant does not meet with success, TeX takes the largest delimiter encountered in this search; if no delimiter at all was found (which can happen if the xyy part is also 000), an empty box of width `\nulldelimiterspace` is taken.

Investigating a variant means, in sequence,

- if the current style (see page 192) is scriptscriptstyle the `\scriptscriptfont` of the family is tried;
- if the current style is scriptstyle or smaller the `\scriptfont` of the family is tried;
- otherwise the `\textfont` of the family is tried.

The plain format puts the cmex10 font in all three styles of family 3.

Looking for a delimiter at a certain position in a certain font means

- if the character is large enough, accept it;
- if the character is extendable, accept it;
- otherwise, if the character has a successor, that is, it is part of a chain of increasingly bigger delimiters in the same font, try the successor.

Information about successors and extensibility of a delimiter is coded in the font metric file of the font. An extendable character has a top, a bottom, possibly a mid piece, and a piece which is repeated directly below the top piece, and directly above the bottom piece if there is a mid piece.

21.2.4 \big, \Big, \bigg, and \Bigg delimiter macros

In order to be able to use a delimiter outside the `\left`...`\right` context, or to specify a delimiter of a different size than TeX would have chosen, four macros for 'big' delimiters exist: `\big`, `\Big`, `\bigg`, and `\Bigg`. These can be used with anything that can follow `\left` or `\right`.

Twelve further macros (for instance `\bigl`, `\bigm`, and `\bigr`) force such delimiters in the context of an opening symbol, a binary relation, and a closing symbol respectively:

```
\def\bigl{\mathopen\big}
\def\bigm{\mathrel\big}  \def\bigr{\mathclose\big}
```

The 'big' macros themselves put the requested delimiter and a null delimiter around an empty vertical box:

```
\def\big#1{{\nulldelimiterspace=0pt \mathsurround=0pt
            \hbox{$\left#1\vbox to 8.5pt{}\right.$}}}
```

As an approximate measure, the Big delimiters are one and a half times as large (11.5pt) as big delimiters; bigg ones are twice (14.5pt), and Bigg ones are two and a half times as large (17.5pt).

21.3 RADICALS

A radical is a compound of a left delimiter and an overlined math expression. The overlined expression is set in the cramped version of the surrounding style (see page 192).

In the plain format and the Computer Modern math fonts there is only one radical: the square root construct

```
\def\sqrt{\radical"270370 }
```

The control sequence \radical is followed by a ⟨24-bit number⟩ which specifies a small and a large variant of the left delimiter as was explained above. Joining the delimiter and the rule is done by letting the delimiter have a large depth, and a height which is equal to the desired rule thickness. The rule can then be placed on the current baseline. After the delimiter and the ruled expression have been joined the whole is shifted vertically to achieve the usual vertical centring (see Chapter 23).

21.4 MATH ACCENTS

Accents in math mode are specified by

\mathaccent⟨15-bit number⟩⟨math field⟩

Representing the 15-bit number as "xyzz, only the family y and the character position zz are used: an accented expression acts as \mathord expression (see Chapter 23).

In math mode whole expressions can be accented, whereas in text mode only characters can be accented. Thus in math mode accents can be stacked. However, the top accent may (or, more likely, will) not be properly positioned horizontally. Therefore the plain format has a macro \skew that effectively shifts the top accent. Its definition is

```
\def\skew#1#2#3{{#2{#3\mkern#1mu}\mkern-#1mu}{}}
```

and it is used for instance like

```
$\skew4\hat{\hat x}$
```

which gives $\hat{x}$.

For the correct positioning of accents over single characters the symbol and extension font have a \skewchar: this is the largest accent that adds to the width of an accented character. Positioning of any accent is based on the width of the character to be accented, followed by the skew character.

The skew characters of the Computer Modern math italic and symbol fonts are character "7F, '⁀', and "30, '′', respectively. The \defaultskewchar value is assigned to the \skewchar when a font is loaded. In plain TeX this is -1, so fonts ordinarily have no \skewchar.

Math accents can adapt themselves to the size of the accented expression: TeX will look for a successor of an accent in the same way that it looks for a successor of a delimiter. In the Computer Modern math fonts this mechanism is used in the \widehat and \widetilde macros. For example,

    \widehat x, \widehat{xy}, \widehat{xyz}

give

$\hat{x}, \widehat{xy}, \widehat{xyz}$

respectively.

CHAPTER 22

Fonts in Formulas

For math typesetting a single current font is not sufficient, as it is for text typesetting. Instead TEX uses several font families, and each family can contain three fonts. This chapter explains how font families are organized, and how TEX determines from what families characters should be taken.

\fam   The number of the current font family.
\newfam   Allocate a new math font family.
\textfont   Access the textstyle font of a family.
\scriptfont   Access the scriptstyle font of a family.
\scriptscriptfont   Access the scriptscriptstyle font of a family.

22.1   DETERMINING THE FONT OF A CHARACTER IN MATH MODE

The characters in math formulas can be taken from several different fonts (or better, font families) without any user commands. For instance, in plain TEX math formulas use the roman font, the math italic font, the symbol font and the math extension font.

In order to determine from which font a character is to be taken, TEX considers for each character in a formula its \mathcode (this is treated in Chapter 21). A \mathcode is a 15-bit number of the form "xyzz, where the hex digits have the following meaning:

  x: class,
  y: family,
  zz: position in font.

In general only the family determines from what font a character is to be taken. The class of a math character is mostly used to control spacing and other aspects of typesetting. Typical classes include 'relation', 'operator', 'delimiter'.

Class 7 is special in this respect: it is called 'variable family'. If a character has a \mathcode of the form "7yzz it is taken from family y, unless the parameter \fam has a value in the range 0–15; then it is taken from family \fam.

22.2 INITIAL FAMILY SETTINGS

Both lowercase and uppercase letters are defined by IniTeX to have math codes "71zz, which means that they are of variable family, initially from family 1. As TeX sets `fam=-1`, that is, an invalid value, when a formula starts, characters are indeed taken from family 1, which in plain TeX is math italic.

Digits have math code "70zz so they are initially from family 0, in plain TeX the roman font. All other character codes have a mathcode assigned by IniTeX as

$\mathcode x = x$

which puts them in class 0, ordinary, and family 0, roman in plain TeX.

In plain TeX, commands such as `\sl` then set both a font and a family:

`\def\sl{\fam\slfam\tensl}`

so putting `\sl` in a formula will cause all letters, digits, and uppercase Greek characters, to change to slanted style.

In most cases, any font can be assigned to any family, but two families in TeX have a special meaning: these are families 2 and 3. For instance, their number of `\fontdimen` parameters is different from the usual 7. Family 2 needs 22 parameters, and family 3 needs 13. These parameters have all a very specialized meaning for positioning in math typesetting. Their meaning is explained below, but for the full story the reader is referred to appendix G of *The TeXbook*.

22.3 FAMILY DEFINITION

TeX can access 16 families of fonts in math mode; font families have numbers 0–15. The number of the current family is recorded in the parameter `\fam`.

The macro `\newfam` gives the number of an unused family. This number is assigned using `\chardef` to the control sequence.

Each font family can have a font meant for text style, script style, and scriptscript style. Below it is explained how TeX determines in what style a (sub-)formula is to be typeset.

Fonts are assigned to a family as follows:

```
\newfam\MyFam
\textfont\MyFam=\tfont  \scriptfont\MyFam=\sfont
\scriptscriptfont\MyFam=\ssfont
```

for the text, script, and scriptscript fonts of a family. In general it is not necessary to fill all three members of a family (but it is for family 3). If TeX needs a character from a family member that has not been filled, it uses the `\nullfont` instead, a primitive font that has no characters (nor a `.tfm` file).

22.4 SOME SPECIFIC FONT CHANGES

22.4.1 Change the font of ordinary characters and uppercase Greek

All letters and the uppercase Greek characters are by default in plain TeX of class 7, variable family, so changing `\fam` will change the font from which they are taken. For example

```
{\fam=9 x}
```

gives an x from family 9.

Uppercase Greek characters are defined by `\mathchardef` statements in the plain format as "70zz, that is, variable family, initially roman. Therefore, uppercase Greek character also change with the family.

22.4.2 Change uppercase Greek independent of text font

In the Computer Modern font layout, uppercase Greek letters are part of the roman font; see page 290. Therefore, introducing another text font (with another layout) will change the uppercase Greek characters (or even make them disappear). One way of remedying this is by introducing a new family in which the cmr font, which contains the uppercase Greek, resides. The control sequences accessing these characters then have to be redefined:

```
\newfam\Kgreek
\textfont\Kgreek=cmr10 ...
\def\hex#1{\ifcase#1\or 1\or 2\or 3\or 4\or 5\or 6\or
    7\or 8\or 9\or A\or B\or C\or D\or E\or F\fi}
\mathchardef\Gamma="0\hex\Kgreek00 % was: "0100
\mathchardef\Beta ="0\hex\Kgreek01 % was: "0101
\mathchardef\Gamma ...
```

Note, by the way, the absence of a either a space or a `\relax` token after `#1` in the definition of `\hex`. This implies that this macro can only be called with an argument that is a control sequence.

22.4.3 Change the font of lowercase Greek and mathematical symbols

Lowercase Greek characters have math code "01zz, meaning they are always from the math italic family. In order to change this one might redefine them, for instance `\mathchardef\alpha="710B`, to make them variable family. This is not done in plain TeX, because the Computer Modern roman font does not have Greek lowercase, although it does have the uppercase characters.

Another way is to redefine them like `\mathchardef\alpha="0n0B` where n is the (hexadecimal) number of a family compatible with math italic, containing for instance a bold math italic font.

22.5 ASSORTED REMARKS

22.5.1 New fonts in formulas

There are two ways to access a font inside mathematics. After `\font\newfont=....` it is not possible to get the 'a' of the new font by `$...{\newfont a}...$` because TeX does not look at the current font in math mode. What does work is

```
$ ... \hbox{\newfont a} ...$
```

but this precludes the use of the new font in script and scriptscript styles.

The proper solution takes a bit more work:

```
\font\newtextfont=...
\font\newscriptfont=... \font\newsscriptfont=...
\newfam\newfontfam
\textfont\newfontfam=\newtextfont
\scriptfont\newfontfam=\newscriptfont
\scriptscriptfont\newfontfam=\newsscriptfont
\def\newfont{\newtextfont \fam=\newfontfam}
```

after which the font can be used as

```
$... {\newfont a_{b_c}} ...$
```

in all three styles.

22.5.2 Evaluating the families

TeX will only look at what is actually in the `\textfont` et cetera of the various families at the end of the whole formula. Switching fonts in the families is thus not possible inside a single formula. The number of 16 families may therefore turn out to be restrictive for some applications.

CHAPTER 23

Mathematics Typesetting

TeX has two math modes, display and non-display, and four styles, display, text, script, and scriptscript style, and every object in math mode belongs to one of eight classes. This chapter treats these concepts.

\everymath   Token list inserted at the start of a non-display math formula.
\everydisplay   Token list inserted at the start of a display math formula.
\displaystyle   Select the display style of math typesetting.
\textstyle   Select the text style of math typesetting.
\scriptstyle   Select the script style of math typesetting.
\scriptscriptstyle   Select the scriptscript style of math typesetting.
\mathchoice   Give four variants of a formula for the four styles of math typesetting.
\mathord   Let the following character or subformula function as an ordinary object.
\mathop   Let the following character or subformula function as a large operator.
\mathbin   Let the following character or subformula function as a binary operation.
\mathrel   Let the following character or subformula function as a relation.
\mathopen   Let the following character or subformula function as a opening symbol.
\mathclose   Let the following character or subformula function as a closing symbol.
\mathpunct   Let the following character or subformula function as a punctuation symbol.
\mathinner   Let the following character or subformula function as an inner formula.
\mathaccent   Place an accent in math mode.
\vcenter   Construct a vertical box, vertically centred on the math axis.
\limits   Place limits over and under a large operator.
\nolimits   Place limits of a large operator as subscript and superscript expressions.
\displaylimits   Restore default placement for limits.
\scriptspace   Extra space after subscripts and superscripts. Plain TeX default: 0.5pt

`\nonscript`   Cancel the next glue item if it occurs in scriptstyle or scriptscriptstyle.
`\mkern`   Insert a kern measured in mu units.
`\mskip`   Insert glue measured in mu units.
`\muskip`   Prefix for skips measured in mu units.
`\muskipdef`   Define a control sequence to be a synonym for a `\muskip` register.
`\newmuskip`   Allocate a new muskip register.
`\thinmuskip`   Small amount of mu glue.
`\medmuskip`   Medium amount of mu glue.
`\thickmuskip`   Large amount of mu glue.
`\mathsurround`   Kern amount placed before and after in-line formulas.
`\over`   Fraction.
`\atop`   Place objects over one another.
`\above`   Fraction with specified bar width.
`\overwithdelims`   Fraction with delimiters.
`\atopwithdelims`   Place objects over one another with delimiters.
`\abovewithdelims`   Generalized fraction with delimiters.
`\underline`   Underline the following ⟨math symbol⟩ or group.
`\overline`   Overline the following ⟨math symbol⟩ or group.
`\relpenalty`   Penalty for breaking after a binary relation not enclosed in a subformula. Plain TeX default: 500
`\binoppenalty`   Penalty for breaking after a binary operator not enclosed in a subformula. Plain TeX default: 700
`\allowbreak`   Macro for creating a breakpoint.

23.1   MATH MODES

TeX changes to math mode when it encounters a math shift character, category 3, in the input. After such an opening math shift it investigates (without expansion) the next token to see whether this is another math shift. In the latter case TeX starts processing in display math mode until a closing double math shift is encountered:

   .. $$ *displayed formula* $$ ..

Otherwise it starts processing an in-line formula in non-display math mode:

   .. $ *in-line formula* $ ..

The single math shift character is a ⟨horizontal command⟩.

   Exception: displays are not possible in restricted horizontal mode, so inside an `\hbox` the sequence $$ is an empty math formula and not the start of a displayed formula.

   Associated with the two math modes are two ⟨token parameter⟩ registers (see also Chapter 14): at the start of an in-line formula the `\everymath` tokens are inserted; at the start of a displayed formula the `\everydisplay` tokens are inserted. Display math is treated further in the next chapter.

Math modes can be tested for: \ifmmode is true in display and non-display math mode, and \ifinner is true in non-display mode, but not in display mode.

23.2 STYLES IN MATH MODE

Math formulas are set in any of eight styles:

D display style,
T text style,
S script style,
SS scriptscript style,

and the four 'cramped' variants D', T', S', SS' of these. The cramped styles differ mainly in the fact that superscripts are not raised as far as in the original styles.

23.2.1 Superscripts and subscripts

TeX can typeset a symbol or group as a superscript (or subscript) to the preceding symbol or group, if that preceding item does not already have a superscript (subscript). Superscripts (subscripts) are specified by the syntax

⟨superscript⟩⟨math field⟩

or

⟨subscript⟩⟨math field⟩

where a ⟨superscript⟩ (⟨subscript⟩) is either a character of category 7 (8), or a control sequence \let to such a character. The plain format has the control sequences

```
\let\sp=^  \let\sb=_
```

as implicit superscript and subscript characters.

Specifying a superscript (subscript) expression as the first item in an empty math list is equivalent to specifying it as the superscript (subscript) of an empty expression. For instance,

`$^{...}$`   is equivalent to   `${}^{...}$`

For TeX's internal calculations, superscript and subscript expressions are made wider by \scriptspace; the value of this in plain TeX is 0.5pt.

23.2.2 Choice of styles

Ordering the four styles D, T, S, and SS, and considering the other four as mere variants, the style rules for math mode are as follows:

- In any style superscripts and subscripts are taken from the next smaller style. Exception: in display style they are taken in script style.

- Subscripts are always in the cramped variant of the style; superscripts are only cramped if the original style was cramped.
- In an {..\over..} formula in any style the numerator and denominator are taken from the next smaller style.
- The denominator is always in cramped style; the numerator is only in cramped style if the original style was cramped.
- Formulas under a \sqrt or \overline are in cramped style.

Styles can be forced by the explicit commands \displaystyle, \textstyle, \scriptstyle, and \scriptscriptstyle.

In display style and text style the \textfont of the current family is used, in scriptstyle the \scriptfont is used, and in scriptscriptstyle the \scriptscriptfont is used.

The primitive command

\mathchoice{*D*}{*T*}{*S*}{*SS*}

lets the user specify four variants of a formula for the four styles. TeX constructs all four and inserts the appropriate one.

23.3 CLASSES OF MATHEMATICAL OBJECTS

Objects in math mode belong to one of eight classes. Depending on the class the object may be surrounded by some amount of white space, or treated specially in some way. Commands exist to force symbols, or sequences of symbols, to act as belonging to a certain class. In the hexadecimal representation "xyzz the class is the ⟨3-bit number⟩ x.

This is the list of classes and commands that force those classes. The examples are from the plain format (see the tables starting at page 295).

0. *ordinary*: lowercase Greek characters and those symbols that are 'just symbols'; the command \mathord forces this class.
1. *large operator*: integral and sum signs, and 'big' objects such as \bigcap or \bigotimes; the command \mathop forces this class. Large operators are centred vertically, and they may behave differently in display style from in the other styles; see below.
2. *binary operation*: plus and minus, and things such as \cap or \otimes; the command \mathbin forces this class.
3. *relation* (also called *binary relation*): equals, less than, and greater than signs, subset and superset, perpendicular, parallel; the command \mathrel forces this class.
4. *opening symbol*: opening brace, bracket, parenthesis, angle, floor, ceiling; the command \mathopen forces this class.
5. *closing symbol*: closing brace, bracket, parenthesis, angle, floor, ceiling; the command \mathclose forces this class.
6. *punctuation*: most punctuation marks, but : is a relation, the \colon is a punctuation colon; the command \mathpunct forces this class.

7. *variable family*: symbols in this class change font with the \fam parameter; in plain TeX uppercase Greek letters and ordinary letters and digits are in this class.

There is one further class: the *inner* subformulas. No characters can be assigned to this class, but characters and subformulas can be forced into it by \mathinner. The ⟨generalized fraction⟩s and \left...\right groups are inner formulas. Inner formulas are surrounded by some white space; see the table below.

Other subformulas than those that are inner are treated as ordinary symbols. In particular, subformulas enclosed in braces are ordinary: $a+b$ looks like '$a + b$', but $a{+}b$ looks like '$a+b$'. Note, however, that in ${a+b}$ the whole subformula is treated as an ordinary symbol, not its components; therefore the result is '$a + b$'.

23.4 LARGE OPERATORS AND THEIR LIMITS

The large operators in the Computer Modern fonts come in two sizes: one for text style and one for display style. Control sequences such as \sum are simply defined by \mathchardef to correspond to a position in a font:

`\mathchardef\sum="1350`

but if the current style is display style, TeX looks to see whether that character has a successor in the font.

Large operators in text style behave as if they are followed by \nolimits, which places the limits as sub/superscript expressions after the operator:

$$\sum_{k=1}^{\infty}$$

In display style they behave as if they are followed by \limits, which places the limits over and under the operator:

$$\sum_{k=1}^{\infty}$$

The successor mechanism (see page 183) lets TeX take a larger variant of the delimiter here.

The integral sign has been defined in plain TeX as

`\mathchardef\intop="1352 \def\int{\intop\nolimits}`

which places the limits after the operator, even in display style:

$$\int_0^\infty e^{-x^2}\,dx = \sqrt{\pi}/2$$

With \limits\nolimits or \nolimits\limits the last specification has precedence; the default placement can be restored by \displaylimits. For instance,

`$ ... \sum\limits\displaylimits ... $`

is equivalent to

`$ ... \sum ... $`

and
$$ \ldots \verb|\sum\nolimits\displaylimits| \ldots $$
is equivalent to
$$ \ldots \verb|\sum| \ldots $$

23.5 VERTICAL CENTRING: `\vcenter`

Each formula has an *axis*, which is for an in-line formula about half the x-height of the surrounding text; the exact value is the `\fontdimen22` of the font in family 2, the symbol font, in the current style.

The bar line in fractions is placed on the axis; large operators, delimiters and `\vcenter` boxes are centred on it.

A `\vcenter`box is a vertical box that is arranged so that it is centred on the math axis. It is possible to give a spread or to specification with a `\vcenter` box.

The `\vcenter` box is allowed only in math mode, and it does not behave like other boxes; for instance, it can not be stored in a box register. It does not qualify as a ⟨box⟩. See page 126 for a macro that repairs this.

23.6 MATHEMATICAL SPACING: MU GLUE

Spacing around mathematical objects is measured in mu units. A mu is 1/18th part of `\fontdimen6` of the font in family 2 in the current style, the 'quad' value of the symbol font.

23.6.1 Classification of mu glue

The user can specify mu spacing by `\mkern` or `\mskip`, but most mu glue is inserted automatically by TeX, based on the classes to which objects belong (see above). First, here are some rules of thumb describing the global behaviour.

- A `\thickmuskip` (default value in plain TeX: 5mu plus 5mu) is inserted around (binary) relations, except where these are preceded or followed by other relations or punctuation, and except if they follow an open, or precede a close symbol.
- A `\medmuskip` (default value in plain TeX: 4mu plus 2mu minus 4mu) is put around binary operators.
- A `\thinmuskip` (default value in plain TeX: 3mu) follows after punctuation, and is put around inner objects, except where these are followed by a close or preceded by an open symbol, and except if the other object is a large operator or a binary relation.
- No mu glue is inserted after an open or before a close symbol except where the latter is preceded by punctuation; no mu glue is inserted also before punctuation, except where the preceding object is punctuation or an inner object.

The following table gives the complete definition of mu glue between math objects.

	0: Ord	1: Op	2: Bin	3: Rel	4: Open	5: Close	6: Punct	Inner
0: Ord	0	1	(2)	(3)	0	0	0	(1)
1: Op	1	1	*	(3)	0	0	0	(1)
2: Bin	(2)	(2)	*	*	(2)	*	*	(2)
3: Rel	(3)	(3)	*	0	(2)	*	*	(2)
4: Open	0	0	*	0	0	0	0	0
5: Close	0	1	(2)	(3)	0	0	0	(1)
6: Punct	(1)	(1)	*	(1)	(1)	(1)	(1)	(1)
Inner	(1)	1	(2)	(3)	(1)	0	(1)	(1)

where the symbols have the following meanings:
- 0, no space; 1, thin space; 2, medium space; 3, thick space;
- (·), insert only in text and display mode, not in script or scriptscript mode;
- cases * cannot occur, because a Bin object is converted to Ord if it is the first in the list, preceded by Bin, Op, Open, Punct, Rel, or followed by Close, Punct, and Rel; also, a Rel is converted to Ord when it is followed by Close or Punct.

Stretchable mu glue is set according to the same rules that govern ordinary glue. However, only mu glue on the outer level can be stretched or shrunk; any mu glue enclosed in a group is set at natural width.

23.6.2 Muskip registers

Like ordinary glue, mu glue can be stored in registers, the \muskip registers, of which there are 256 in TeX. The registers are denoted by

\muskip⟨8-bit number⟩

and they can be assigned to a control sequence by

\muskipdef⟨control sequence⟩⟨equals⟩⟨8-bit number⟩

and there is a macro that allocates unused registers:

\newmuskip⟨control sequence⟩

Arithmetic for mu glue exists as for glue; see Chapter 8.

23.6.3 Other spaces in math mode

In math mode space tokens are ignored; however, the math code of the space character is "8000 in plain TeX, so if its category is made 'letter' or 'other character', it will behave like an active character in math mode. See also page 181.

Admissible glue in math mode is of type ⟨mathematical skip⟩, which is either a ⟨horizontal skip⟩ (see Chapter 6) or \mskip⟨muglue⟩. Leaders in math mode can be specified with a ⟨mathematical skip⟩.

A glue item preceded by \nonscript is cancelled if it occurs in scriptstyle or scriptscriptstyle.

Control space functions in math mode as it does in horizontal mode.

In-line formulas are surrounded by kerns of size \mathsurround, the so-called 'math-on' and 'math-off' items. Line breaking can occur at the front of the math-off kern if it is followed by glue.

23.7 GENERALIZED FRACTIONS

Fraction-like objects can be set with six primitive commands of type ⟨generalized fraction⟩. Each of these takes the preceding and the following subformulas and puts them over one another, if necessary with a fraction bar and with delimiters.

\over is the ordinary fraction; the bar thickness is \fontdimen8 of the extension font:

$\pi\over2$ gives '$\frac{\pi}{2}$'

\atop is equivalent to a fraction with zero bar thickness:

$\pi\atop2$ gives '$\genfrac{}{}{0pt}{}{\pi}{2}$'

\above⟨dimen⟩ specifies the thickness of the bar line explicitly:

$\pi\above 1pt 2$ gives '$\frac{\pi}{2}$'

To each of these three there corresponds a \...withdelims variant that lets the user specify delimiters for the expression. For example, the most general command, in terms of which all five others could have been defined, is

\abovewithdelims⟨delim$_1$⟩⟨delim$_2$⟩⟨dimen⟩.

Delimiters in these generalized fractions do not grow with the enclosed expression: in display mode a delimiter is taken which is at least \fontdimen20 high, otherwise it has to be at least \fontdimen21 high. These dimensions are taken from the font in family 2, the symbol font, in the current style.

The control sequences \over, \atop, and \above are primitives, although they could have been defined as \...withdelims.., that is, with two null delimiters. Because of these implied surrounding null delimiters, there is a kern of size \nulldelimiterspace before and after these simple generalized fractions.

23.8 UNDERLINING, OVERLINING

The primitive commands \underline and \overline take a ⟨math field⟩ argument, that is, a ⟨math symbol⟩ or a group, and draw a line under or over it. The result is an 'Under' or 'Over' atom, which is appended to the current math list. The line thickness is font dimension 8 of the extension font, which also determines the clearance between the line and the ⟨math field⟩.

Various other \over... and \under... commands exist in plain TeX; these are all macros that use TeX \halign command.

23.9 LINE BREAKING IN MATH FORMULAS

In-line formulas can be broken after relations and binary operators. The respective penalties are the \relpenalty and the \binoppenalty. However, TeX will only break after such symbols if they are not enclosed in braces. Other breakpoints can be created with \allowbreak, which is an abbreviation for \penalty0.

Unlike in horizontal or vertical mode where putting two penalties in a row is equivalent to just placing the smallest one, in math mode a penalty placed at a break point — that is, after a relation or binary operator — will effectively replace the old penalty by the new one.

23.10 FONT DIMENSIONS OF FAMILIES 2 AND 3

If a font is used in text mode, TeX will look at its first 7 \fontdimen parameters (see page 35), for instance to control spacing. In math, however, more font dimensions are needed. TeX will look at the first 22 parameters of the fonts in family 2, and the first 13 of the fonts in family 3, to control various aspects of math typesetting. The next two subsections have been quoted loosely from Beeton (1991).

23.10.1 Symbol font attributes

Attributes of the font in family 2 mainly specify the initial vertical positioning of parts of fractions, subscripts, superscripts, et cetera. The position determined by applying these attributes may be further modified because of other conditions, for example the presence of a fraction bar.

One text font dimension, number 6, the quad, determines the size of mu glue; see above.

Fraction numerator attributes: minimum shift up, from the main baseline, of the baseline of the numerator of a generalized fraction,

8. num1: for display style,
9. num2: for text style or smaller if a fraction bar is present,
10. num3: for text style or smaller if no fraction bar is present.

Fraction denominator attributes: minimum shift down, from the main baseline, of the baseline of the denominator of a generalized fraction,

11. denom1: for display style,
12. denom2: for text style or smaller.

Superscript attributes: minimum shift up, from the main baseline, of the baseline of a superscript,

13. sup1: for display style,
14. sup2: for text style or smaller, non-cramped,

15. sup3: for text style or smaller, cramped.

Subscript attributes: minimum shift down, from the main baseline, of the baseline of a subscript,

16. sub1: when no superscript is present,
17. sub2: when a superscript is present.

Script adjustment attributes: for use only with non-glyph, that is, composite, objects.

18. sup_drop: maximum distance of superscript baseline below top of nucleus
19. sub_drop: minimum distance of subscript baseline below bottom of nucleus.

Delimiter span attributes: height plus depth of delimiter enclosing a generalized fraction,

20. delim1: in display style,
21. delim2: in text style or smaller.

A parameter with many uses, the height of the math axis,

22. axis_height: the height above the baseline of the fraction bar, and the centre of large delimiters and most operators and relations. This position is used in vertical centring operations.

23.10.2 Extension font attributes

Attributes of the font in family 3 mostly specify the way the limits of large operators are set.

The first parameter, number 8, default_rule_thickness, serves many purposes. It is the thickness of the rule used for overlines, underlines, radical extenders (square root), and fraction bars. Various clearances are also specified in terms of this dimension: between the fraction bar and the numerator and denominator, between an object and the rule drawn by an underline, overline, or radical, and between the bottom of superscripts and top of subscripts.

Minimum clearances around large operators are as follows:

9. big_op_spacing1: minimum clearance between baseline of upper limit and top of large operator; see below.
10. big_op_spacing2: minimum clearance between bottom of large operator and top of lower limit.
11. big_op_spacing3: minimum clearance between baseline of upper limit and top of large operator, taking into account depth of upper limit; see below.
12. big_op_spacing4: minimum clearance between bottom of large operator and top of lower limit, taking into account height of lower limit; see below.
13. big_op_spacing5: clearance above upper limit or below lower limit of a large operator.

The resulting clearance above an operator is the maximum of parameter 7, and parameter 11 minus the depth of the upper limit. The resulting clearance below an operator is the maximum of parameter 10, and parameter 12 minus the height of the lower limit.

23.10.3 Example: subscript lowering

The location of a subscript depends on whether there is a superscript; for instance
$$X_1 + Y_1^2 = 1$$
If you would rather have that look like
$$X_1 + Y_1^2 = 1,$$
it suffices to specify

    \fontdimen16\textfont2=3pt \fontdimen17\textfont2=3pt

which makes the subscript drop equal in both cases.

CHAPTER 24

Display Math

Displayed formulas are set on a line of their own, usually somewhere in a paragraph. This chapter explains how surrounding white space (both above/below and to the left/right) is calculated.

\abovedisplayskip \belowdisplayskip   Glue above/below a display. Plain
   TeX default: 12pt plus 3pt minus 9pt
\abovedisplayshortskip \belowdisplayshortskip   Glue above/below a
   display if the line preceding the display was short. Plain TeX defaults: 0pt
   plus 3pt and 7pt plus 3pt minus 4pt respectively.
\predisplaypenalty \postdisplaypenalty   Penalty placed in the vertical list
   above/below a display. Plain TeX defaults: 10 000 and 0 respectively.
\displayindent   Distance by which the box, in which the display is centred, is
   indented owing to hanging indentation.
\displaywidth   Width of the box in which the display is centred.
\predisplaysize   Effective width of the line preceding the display.
\everydisplay   Token list inserted at the start of a display.
\eqno   Place a right equation number in a display formula.
\leqno   Place a left equation number in a display formula.

24.1 DISPLAYS

TeX starts building a display when it encounters two math shift characters (characters of category 3, $ in plain TeX) in a row. Another such pair (possibly followed by one optional space) indicates the end of the display.

Math shift is a ⟨horizontal command⟩, but displays are only allowed in unrestricted horizontal mode ($$ is an empty math formula in restricted horizontal mode). Displays themselves, however, are started in the surrounding (possibly internal) vertical mode in order to calculate quantities such as \prevgraf; the result of the display is appended to the vertical list.

The part of the paragraph above the display is broken into lines as an independent paragraph (but \prevgraf is carried over; see below), and the remainder of the paragraph is set, starting with an empty list and \spacefactor equal to 1000. The \everypar tokens are not inserted for the part of the paragraph after the display, nor is \parskip glue inserted.

Right at the beginning of the display the \everydisplay token list is inserted (but after the calculation of \displayindent, \displaywidth, and \predisplaysize). See page 204 for an example of the use of \everydisplay.

The page builder is exercised before the display (but after the \everydisplay tokens have been inserted), and after the display finishes.

The 'display style' of math typesetting was treated in Chapter 22.

24.2 DISPLAYS IN PARAGRAPHS

Positioning of a display in a paragraph may be influenced by hanging indentation or a \parshape specification. For this, TeX uses the \prevgraf parameter (see Chapter 18), and acts as if the display is three lines deep.

If n is the value of \prevgraf when the display starts – so there are n lines of text above the display – \prevgraf is set to to $n+3$ when the paragraph resumes. The display occupies, as it were, lines $n+1$, $n+2$, and $n+3$. The shift and line width for the display are those that would hold for line $n+2$.

The shift for the display is recorded in \displayindent; the line width is recorded in \displaywidth. These parameters (and the \predisplaysize explained below) are set immediately after the $$ has been scanned. Usually they are equal to zero and \hsize respectively. The user can change the values of these parameters; TeX will use the values that hold after the math list of the display has been processed.

Note that a display is vertical material, and therefore not influenced by settings of \leftskip and \rightskip.

24.3 VERTICAL MATERIAL AROUND DISPLAYS

A display is preceded in the vertical list by

- a penalty of size \predisplaypenalty (plain TeX default 10 000), and
- glue of size \abovedisplayskip or \abovedisplayshortskip; this glue is omitted in cases where a \leqno equation number is set on a line of its own (see below).

A display is followed by

- a penalty of size \postdisplaypenalty (default 0), and possibly
- glue of size \belowdisplayskip or \belowdisplayshortskip; this glue is omitted in cases where an \eqno equation number is set on a line of its own (see below).

The 'short' variants of the glue are taken if there is no \leqno left equation number, and if the last line of the paragraph above the display is short enough for the display to be raised a bit without coming too close to that line. In order to decide this, the effective width of the preceding line is saved in \predisplaysize.

This value is calculated immediately after the opening $$ of the display has been scanned, together with the \displaywidth and \displayindent explained above.

Remembering that the part of the paragraph above the display has already been broken into lines, the following method for finding the effective width of the last line ensues. TeX takes the last box of the list, which is a horizontal box containing the last line, and locates the right edge of the last box in it. The \predisplaysize is then the place of that rightmost edge, plus any amount by which the last line was shifted, plus two ems in the current font.

There are two exceptions to this. The \predisplaysize is taken to be −\maxdimen if there was no previous line, that is, the display started the paragraph, or it followed another display; \predisplaysize is taken to be \maxdimen if the glue in the last line was not set at its natural width, which may happen if the \parfillskip contained only finite stretch. The reason for the last clause is that glue setting is slightly machine-dependent, and such dependences should be kept out of TeX's global decision processes.

24.4 GLUE SETTING OF THE DISPLAY MATH LIST

The display has to fit in \displaywidth, but in addition to the formula there may be an equation number. The minimum separation between the formula and the equation number should be one em in the symbol font, that is, \fontdimen6\textfont2.

If the formula plus any equation number and separation fit into \displaywidth, the glue in the formula is set at its natural width. If it does not fit, but the formula contains enough shrink, it is shrunk. Otherwise TeX puts any equation number on a line of its own, and the glue in the formula is set to fit it in \displaywidth. With the equation number on a separate line the formula may now very well fit in the display width; however, if it was a very long formula the box in which it is set may still be overfull. TeX nevers breaks a displayed formula.

24.5 CENTRING THE DISPLAY FORMULA: DISPLACEMENT

Based on the width of the box containing the formula − which may not really 'contain' it; it may be overfull − TeX tries to centre the formula in the \displaywidth, that is, without taking the equation number into account. Initially, a displacement is calculated that is half the difference between \displaywidth and the width of the formula box.

However, if there is an equation number that will not be put on a separate line and the displacement is less than twice the width of the equation number, a new displacement is calculated. This new displacement is zero if the formula started with glue; otherwise it is such that the formula box is centred in the space left by the equation number.

If there was no equation number, or if the equation number will be put on a separate line, the formula box is now placed, shifted right by \displayindent plus the displacement calculated above.

24.6 EQUATION NUMBERS

The user can specify a equation number for a display by ending it with

`\eqno`⟨math mode material⟩`$$`

for an equation number placed on the right, or

`\leqno`⟨math mode material⟩`$$`

for an equation number placed on the left.

24.6.1 Ordinary equation numbers

Above it was described how TeX calculates a displacement from the display formula and the equation number, if this is to be put on the same line as the formula.

If the equation number was a `\leqno` number, TeX places a box containing

- the equation number,
- a kern with the size of the displacement calculated, and
- the formula.

This box is shifted right by `\displayindent`.

If the equation number was an `\eqno` number, TeX places a box containing

- the formula,
- a kern with the size of the displacement calculated, and
- the equation number.

This box is shifted right by `\displayindent` plus the displacement calculated.

24.6.2 The equation number on a separate line

Since displayed formulas may become rather big, TeX can decide (as was described above) that any equation number should be placed on a line of its own. A left-placed equation number is then to be placed above the display, in a box that is shifted right by `\displayindent`; a right-placed equation number will be placed below the display, in a box that is shifted to the right by `\displayindent` plus `\displaywidth` minus the width of the equation number box.

In both cases a penalty of 10 000 is placed between the equation number box and the formula.

TeX does not put extra glue above a left-placed equation number or below a right-placed equation number; TeX here relies on the baselineskip mechanism.

24.7 NON-CENTRED DISPLAYS

As a default, TeX will centre displays. In order to get non-centred displays some macro trickery is needed.

One approach would be to write a macro `\DisplayEquation` that would basically look like

```
\def\DisplayEquation#1{%
    \par \vskip\abovedisplayskip
    \hbox{\kern\parindent$\displaystyle#1$}
    \vskip\belowdisplayskip \noindent}
```

but it would be nicer if one could just write

```
$$ ... \eqno ... $$
```

and having this come out as a left-aligning display.

Using the `\everydisplay` token list, the above idea can be realized. The basic idea is to write

```
\everydisplay{\IndentedDisplay}
\def\IndentedDisplay#1$${ ...
```

so that the macro `\IndentedDisplay` will receive the formula, including any equation number. The first step is now to extract an equation number if it is present. This makes creative use of delimited macro parameters.

```
\def\ExtractEqNo#1\eqno#2\eqno#3\relax
    {\def\Equation{#1}\def\EqNo{#2}}
\def\IndentedDisplay#1$${%
    \ExtractEqNo#1\eqno\eqno\relax
```

Next the equation should be set in the available space `\displaywidth`:

```
    \hbox to \displaywidth
        {\kern\parindent
         $\displaystyle\Equation$\hfil$\EqNo$}$$
    }
```

Note that the macro ends in the closing `$$` to balance the opening dollars that caused insertion of the `\everydisplay` tokens. This also means that the box containing the displayed material will automatically be surrounded by `\abovedisplayskip` and `\belowdisplayskip` glue. There is no need to use `\displayindent` anywhere in this macro, because TeX itself will shift the display appropriately.

CHAPTER 25

Alignment

TeX provides a general alignment mechanism for making tables.

`\halign`   Horizontal alignment.
`\valign`   Vertical alignment.
`\omit`   Omit the template for one alignment entry.
`\span`   Join two adjacent alignment entries.
`\multispan`   Macro to join a number of adjacent alignment entries.
`\tabskip`   Amount of glue in between columns (rows) of an `\halign` (`\valign`).
`\noalign`   Specify vertical (horizontal) material to be placed in between rows (columns) of an `\halign` (`\valign`).
`\cr`   Terminate an alignment line.
`\crcr`   Terminate an alignment line if it has not already been terminated by `\cr`.
`\everycr`   Token list inserted after every `\cr` or non-redundant `\crcr`.
`\centering`   Glue register in plain TeX for centring `\eqalign` and `\eqalignno`.
   Value: `0pt plus 1000pt minus 1000pt`
`\hideskip`   Glue register in plain TeX to make alignment entries invisible.
   Value: `-1000pt plus 1fill`
`\hidewidth`   Macro to make preceding or following entry invisible.

25.1   INTRODUCTION

TeX has a sophisticated alignment mechanism, based on templates, with one template entry per column or row. The templates may contain any common elements of the table entries, and in general they contain instructions for typesetting the entries. TeX first calculates widths (for `\halign`) or heights (for `\valign`) of all entries; then it typesets the whole alignment using in each column (row) the maximum width (height) of entries in that column (row).

25.2   HORIZONTAL AND VERTICAL ALIGNMENT

The two alignment commands in TeX are

`\halign`⟨box specification⟩{⟨alignment material⟩}

for horizontal alignment of columns, and

> \valign⟨box specification⟩{⟨alignment material⟩}

for vertical alignment of rows. \halign is a ⟨vertical command⟩, and \valign is a ⟨horizontal command⟩.

The braces induce a new level of grouping; they can be implicit.

The discussion below will mostly focus on horizontal alignments, but, replacing 'column' by 'row' and vice versa, it applies to vertical alignments too.

25.2.1 Horizontal alignments: \halign

Horizontal alignments yield a list of horizontal boxes, the rows, which are placed on the surrounding vertical list. The page builder is exercised after the alignment rows have been added to the vertical list. The value of \prevdepth that holds before the alignment is used for the baselineskip of the first row, and after the alignment \prevdepth is set to a value based on the last row.

Each entry is processed in a group of its own, in restricted horizontal mode.

A special type of horizontal alignment exists: the display alignments, specified as

> $$⟨assignments⟩\halign⟨box specification⟩{...}⟨assignments⟩$$

Such an alignment is shifted by \displayindent (see Chapter 24) and surrounded by \abovedisplayskip and \belowdisplayskip glue.

25.2.2 Vertical alignments: \valign

Vertical alignments are 'rotated' horizontal alignments: they are placed on the surrounding horizontal lists, and yield a row of columns. The \spacefactor value is treated the same way as the \prevdepth for horizontal alignments: the value current before the alignment is used for the first column, and the value reached after the last column is used after the alignment. In between columns the \spacefactor value is 1000.

Each entry is in a group of its own, and it is processed in internal vertical mode.

25.2.3 Material between the lines: \noalign

Material that has to be contained in the alignment, but should not be treated as an entry or series of entries, can be given by

> \noalign⟨filler⟩{⟨vertical mode material⟩}

for horizontal alignments, and

> \noalign⟨filler⟩{⟨horizontal mode material⟩}

for vertical alignments.

Examples are

```
\noalign{\hrule}
```

for drawing a horizontal rule between two lines of an `\halign`, and

```
\noalign{\penalty100}
```

for discouraging a page break (or line break) in between two rows (columns) of an `\halign` (`\valign`).

25.2.4 Size of the alignment

The ⟨box specification⟩ can be used to give the alignment a predetermined size: for instance

```
\halign to \hsize{ ... }
```

Glue contained in the entries of the alignment has no role in this; any stretch or shrink required is taken from the `\tabskip` glue. This is explained below.

25.3 THE PREAMBLE

Each line in an alignment is terminated by `\cr`; the first line is called the *template line*. It is of the form

$$u_1 \# v_1 \& \ldots \& u_n \# v_n \text{\cr}$$

where each u_i, v_i is a (possibly empty) arbitrary sequence of tokens, and the template entries are separated by the *alignment tab character* (`&` in plain TEX), that is, any character of category 4.

A $u_i \# v_i$ sequence is the template that will be used for the i th column: whatever sequence α_i the user specifies as the entry for that column will be inserted at the parameter character. The sequence $u_i \alpha_i v_i$ is then processed to obtain the actual entry for the i th column on the current line. See below for more details.

The length n of the template line need not be equal to the actual number of columns in the alignment: the template is used only for as many items as are specified on a line. Consider as an example

```
\halign{a#&b#&c#\cr 1&2\cr 1\cr}
```

which has a three-item template, but the rows have only one or two items. The output of this is

a1b2
a1

25.3.1 Infinite preambles

For the case where the number of columns is not known in advance, for instance if the alignment is to be used in a macro where the user will specify the columns, it is possible to specify that a trailing piece of the preamble can be repeated arbitrarily many times. By preceding it with &, an entry can be marked as the start of this repeatable part of the preamble. See the example of \matrix below.

When the whole preamble is to be repeated, there will be an alignment tab character at the start of the first entry:

\halign{& ... & ... \cr ... }

If a starting portion of the preamble is to be exempted from repetition, a double alignment tab will occur:

\halign{ ... & ... & ... && ... & ... \cr ... }

The repeatable part need not be used an integral number of times. The alignment rows can end at any time; the rest of the preamble is then not used.

25.3.2 Brace counting in preambles

Alignments may appear inside alignments, so TeX uses the following rule to determine to which alignment an & or \cr control sequence belongs:

> All tab characters and \cr tokens of an alignment should be on the same level of grouping.

From this it follows that tab characters and \cr tokens can appear inside an entry if they are nested in braces. This makes it possible to have nested alignments.

25.3.3 Expansion in the preamble

All tokens in the preamble – apart from the tab characters – are stored for insertion in the entries of the alignment, but a token preceded by \span is expanded while the preamble is scanned. See below for the function of \span in the rest of the alignment.

25.3.4 \tabskip

Entries in an alignment are set to take the width of the largest element in their column. Glue for separating columns can be specified by assigning to \tabskip. TeX inserts this glue in between each pair of columns, and before the first and after the last column.

The value of \tabskip that holds outside the alignment is used before the first column, and after all subsequent columns, unless the preamble contains assignments to \tabskip. Any assignment to \tabskip is executed while TeX is scanning the preamble; the value that holds when a tab character is reached will be used at that place in each row, and after all subsequent columns, unless further assignments occur. The value of \tabskip that holds when \cr is reached is used after the last column.

Assignments to \tabskip in the preamble are local to the alignment, but not to the entry where they are given. These assignments are ordinary glue assignments: they remove any optional trailing space.

As an example, in the following table there is no tabskip glue before the first and after the last column; in between all columns there is stretchable tabskip.

```
\tabskip=0pt \halign to \hsize{
    \vrule#\tabskip=0pt plus 1fil\strut&
    \hfil#\hfil& \vrule## \hfil#\hfil& \vrule## \hfil#\hfil&
    \tabskip=0pt\vrule#\cr
\noalign{\hrule}
    &\multispan5\hfil Just a table\hfil&\cr
\noalign{\hrule}
    &one&&two&&three&\cr &a&&b&&c&\cr
\noalign{\hrule}
    }
```

The result of this is

	Just a table	
one	two	three
a	b	c

All of the vertical rules of the table are in a separate column. This is the only way to get the space around the items to stretch.

25.4 THE ALIGNMENT

After the template line any number of lines terminated by \cr can follow. TeX reads all of these lines, processing the entries in order to find the maximal width (height) in each column (row). Because all entries are kept in memory, long tables can overflow TeX's main memory. For such tables it is better to write a special-purpose macro.

25.4.1 Reading an entry

Entries in an alignment are composed of the constant u and v parts of the template, and the variable α part. Basically TeX forms the sequence of tokens $u\alpha v$ and processes this. However, there are two special cases where TeX has to expand before it forms this sequence.

Above, the \noalign command was described. Since this requires a different treatment from other alignment entries, TeX expands, after it has read a \cr, the first token of the first α string of the next line to see whether that is or expands to \noalign. Similarly, for all entries in a line the first token is expanded to see whether it is or expands to \omit. This control sequence will be described below.

Entries starting with an \if... conditional, or a macro expanding to one, may be misinterpreted owing to this premature expansion. For example,

```
\halign{$#$\cr \ifmmode a\else b\fi\cr}
```

will give

> *b*

because the conditional is evaluated before math mode has been set up. The solution is, as in many other cases, to insert a `\relax` control sequence to stop the expansion. Here the `\relax` has to be inserted at the start of the alignment entry.

If neither `\noalign` nor `\omit` (see below) is found, TeX will process an input stream composed of the *u* part, the α tokens (which are delimited by either `&` or `\span`, see below), and the *v* part.

Entries are delimited by `&`, `\span`, or `\cr`, but only if such a token occurs on the same level of grouping. This makes it possible to have an alignment as an entry of another alignment.

25.4.2 Alternate specifications: `\omit`

The template line will rarely be sufficient to describe all lines of the alignment. For lines where items should be set differently the command `\omit` exists: if the first token in an entry is (or expands to) `\omit` the trivial template `#` is used instead of what the template line specifies.

Example
The following alignment uses the same template for all columns, but in the second column an `\omit` command is given.

```
\tabskip=1em
\halign{&$<#>$\cr a&\omit (b)&c \cr}
```

The output of this is

> $<a>$ (b) $<c>$

25.4.3 Spanning across multiple columns: `\span`

Sometimes it is desirable to have material spanning several columns. The most obvious example is that of a heading above a table. For this TeX provides the `\span` command.

Entries are delimited either by `&`, by `\cr`, or by `\span`. In the last case TeX will omit the tabskip glue that would normally follow the entry thus delimited, and it will typeset the material just read plus the following entry in the joint space available.

As an example,

```
\tabskip=1em
\halign{&#\cr a&b&c&d\cr a&\hrulefill\span\hrulefill&d\cr}
```

gives

> a b c d
> a ___   d

Note that there is no tabskip glue in between the two spanned columns, but there is tabskip glue before the first column and after the last.

Using the `\omit` command this same alignment could have been generated as

```
\halign{&#\cr a&b&c&d\cr a&\hrulefill\span\omit&d\cr}
```

The `\span\omit` combination is used in the plain TeX macro `\multispan`: for instance

```
\multispan4   gives   \omit\span\omit\span\omit\span\omit
```

which spans across three tabs, and removes the templates of four entries. Repeating the above example once again:

```
\halign{&#\cr a&b&c&d\cr a&\multispan2\hrulefill&d\cr}
```

The argument of `\multispan` is a single token, not a number, so in order to span more than 9 columns the argument should be enclosed in braces, for instance `\multispan{12}`. Furthermore, a space after a single-digit argument will wind up in the output.

For a 'low budget' solution to spanning columns plain TeX has the macro `\hidewidth`, defined by

```
\newskip\hideskip \hideskip=-1000pt plus 1fill
\def\hidewidth{\hskip\hideskip}
```

Putting `\hidewidth` at the beginning or end of an alignment entry will make its width zero, with the material in the entry sticking out to the left or right respectively.

25.4.4 Rules in alignments

Horizontal rules inside a horizontal alignment will mostly be across the width of the alignment. The easiest way to attain this is to use

```
\noalign{\hrule}
```

lines inside the alignment. If the alignment is contained in a vertical box, lines above and below the alignment can be specified with

```
\vbox{\hrule \halign{...} \hrule}
```

The most general way to get horizontal lines in an alignment is to use

```
\multispan n\hrulefill
```

which can be used to underline arbitrary adjacent columns.

Vertical rules in alignments take some more care. Since a horizontal alignment breaks up into horizontal boxes that will be placed on a vertical list, TeX will insert baselineskip glue in between the rows of the alignment. If vertical rules in adjacent rows are to abut, it is necessary to prevent baselineskip glue, for instance by the `\offinterlineskip` macro.

In order to ensure that rows will still be properly spaced it is then necessary to place a *strut* somewhere in the preamble. A strut is an invisible object with a certain height and depth. Putting that in the preamble guarantees that every line will have at least that height and depth. In the plain format \strut is defined statically as

```
\vrule height8.5pt depth3.5pt width0pt
```

so this must be changed when other fonts or sizes are used.

It is a good idea to use a whole column for a vertical rule, that is, to write

```
\vrule#&
```

in the preamble and to leave the corresponding entry in the alignment empty. Omitting the vertical rule can then be done by specifying \omit, and the size of the rule can be specified explicitly by putting, for instance, height 15pt in the entry instead of leaving it empty. Of course, tabskip glue will now be specified to the left and right of the rule, so some extra tabskip assignments may be needed in the preamble.

25.4.5 End of a line: \cr and \crcr

All lines in an alignment are terminated by the \cr control sequence, including the last line. TeX is not able to infer from a closing brace in the α part that the alignment has ended, because an unmatched closing brace is perfectly valid in an alignment entry; it may match an opening brace in the u part of the corresponding preamble entry.

TeX has a primitive command \crcr that is equivalent to \cr, but it has no effect if it immediately follows a \cr. Consider as an example the definition in plain TeX of \cases:

```
\def\cases#1{%
    \left\{\,\vcenter{\normalbaselines\m@th
        \ialign{ $##\hfil$& \quad##\hfil \crcr #1\crcr}}%
    \right.}
```

Because of the \crcr after the user argument #1, the following two applications of this macro

```
\cases{1&2\cr 3&4}    and    \cases{1&2\cr 3&4\cr}
```

both work. In the first case the \crcr in the macro definition ends the last line; in the second case the user's \cr ends the line, and the \crcr is redundant.

After \cr and after a non-redundant \crcr the ⟨token parameter⟩ \everycr is inserted. This includes the \cr terminating the template line.

25.5   EXAMPLE: MATH ALIGNMENTS

The plain format has several alignment macros that function in math mode. One example is \matrix, defined by

```
\def\matrix#1{\null\,\vcenter{\normalbaselines\m@th
    \ialign{\hfil$##$\hfil && \quad\hfil$##$\hfil\crcr
        \mathstrut\crcr
        \noalign{\kern-\baselineskip}
          #1\crcr
        \mathstrut\crcr
        \noalign{\kern-\baselineskip}}}\,}
```

This uses a repeating (starting with &&) second preamble entry; each entry is centred by an \hfil before and after it, and there is a \quad of space in between columns. Tabskip glue was not used for this, because there should not be any glue preceding or following the matrix.

The combination of a \mathstrut and \kern-\baselineskip above and below the matrix increases the vertical size such that two matrices with the same number of rows will have the same height and depth, which would not otherwise be the case if one of them had subscripts in the last row, but the other not. The \mathstrut causes interline glue to be inserted and, because it has a size equal to \baselineskip, the negative kern will effectively leave only the interline glue, thereby buffering any differences in the first and last line. Only to a certain point, of course: objects bigger than the opening brace will still result in a different height or depth of the matrix.

Another, more complicated, example of an alignment for math mode is \eqalignno.

```
\def\eqalignno#1{\displ@y \tabskip\centering
  \halign to\displaywidth{
    \hfil$\@lign\displaystyle{##}$%     -- first column
        \tabskip\z@skip
    &$\@lign\displaystyle{{}##}$\hfil%  -- second column
        \tabskip\centering
    &\llap{$\@lign##$}%                 -- third column
        \tabskip\z@skip\crcr   %  end of the preamble
    #1\crcr}}
```

Firstly, the tabskip is set to zero after the equation number, so this number is set flush with the right margin. Since it is placed by \llap, its effective width is zero. Secondly, the tabskip between the first and second columns is also zero, and the tabskip before the first column and after the second is \centering, which is 0pt plus 1000pt minus 1000pt, so the first column and second are jointly centred in the \hsize. Note that, because of the minus 1000pt, these two columns will happily go outside the left and right margins, overwriting any equation numbers.

CHAPTER 26

Page Shape

This chapter treats some of the parameters that determine the size of the page and how it appears on paper.

\topskip Minimum distance between the top of the page box and the baseline of the first box on the page. Plain TeX default: 10pt
\hoffset \voffset Distance by which the page is shifted right/down with respect to the reference point.
\vsize Height of the page box. Plain TeX default: 8.9in
\maxdepth Maximum depth of the page box. Plain TeX default: 4pt
\splitmaxdepth Maximum depth of a box split off by a \vsplit operation.
Plain TeX default: \maxdimen

26.1   THE REFERENCE POINT FOR GLOBAL POSITIONING

It is a TeX convention, to which output device drivers must adhere, that the top left point of the page is one inch from the page edges. Unfortunately this may lead to lots of trouble, for instance if a printer (or the page description language it uses) takes, say, the *lower* left corner as the reference point, and is factory set to US paper sizes, but is used with European standard A4 paper.

The page is shifted on the paper if one assigns non-zero values to \hoffset or \voffset: positive values shift to the right and down respectively.

26.2   \topskip

The \topskip ensures to a certain point that the first baseline of a page will be at the same location from page to page, even if font sizes are switched between pages or if the first line has no ascenders.

Before the first box on each page some glue is inserted. This glue has the same stretch and shrink as \topskip, but the natural size is the natural size of \topskip minus the height of the first box, or zero if this would be negative.

Plain TeX sets \topskip to 10pt. Thus the top lines of pages will have their baselines at the same place if the top portion of the characters is ten point or less. For the Computer Modern fonts this condition is satisfied if the font size is less than (about) 13 points; for larger fonts the baseline of the top line will drop.

The height of the page box for a page containing only text (and assuming a zero \parskip) will be the \topskip plus a number of times the \baselineskip. Thus one can define a macro to compute the \vsize from the number of lines on a page:

```
\def\HeightInLines#1{\count@=#1\relax
    \advance\count@ by -1\relax
    \vsize=\baselineskip
    \multiply\vsize by \count@
    \advance\vsize by \topskip}
```

Calculating the \vsize this way will prevent underfull boxes for text-only pages.

In cases where the page does not start with a line of text (for instance a rule), the topskip may give unwanted effects. To prevent these, start the page with

```
\hbox{}\kern-\topskip
```

followed by what you wanted on top.

Analogous to the \topskip, there is a \splittopskip for pages generated by a \vsplit operation; see the next chapter.

26.3 PAGE HEIGHT AND DEPTH

TeX tries to build pages as a \vbox of height \vsize; see also \pagegoal in the next chapter.

If the last item on a page has an excessive depth, that page would be noticeably longer than other pages. To prevent this phenomenon TeX uses \maxdepth as the maximum depth of the page box. If adding an item to the page would make the depth exceed this quantity, then the reference point of the page is moved down to make the depth exactly \maxdepth.

The 'raggedbottom' effect is obtained in plain TeX by giving the \topskip some finite stretchability: 10pt plus 60pt. Thus the natural height of box 255 can vary when it reaches the output routine. Pages are then shipped out (more or less) as

```
\dimen0=\dp255 \unvbox255
\ifraggedbottom \kern-\dimen0 \vfil \fi
```

The \vfil causes the topskip to be set at natural width, so the effect is one of a fixed top line and a variable bottom line of the page.

Before \box255 is unboxed in the plain TeX output routine, \boxmaxdepth is set to \maxdepth so that this box will made under the same assumptions that the page builder used when putting together \box255.

The depth of box split off by a \vsplit operation is controlled by the \split-maxdepth parameter.

CHAPTER 27

Page Breaking

This chapter treats the 'page builder': the part of TeX that decides where to break the main vertical list into pages. The page builder operates before the output routine, and it hands its result in \box255 to the output routine.

\vsplit Split of a top part of a box. This is comparable with page breaking.

\splittopskip Minimum distance between the top of what remains after a \vsplit operation, and the first item in that box. Plain TeX default: 10pt

\pagegoal Goal height of the page box. This starts at \vsize, and is diminished by heights of insertion items.

\pagetotal Accumulated natural height of the current page.

\pagedepth Depth of the current page.

\pagestretch Accumulated zeroth-order stretch of the current page.

\pagefilstretch Accumulated first-order stretch of the current page.

\pagefillstretch Accumulated second-order stretch of the current page.

\pagefilllstretch Accumulated third-order stretch of the current page.

\pageshrink Accumulated shrink of the current page.

\outputpenalty Value of the penalty at the current page break, or 10 000 if the break was not at a penalty.

\interlinepenalty Penalty for breaking a page between lines of a paragraph. Plain TeX default: 0

\clubpenalty Additional penalty for breaking a page after the first line of a paragraph. Plain TeX default: 150

\widowpenalty Additional penalty for breaking a page before the last line of a paragraph. Plain TeX default: 150

\displaywidowpenalty Additional penalty for breaking a page before the last line above a display formula. Plain TeX default: 50

\brokenpenalty Additional penalty for breaking a page after a hyphenated line. Plain TeX default: 100

\penalty Place a penalty on the current list.

\lastpenalty If the last item on the list was a penalty, the value of this.

\unpenalty Remove the last item of the current list if this was a penalty.

27.1 THE CURRENT PAGE AND THE RECENT CONTRIBUTIONS

The main vertical list of TeX is divided in two parts: the 'current page' and the list of 'recent contributions'. Any material that is added to the main vertical list is appended to the recent contributions; the act of moving the recent contributions to the current page is known as 'exercising the page builder'.

Every time something is moved to the current page, TeX computes the cost of breaking the page at that point. If it decides that it is past the optimal point, the current page up to the best break so far is put in \box255 and the remainder of the current page is moved back on top of the recent contributions. If the page is broken at a penalty, that value is recorded in \outputpenalty, and a penalty of size 10 000 is placed on top of the recent contributions; otherwise, \outputpenalty is set to 10 000.

If the current page is empty, discardable items that are moved from the recent contributions are discarded. This is the mechanism that lets glue disappear after a page break and at the top of the first page. When the first non-discardable item is moved to the current page, the \topskip glue is inserted; see the previous chapter.

The workings of the page builder can be made visible by setting \tracing-pages to some positive value (see Chapter 34).

27.2 ACTIVATING THE PAGE BUILDER

The page builder comes into play in the following circumstances.

- Around paragraphs: after the \everypar tokens have been inserted, and after the paragraph has been added to the vertical list. See the end of this chapter for an example.
- Around display formulas: after the \everydisplay tokens have been inserted, and after the display has been added to the list.
- After \par commands, boxes, insertions, and explicit penalties in vertical mode.
- After an output routine has ended.

In these places the page builder moves the recent contributions to the current page. Note that TeX need not be in vertical mode when the page builder is exercised. In horizontal mode, activating the page builder serves to move preceding vertical glue (for example, \parskip, \abovedisplayskip) to the page.

The \end command – which is only allowed in external vertical mode – terminates a TeX job, but only if the main vertical list is empty and \deadcycles = 0. If this is not the case the combination

$$\hbox{}\vfill\penalty-2^{30}$$

is appended, which forces the output routine to act.

27.3 PAGE LENGTH BOOKKEEPING

The height and depth of the page box that reaches the output routine are determined by \vsize, \topskip, and \maxdepth as described in the previous chapter. TeX places the \topskip glue when the first box is placed on the current page; the \vsize and \maxdepth are read when the first box or insertion occurs on the page. Any subsequent changes to these parameters will not be noticeable until the next page or, more strictly, until after the output routine has been called.

After the first box, rule, or insertion on the current page the \vsize is recorded in \pagegoal, and its value is not looked at until \output has been active. Changing \pagegoal does have an effect on the current page. When the page is empty, the pagegoal is \maxdimen, and \pagetotal is zero.

Accumulated dimensions and stretch are available in the parameters \pagetotal, \pagedepth, \pagestretch, \pagefilstretch, \pagefillstretch, \pageshrink, and \pagefilllstretch. They are set by the page builder. The stretch and shrink parameters are updated every time glue is added to the page. The depth parameter becomes zero if the last item was kern or glue.

These parameters are ⟨special dimen⟩s; an assignment to any of them is an ⟨intimate assignment⟩, and it is automatically global.

27.4 BREAKPOINTS

27.4.1 Possible breakpoints

Page breaks can occur at the same kind of locations where line breaks can occur:
- at glue that is preceded by a non-discardable item;
- at a kern that is immediately followed by glue;
- at a penalty.

TeX inserts interline glue and various sorts of interline penalties when the lines of a paragraph are added to the vertical list, so there will usually be sufficient breakpoints on the page.

27.4.2 Breakpoint penalties

If TeX decides to break a page at a penalty item, this penalty will, most of the time, be one that has been inserted automatically between the lines of a paragraph.

If the last item on a list (not necessarily a vertical list) is a penalty, the value of this is recorded in the parameter \lastpenalty. If the item is other than a penalty, this parameter has the value zero. The last penalty of a list can be removed with the command \unpenalty. See Section 5.9.6 for an example.

Here is a list of such penalties:

\interlinepenalty   Penalty for breaking a page between lines of a paragraph.
    In plain TeX this is zero, so no penalty is added in between lines. TeX can
    then find a valid breakpoint at the \baselineskip glue.

\clubpenalty Extra penalty for breaking a page after the first line of
a paragraph. In plain TeX this is 150. This amount, and the following
penalties, are added to the \interlinepenalty, and a penalty of the
resulting size is inserted after the \hbox containing the first line of a
paragraph instead of the \interlinepenalty.

\widowpenalty Extra penalty for breaking a page before the last line of a
paragraph. In plain TeX this is 150.

\displaywidowpenalty Extra penalty for breaking a page before the last line
above a display formula. The default value in plain TeX is 50.

\brokenpenalty Extra penalty for breaking a page after a hyphenated line.
The default value in plain TeX is 100.

If the resulting penalty is zero, it is not placed.

Penalties can also be inserted by the user. For instance, the plain format has macros to encourage (possibly, force) or prohibit page breaks:

```
\def\break{\penalty-10000 }        % force break
\def\nobreak{\penalty10000 }       % prohibit break
\def\goodbreak{\par\penalty-500 }  % encourage page break
```

Also, \vadjust{\penalty ... } is a way of getting penalties in the vertical list. This can be used to discourage or encourage page breaking after a certain line of a paragraph.

27.4.3 Breakpoint computation

Whenever an item is moved to the current page, TeX computes the penalty p and the badness b associated with breaking the page at that place. From the penalty and the badness the cost c of breaking is computed.

The place of least cost is remembered, and when the cost is infinite, that is, the page is overfull, or when the penalty is $p \leq -10\,000$, the current page is broken at the (last remembered) place of least cost. The broken off piece is then put in \box255 and the output routine token list is inserted. Box 255 is always given a height of \vsize, regardless of how much material it has.

The badness calculation is based on the amount of stretching or shrinking that is necessary to fit the page in a box with height \vsize and maximum depth \maxdepth. This calculation is the same as for line breaking (see Chapter 8). Badness is a value $0 \leq b \leq 10\,000$, except when pages are overfull; then $b = \infty$.

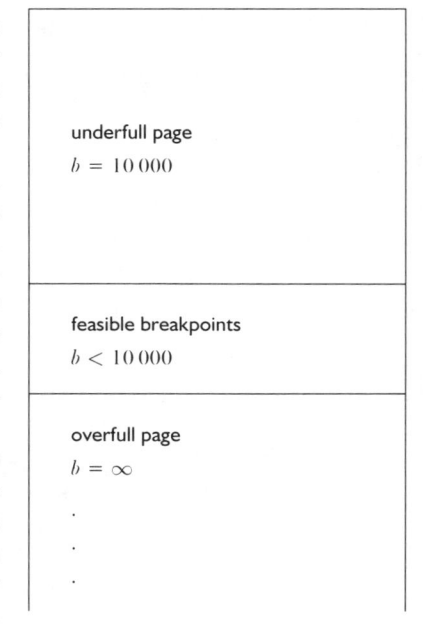

underfull page
$b = 10\,000$

feasible breakpoints
$b < 10\,000$

overfull page
$b = \infty$

Some penalties are implicitly inserted by TeX, for instance the \interlinepenalty which is put in between every pair of lines of a paragraph. Other penalties can be explicitly inserted by the user or a user macro. A penalty value $p \geq 10\,000$ inhibits breaking; a penalty $p \leq -10\,000$ (in external vertical mode) forces a page break, and immediately activates the output routine.

Cost calculation proceeds as follows:

1. When a penalty is so low that it forces a page break and immediate invocation of the output routine, but the page is not overfull, that is

    $b < \infty$ and $p \leq -10\,000$

    the cost is equal to the penalty: $c = p$.

2. When penalties do not force anything, and the page is not overfull, that is

    $b < \infty$ and $|p| < 10\,000$

    the cost is $c = b + p$.

3. For pages that are very bad, that is

    $b = 10\,000$ and $|p| < 10\,000$

    the cost is $c = 10\,000$.

4. An overfull page, that is

    $b = \infty$ and $p < 10\,000$

    gives infinite cost: $c = \infty$. In this case TeX decides that the optimal break point must have occurred earlier, and it invokes the output routine. Values of \insertpenalties (see Chapter 29) that exceed 10 000 also give infinite cost.

The fact that a penalty $p \leq -10\,000$ activates the output routine is used extensively in the LaTeX output routine: the excess $|p| - 10\,000$ is a code indicating the reason for calling the output routine; see also the second example in the next chapter.

27.5 \vsplit

The page-breaking operation is available to the user through the \vsplit operation.

Example

    \box1 = \vsplit2 to \dimen3

assigns to box 1 the top part of size \dimen3 of box 2. This material is actually removed from box 2. Compare this with splitting off a chunk of size \vsize from the current page.

The extracted result of

    \vsplit⟨8-bit number⟩to⟨dimen⟩

is a box with the following properties.

- Height equal to the specified ⟨dimen⟩; TeX will go through the original box register (which must contain a vertical box) to find the best breakpoint. This may result in an underfull box.
- Depth at most `\splitmaxdepth`; this is analogous to the `\maxdepth` for the page box, rather than the `\boxmaxdepth` that holds for any box.
- A first and last mark in the `\splitfirstmark` and `\splitbotmark` registers.

The remainder of the `\vsplit` operation is a box where

- all discardables have been removed from the top;
- glue of size `\splittopskip` has been inserted on top; if the box being split was box 255, it already had `\topskip` glue on top;
- its depth has been forced to be at most `\splitmaxdepth`.

The bottom of the original box is always a valid breakpoint for the `\vsplit` operation. If this breakpoint is taken, the remainder box register is void. The extracted box can be empty; it is only void if the original box was void, or not a vertical box.

Typically, the `\vsplit` operation is used to split off part of `\box255`. By setting `\splitmaxdepth` equal to `\boxmaxdepth` the result is something that could have been made by TeX's page builder. After pruning the top of `\box255`, the mark registers `\firstmark` and `\botmark` contain the first and last marks on the remainder of box 255. See the next chapter for more information on marks.

27.6 EXAMPLES OF PAGE BREAKING

27.6.1 Filling up a page

Suppose a certain vertical box is too large to fit on the remainder of the page. Then

```
\vfil\vbox{ ... }
```

is the wrong way to fill up the page and push the box to the next. TeX can only break at the start of the glue, and the `\vfil` is discarded after the break: the result is an underfull, or at least horribly stretched, page. On the other hand,

```
\vfil\penalty0 % or any other value
\vbox{ ... }
```

is the correct way: TeX will break at the penalty, and the page will be filled.

27.6.2 Determining the breakpoint

In the following examples the `\vsplit` operation is used, which has the same mechanism as page breaking.

Let the macros and parameter settings

```
\offinterlineskip \showboxdepth=1
\def\High{\hbox{\vrule height5pt}}
\def\HighAndDeep{\hbox{\vrule height2.5pt depth2.5pt}}
```

be given.

First let us consider an example where a vertical list is simply stretched in order to reach a break point.

```
\splitmaxdepth=4pt
\setbox1=\vbox{\High \vfil \HighAndDeep}
\setbox2=\vsplit1 to 9pt
```

gives

```
> \box2=
\vbox(9.0+2.5)x0.4, glue set 1.5fil
.\hbox(5.0+0.0)x0.4 []
.\glue 0.0 plus 1.0fil
.\glue(\lineskip) 0.0
.\hbox(2.5+2.5)x0.4 []
```

The two boxes together have a height of 7.5pt, so the glue has to stretch 1.5pt. Next, we decrease the allowed depth of the resulting list.

```
\splitmaxdepth=2pt
\setbox1=\vbox{\High \vfil \HighAndDeep}
\setbox2=\vsplit1 to 9pt
```

gives

```
> \box2=
\vbox(9.0+2.0)x0.4, glue set 1.0fil
.\hbox(5.0+0.0)x0.4 []
.\glue 0.0 plus 1.0fil
.\glue(\lineskip) 0.0
.\hbox(2.5+2.5)x0.4 []
```

The reference point is moved down half a point, and the stretch is correspondingly diminished, but this motion cannot lead to a larger dimension than was specified.

As an example of this, consider the sequence

```
\splitmaxdepth=3pt
\setbox1=\vbox{\High \kern1.5pt \HighAndDeep}
\setbox2=\vsplit1 to 9pt
```

This gives a box exactly 9 points high and 2.5 points deep. Setting `\splitmaxdepth=2pt` does not increase the height by half a point; instead, an underfull box results because an earlier break is taken.

Sometimes the timing of actions is important. TeX first locates a breakpoint that will lead to the requested height, then checks whether accommodating the `\maxdepth` or `\splitmaxdepth` will not violate that height.

Consider an example of this timing: in

```
\splitmaxdepth=4pt
\setbox1=\vbox{\High \vfil \HighAndDeep}
\setbox2=\vsplit1 to 7pt
```

the result is *not* a box of 7 points high and 3 points deep. Instead,

```
> \box2=
\vbox(7.0+0.0)x0.4
.\hbox(5.0+0.0)x0.4 []
```

which is an underfull box.

27.6.3 The page builder after a paragraph

After a paragraph, the page builder moves material to the current page, but it does not decide whether a breakpoint has been found yet.

Example

```
\output{\interrupt \plainoutput}% show when you're active
\def\nl{\hfil\break}\vsize=22pt % make pages of two lines
a\nl b\nl c\par \showlists      % make a 3-line paragraph
```

will report

```
### current page:
[...]
total height 34.0
 goal height 22.0
prevdepth 0.0, prevgraf 3 lines
```

Even though more than enough material has been gathered, \output is only invoked when the next paragraph starts: typing a d gives

```
! Undefined control sequence.
<output> {\interrupt
                \plainoutput }
<to be read again>
                d
```

when \output is inserted after \everypar.

CHAPTER 28

Output Routines

The final stages of page processing are performed by the output routine. The page builder cuts off a certain portion of the main vertical list and hands it to the output routine in \box255. This chapter treats the commands and parameters that pertain to the output routine, and it explains how output routines can receive information through marks.

\output   Token list with instructions for shipping out pages.
\shipout   Ship a box to the dvi file.
\mark   Specify a mark text.
\topmark   The last mark on the previous page.
\botmark   The last mark on the current page.
\firstmark   The first mark on the current page.
\splitbotmark   The last mark on a split-off page.
\splitfirstmark   The first mark on a split-off page.
\deadcycles   Counter that keeps track of how many times the output routine has been called without a \shipout taking place.
\maxdeadcycles   The maximum number of times that the output routine is allowed to be called without a \shipout occurring.
\outputpenalty   Value of the penalty at the current page break, or 10 000 if the break was not at a penalty.

28.1   THE \output TOKEN LIST

Common parlance has it that 'the output routine is called' when TEX has found a place to break the main vertical list. Actually, \output is not a macro but a token list that is inserted into TEX's command stream.

Insertion of the \output token list happens inside a group that is implicitly opened. Also, TEX enters internal vertical mode. Because of the group, non-local assignments (to the page number, for instance) have to be prefixed with \global. The vertical mode implies that during the workings of the output routine spaces are mostly harmless.

The \output token list belongs to the class of the ⟨token parameter⟩s. These behave the same as \toks*nnn* token lists; see Chapter 14. Assigning an output routine can therefore take the following forms:

\output⟨equals⟩⟨general text⟩   or   \output⟨equals⟩⟨filler⟩⟨token variable⟩

28.2 OUTPUT AND \box255

TeX's page builder breaks the current page at the optimal point, and stores everything above that in \box255; then, the \output tokens are inserted into the input stream. Any remaining material on the main vertical list is pushed back to the recent contributions. If the page is broken at a penalty, that value is recorded in \outputpenalty, and a penalty of size 10 000 is placed on top of the recent contributions; otherwise, \outputpenalty is set to 10 000. When the output routine is finished, \box255 is supposed to be empty. If it is not, TeX gives an error message.

Usually, the output routine will take the pagebox, append a headline and/or footline, maybe merge in some insertions such as footnotes, and ship the page to the dvi file:

```
\output={\setbox255=\vbox
        {\someheadline
         \vbox to \vsize{\unvbox255 \unvbox\footins}
         \somefootline}
      \shipout\box255}
```

When box 255 reaches the output routine, its height has been set to \vsize. However, the material in it can have considerably smaller height. Thus, the above output routine may lead to underfull boxes. This can be remedied with a \vfil.

The output routine is under no obligation to do anything useful with \box255; it can empty it, or unbox it to let TeX have another go at finding a page break. The number of times that the output routing postpones the \shipout is recorded in \deadcycles: this parameter is set to 0 by \shipout, and increased by 1 just before every \output.

When the number of dead cycles reaches \maxdeadcycles, TeX gives an error message, and performs the default output routine

```
\shipout\box255
```

instead of the routine it was about to start. The LaTeX format has a much higher value for \maxdeadcycles than plain TeX, because the output routine in LaTeX is often called for intermediate handling of floats and marginal notes.

The \shipout command can send any ⟨box⟩ to the dvi file; this need not be box 255, or even a box containing the current page. It does not have to be called inside the output routine, either.

If the output routine produces any material, for instance by calling

```
\unvbox255
```

this is put on top of the recent contributions.

After the output routine finishes, the page builder is activated. In particular, because the current page has been emptied, the \vsize is read again. Changes made to this parameter inside the output routine (using \global) will therefore take effect.

28.3 MARKS

Information can be passed to the output routine through the mechanism of 'marks'. The user can specify a token list with

>   \mark{⟨mark text⟩}

which is put in a mark item on the current vertical list. The mark text is subject to expansion as in \edef.

If the mark is given in horizontal mode it migrates to the surrounding vertical lists like an insertion item (see page 59); however, if this is not the external vertical list, the output routine will not find the mark.

Marks are the main mechanism through which the output routine can obtain information about the contents of the currently broken off page, in particular its top and bottom. TeX sets three variables:

\botmark   the last mark occurring on the current page;
\firstmark   the first mark occurring on the current page;
\topmark   the last mark of the previous page, that is, the value of \botmark on the previous page.

If no marks have occurred yet, all three are empty; if no marks occurred on the current page, all three mark variables are equal to the \botmark of the previous page.

For boxes generated by a \vsplit command (see previous chapter), the \splitbotmark and \splitfirstmark contain the marks of the split-off part; \firstmark and \botmark reflect the state of what remains in the register.

Example
Marks can be used to get a section heading into the headline or footline of the page.

```
\def\section#1{ ... \mark{#1} ... }
\def\rightheadline{\hbox to \hsize
    {\headlinefont \botmark\hfil\pagenumber}}
\def\leftheadline{\hbox to \hsize
    {\headlinefont \pagenumber\hfil\firstmark}}
```

This places the title of the first section that starts on a left page in the left headline, and the title of the last section that starts on the right page in the right headline. Placing the headlines on the page is the job of the output routine; see below.

It is important that no page breaks can occur in between the mark and the box that places the title:

```
\def\section#1{ ...
    \penalty\beforesectionpenalty
    \mark{#1}
    \hbox{ ... #1 ...}
    \nobreak
```

```
\vskip\aftersectionskip
\noindent}
```

Let us consider another example with headlines: often a page looks better if the headline is omitted on pages where a chapter starts. This can be implemented as follows:

```
\def\chapter#1{ ... \def\chtitle{#1}\mark{1}\mark{0} ... }
\def\theheadline{\expandafter\ifx\firstmark1
    \else \chapheadline \fi}
```

Only on the page where a chapter starts will the mark be 1, and on all other pages a headline is placed.

28.4 ASSORTED REMARKS

28.4.1 Hazards in non-trivial output routines

If the final call to the output routine does not perform a \shipout, TeX will call the output routine endlessly, since a run will only stop if both the vertical list is empty, and \deadcycles is zero. The output routine can set \deadcycles to zero to prevent this.

28.4.2 Page numbering

The page number is not an intrinsic property of the output routine; in plain TeX it is the value of \count0. The output routine is responsible for increasing the page number when a shipout of a page occurs.

Apart from \count0, counter registers 1–9 are also used for page identification: at shipout TeX writes the values of these ten counters to the dvi file (see Chapter 33). Terminal and log file output display only the non-zero counters, and the zero counters for which a non-zero counter with a higher number exists, that is, if \count0 = 1 and \count3 = 5 are the only non-zero counters, the displayed list of counters is [1.0.0.5].

28.4.3 Headlines and footlines in plain TeX

Plain TeX has token lists \headline and \footline; these are used in the macros \makeheadline and \makefootline. The page is shipped out as (more or less)

```
\vbox{\makeheadline\pagebody\makefootline}
```

Both headline and footline are inserted inside a \line. For non-standard headers and footers it is easier to redefine the macros \makeheadline and \makefootline than to tinker with the token lists.

28.4.4 Example: no widow lines

Suppose that one does not want to allow widow lines, but pages have in general no stretch or shrink, for instance because they only contain plain text. A solution would be to increase the page length by one line if a page turns out to be broken at a widow line.

TeX's output routine can perform this sort of trick: if the \widowpenalty is set to some recognizable value, the output routine can see by the \outputpenalty if a widow line occurred. In that case, the output routine can temporarily increase the \vsize, and let the page builder have another go at finding a break point.

Here is the skeleton of such an output routine. No headers or footers are provided for.

```
\newif\ifLargePage  \widowpenalty=147
\newdimen\oldvsize  \oldvsize=\vsize
\output={
    \ifLargePage \shipout\box255
        \global\LargePagefalse
        \global\vsize=\oldvsize
    \else \ifnum \outputpenalty=\widowpenalty
            \global\LargePagetrue
            \global\advance\vsize\baselineskip
            \unvbox255 \penalty\outputpenalty
        \else  \shipout\box255
    \fi   \fi}
```

The test \ifLargePage is set to true by the output routine if the \outputpenalty equals the \widowpenalty. The page box is then \unvboxed, so that the page builder will tackle the same material once more.

28.4.5 Example: no indentation top of page

Some output routines can be classified as abuse of the output routine mechanism. The output routine in this section is a good example of this.

It is imaginable that one wishes paragraphs not to indent if they start at the top of a page. (There are plenty of objections to this layout, but occasionally it is used.) This problem can be solved using the output routine to investigate whether the page is still empty and, if so, to give a signal that a paragraph should not indent.

Note that we cannot use the fact here that the page builder comes into play after the insertion of \everypar: even if we could force the output routine to be activated here, there is no way for it to remove the indentation box.

The solution given here lets the \everypar terminate the paragraph immediately with

```
\par\penalty-\specialpenalty
```

which activates the output routine. Seeing whether the pagebox is empty (after removing the empty line and any \parskip glue), the output routine then can set a switch signalling whether the retry of the paragraph should indent.

There are some minor matters in the following routines, the sense of which is left for the reader to ponder.

```
\mathchardef\specialpenalty=10001
\newif\ifPreventSwitch
\newbox\testbox
\topskip=10pt

\everypar{\begingroup \par
    \penalty-\specialpenalty
    \everypar{\endgroup}\parskip0pt
    \ifPreventSwitch \noindent \else \indent \fi
    \global\PreventSwitchfalse
    }
\output{
    \ifnum\outputpenalty=-\specialpenalty
        \setbox\testbox\vbox{\unvbox255
                {\setbox0=\lastbox}\unskip}
        \ifdim\ht\testbox=0pt \global\PreventSwitchtrue
        \else \topskip=0pt \unvbox\testbox \fi
    \else \shipout\box255 \global\advance\pageno1 \fi}
```

28.4.6 More examples of output routines

A large number of examples of output routines can be found in Salomon (1990a) and Salomon (1990b).

CHAPTER 29

Insertions

Insertions are TeX's way of handling floating information. TeX's page builder calculates what insertions and how many of them will fit on the page; these insertion items are then placed in insertion boxes which to be handled by the output routine.

\insert   Start an insertion item.
\newinsert   Allocate a new insertion class.
\insertpenalties   Total of penalties for split insertions. Inside the output routine, the number of held-over insertions.
\floatingpenalty   Penalty added when an insertion is split.
\holdinginserts   (TeX3 only) If this is positive, insertions are not placed in their boxes at output time.
\footins   Number of the footnote insertion class in plain TeX.
\topins   Number of the top insertion class.
\topinsert   Plain TeX macro to start a top insert.
\pageinsert   Plain TeX macro to start an insert that will take up a whole page.
\midinsert   Plain TeX macro that places its argument if there is space, and converts it into a top insert otherwise.
\endinsert   Plain TeX macro to wind up an insertion item that started with \topinsert, \midinsert, or \pageinsert.

29.1 INSERTION ITEMS

Insertions contain floating information. Handling insertions is a strange interplay between the user, TeX's internal workings, and the output routine. First the user specifies an insertion, which is a certain amount of vertical material; then TeX's page builder decides what insertions should go on the current page and puts these insertions in insertion boxes; finally, the output routine has to do something with these boxes.

An insertion item looks like

\insert⟨8-bit number⟩{⟨vertical mode material⟩}

where the 8-bit number should not be 255, because \box255 is used by TeX for passing the page to the output routine.

The braces around the vertical mode material in an insertion item can be implicit; they imply a new level of grouping. The vertical mode material is processed in internal vertical mode.

Values of \splittopskip, \splitmaxdepth, and \floatingpenalty are relevant for split insertions (see below); the values that are current just before the end of the group are used.

Insertion items can appear in vertical mode, horizontal mode, and math mode. For the latter two modes they have to migrate to the surrounding vertical list (see page 59). After an insertion item is put on the vertical list the page builder is exercised.

29.2 INSERTION CLASS DECLARATION

In the plain format the number for a new insertion class is allocated by \newinsert:

```
\newinsert\myinsert % new insertion class
```

which uses \chardef to assign a number to the control sequence.

Insertion classes are allocated numbering from 254 downward. As box 255 is used for output, this allocation scheme leaves \skip255, \dimen255, and \count255 free for scratch use.

29.3 INSERTION PARAMETERS

For each insertion class n four registers are allocated:

- \box n When the output routine is active this box contains the insertion items of class n that should be placed on the current page.
- \dimen n This is the maximum space allotted for insertions of class n per page. If this amount would be exceeded TeX will split insertions.
- \skip n Glue of this size is added the first time an insertion item of class n is added to the current page. This is useful for such phenomena as a rule separating the footnotes from the text of the page.
- \count n Each insertion item is a vertical list, so it has a certain height. However, the effective height, the amount of influence it has on the text height of the page, may differ from this real height. The value of \count n is then 1000 times the factor by which the height should be multiplied to obtain the effective height.

Consider the following examples:

- Marginal notes do not affect the text height, so the factor should be 0.
- Footnotes set in double column mode affect the page by half of their height: the count value should by 500.
- Conversely, footnotes set at page width underneath a page in double column mode affect both columns, so – provided that the double column

mode is implemented by applying \vsplit to a double-height column – the count value should be 2000.

29.4 MOVING INSERTION ITEMS FROM THE CONTRIBUTIONS LIST

The most complicated issue with insertions is the algorithm that adds insertion items to the main vertical list, and calculates breakpoints if necessary.

TeX never changes the \vsize, but it diminishes the \pagegoal by the (effective) heights of the insertion items that will appear before a page break. Thus the output routine will receive a \box255 that has height \pagegoal, not necessarily \vsize.

1. When the first insertion of a certain class n occurs on the current page TeX has to account for the quantity \skip$n$. This step is executed only if no earlier insertion item of this class occurs on the vertical list – this includes insertions that were split – but \box$n$ need not be empty at this time.

    If \box$n$ is not empty, its height plus depth is multiplied by \count$n$/1000 and the result is subtracted from \pagegoal. Then the \pagegoal is diminished by the natural component of \skip$n$. Any stretch and shrink of \skip$n$ are incorporated in \pagestretch and \pageshrink respectively.

2. If there is a split insertion of class n on the page – this case and the previous step in the algorithm are mutually exclusive – the \floatingpenalty is added to \insertpenalties. A split insertion is an insertion item for which a breakpoint has been calculated as it will not fit on the current page in its entirety. Thus the insertion currently under consideration will certainly not wind up on the current page.

3. After the preliminary action of the two previous points TeX will place the actual insertion item on the main vertical list, at the end of the current contributions. First it will check whether the item will fit without being split.

    There are two conditions to be checked:

    - adding the insertion item (plus all previous insertions of that class) to \box$n$ should not let the height plus depth of that box exceed \dimen$n$, and
    - either the effective height of the insertion is negative, or \pagetotal plus \pagedepth minus \pageshrink plus the effective size of the insertion should be less than \pagegoal.

    If these conditions are satisfied, \pagegoal is diminished by the effective size of the insertion item, that is, by the height plus depth, multiplied by \count$n$/1000.

4. Insertions that fail on one of the two conditions in the previous step of the algorithm will be considered for splitting. TeX will calculate the size of the maximal portion to be split off the insertion item, such that

    a. adding this portion together with earlier insertions of this class to \box$n$ will not let the size of the box exceed \dimen$n$, and

b. the effective size of this portion, added to \pagetotal plus \pagedepth, will not exceed \pagegoal. Note that \pageshrink is not taken into account this time, as it was in the previous step.

Once this maximal size to be split off has been determined, TeX locates the least-cost breakpoint in the current insertion item that will result in a box with a height that is equal to this maximal size. The penalty associated with this breakpoint is added to \insertpenalties, and \pagegoal is diminished by the effective height plus depth of the box to be split off the insertion item.

29.5 INSERTIONS IN THE OUTPUT ROUTINE

When the output routine comes into action – more precisely: when TeX starts processing the tokens in the \output token list – all insertions that should be placed on the current page have been put in their boxes, and it is the responsibility of the output routine to put them somewhere in the box that is going to be shipped out.

Example
The plain TeX output routine handles top inserts and footnotes by packaging the following sequence:

```
\ifvoid\topins \else \unvbox\topins \fi
\pagebody
\ifvoid\footins \else \unvbox\footins \fi
```

Unboxing the insertion boxes makes the glue on various parts of the page stretch or shrink in a uniform manner.

With TeX3 the insertion mechanism has been extended slightly: the parameter \holdinginserts can be used to specify that insertions should not yet be placed in their boxes. This is very useful if the output routine wants to recalculate the \vsize, or if the output routine is called to do other intermediate calculations instead of ejecting a page.

During the output routine the parameter \insertpenalties holds the number of insertion items that are being held over for the next page. In the plain TeX output routine this is used after the last page:

```
\def\dosupereject{\ifnum\insertpenalties>0
    % something is being held over
  \line{}\kern-\topskip\nobreak\vfill\supereject\fi}
```

29.6 PLAIN TeX INSERTIONS

The plain TeX format has only two insertion classes: the footnotes and the top inserts. The macro \pageinsert generates top inserts that are stretched to be exactly \vsize high. The \midinsert macro tests whether the vertical material specified by the user fits on the page; if so, it is placed there; if not, it is converted to a top insert.

Footnotes are allowed to be split, but once one has been split no further footnotes should appear on the current page. This effect is attained by setting

`\floatingpenalty=20000`

The `\floatingpenalty` is added to `\insertpenalties` if an insertion follows a split insertion of the same class. However, `\floatingpenalty` $> 10\,000$ has infinite cost, so TeX will take an earlier breakpoint for splitting off the page from the vertical list.

Top inserts essentially contain only a vertical box which holds whatever the user specified. Thus such an insert cannot be split. However, the `\endinsert` macro puts a `\penalty100` on top of the box, so the insertion can be split with an empty part before the split. The effect is that the whole insertion is carried over to the next page. As the `\floatingpenalty` for top inserts is zero, arbitrarily many of these inserts can be moved forward until there is a page with sufficient space.

Further examples of insertion macros can be found in Salomon (1990c).

CHAPTER

30

File Input and Output

This chapter treats the various ways in which TeX can read from and write to external files.

\input   Read a specified file as TeX input.
\endinput   Terminate inputting the current file after the current line.
\pausing   Specify that TeX should pause after each line that is read from a file.
\inputlineno   Number of the current input line.
\write   Write a ⟨general text⟩ to the terminal or to a file.
\read   Read a line from a stream into a control sequence.
\newread \newwrite   Macro for allocating a new input/output stream.
\openin \closein   Open/close an input stream.
\openout \closeout   Open/close an output stream.
\ifeof   Test whether a file has been fully read, or does not exist.
\immediate   Prefix to have output operations executed right away.
\escapechar   Number of the character that is used when control sequences are being converted into character tokens. IniTeX default: 92.
\newlinechar   Number of the character that triggers a new line in \write statements.

30.1   INCLUDING FILES: \input AND \endinput

Large documents can be segmented in TeX by putting parts in separate files, and loading these with \input into the master file. The exact syntax for file names is implementation dependent; most of the time a .tex file extension is assumed if no explicit extension is given. File names can be delimited with a space or with \relax. The \input command is expandable.

If TeX encounters in an input file the \endinput statement, it acts as if the file ends after the line on which the statement occurs. Any statements on the same line as \endinput are still executed. The \endinput statement is expandable.

30.2   FILE I/O

TeX supports input and output streams for reading and writing files one line at a time.

30.2.1 Opening and closing streams

TeX supports up to 16 simultaneous input and 16 output streams. The plain TeX macros \newread and \newwrite give the number of an unused stream. This number is assigned by a \chardef command. Input streams are completely independent of output streams.

Input streams are opened by

\openin⟨4-bit number⟩⟨equals⟩⟨filename⟩

and closed by

\closein⟨4-bit number⟩

Output streams are opened by

\openout⟨4-bit number⟩⟨equals⟩⟨filename⟩

and closed by

\closeout⟨4-bit number⟩

If an output file does not yet exist, it is created by \openout; if it did exist, an \openout will cause it to be overwritten.

The output operations \openout, \closeout, and \write can all three be prefixed by \immediate; see below.

30.2.2 Input with \read

In addition to the \input command, which reads a whole file, TeX has the \read operation, which reads one line from a file (or from the user terminal). The syntax of the read command is

\read⟨number⟩to⟨control sequence⟩

The effect of this statement is that one input line is read from the designated stream, and the control sequence is defined as a macro without parameters, having that line as replacement text.

If the input line is not balanced with respect to braces, TeX will read more than one line, continuing for as long as is necessary to get a balanced token list. TeX implicitly appends an empty line to each input stream, so the last \read operation on a stream will always yield a single \par token.

Read operations from any stream outside the range 0–15 – or streams not associated with an open file, or on which the file end has been reached – read from the terminal. If the stream number is positive the user is prompted with the name of the control sequence being defined by the \read statement.

Example

    \read16 to \data

displays a prompt

    \data=

and typing 'my name' in response makes the read statement equivalent to

```
\def\data{my name }
```

The space at the end of the input derives from the line end; to prevent this one could write

```
{\endlinechar=-1 \global\read16 to \data}
```

30.2.3 Output with \write

TeX's `\write` command

```
\write⟨number⟩⟨general text⟩
```

writes a balanced token list to a file which has been opened by `\openout`, to the log file, or to the terminal.

Write operations to a stream outside 0–15 – or to a stream that is not associated with an open file – go to the log file; if the stream number is positive they go to the log file as well as to the terminal.

The token list argument of `\write`, defined as

⟨general text⟩ ⟶ ⟨filler⟩{⟨balanced text⟩⟨right brace⟩

can have an implicit opening brace. This argument is expanded as if it were the replacement text of an `\edef`, so, for instance, any macros and conditionals appearing are expanded. No commands are executed, however. This expansion occurs at the time of shipping out; see below. Until that time the argument token list is stored in a whatsit item on the current list. See further Chapter 12 for a discussion of expansion during writing.

A control sequence output by `\write` (or `\message`) is represented with a trailing space, and using character number `\escapechar` for the escape character. The IniTeX default for this is 92, the code for the backslash. The trailing space can be prevented by prefixing the control sequence with `\string`.

30.3 WHATSITS

There is an essential difference in execution between input and output: operations concerning output (`\openout`, `\closeout`, `\write`) are not executed immediately; instead, they are saved until the box in which they appear is shipped out to the `dvi` file.

Writes and the other two output operations are placed in 'whatsit' items on whichever list is currently being built. The actual operation occurs when the part of the page that has the item is shipped out to the `dvi` file. This delayed output is made necessary by TeX's asynchronous output routine behaviour. See a worked-out example on page 121.

An `\immediate\write` – or any other `\immediate` output operation – is executed on the spot, and does not place a whatsit item on the current list.

The argument of a \special command (see page 253) is also placed in a whatsit.

Whatsit items in leader boxes are ignored.

30.4 ASSORTED REMARKS

30.4.1 Inspecting input

TeX records the current line number in the current input file in the ⟨internal integer⟩ parameter \inputlineno (in TeX3).

If the parameter \pausing is positive, TeX shows every line that is input on the terminal screen, and gives the user the opportunity to insert commands. These can for instance be \show commands. Inserted commands are treated as if they were directly in the source file: it is for instance not necessary to prefix them with 'i', as would be necessary when TeX pauses for an error.

30.4.2 Testing for existence of files

TeX is not the friendliest of systems when you ask it to input a non-existing file. Therefore the following sequence of commands can be used to prevent trouble:

```
\newread\instream \openin\instream= fname.tex
\ifeof\instream \message{File 'fname' does not exist!}
\else \closein\instream \input fname.tex
\fi
```

Here an input stream is opened with the given file name. The end-of-file test is also true if an input stream does not correspond to a physical file, so if this conditional is not true, the file exists and an \input command can safely be given.

30.4.3 Timing problems

The synchronization between write operations on the one hand, and opening/closing operations of files on the other hand, can be a crucial point. Auxiliary files, such as are used by various formats to implement cross-references, are a good illustration of this.

Suppose that during a run of TeX the auxiliary file is written, and at the end of the run it has to be input again for a variety of purposes (such as seeing whether references have changed). An \input command is executed right away, so the file must have been closed with an \immediate\closeout. However, now it becomes possible that the file is closed before all writes to it have been performed. The following sequence remedies this:

```
\par\vfil\penalty -10000 \immediate\closeout\auxfile
```

The first three commands activate the output routine in order to close off the last page, so all writes will indeed have been performed before the file is closed.

30.4.4 \message versus \immediate\write16

Messages to the user can be given using \message⟨general text⟩, which writes to the terminal. Messages are appended to one another; the line is wrapped when the line length (a TeX compile-time constant) has been reached. A maximum of 1000 characters is written per message; this is not a compile-time constant, but is hard-wired into the TeX program.

Each message given with \immediate\write starts on a new line; the user can force a new line in the message by including the character with number \newlinechar. This parameter has no effect in \message.

30.4.5 Write inside a vertical box

Since a write operation winds up on the vertical list in a whatsit, issuing one at the start of a \vtop will probably influence the height of that box (see Chapter 5). As an example,

```
have the \vtop{\write\terminal{Hello!}\hbox{more text}}
dangling from
```

will have the $\vtop{\text{more text}}$ dangling from the baseline (and when this book is TeXed the message 'Hello!' appears on the screen).

30.4.6 Expansion and spaces in \write and \message

Both \write and \message expand their argument as if it were the replacement text of an \edef. Therefore

```
\def\a{b}\message{\a}
```

will write out 'b'.

Unexpandable control sequences are displayed with a trailing space (and prefixed with the \escapechar):

```
\message{\hbox\vbox!}
```

will write out '\hbox \vbox !'. Undefined control sequences give an error here.

Expandable control sequences can be written out with some care:

```
\message{\noexpand\ifx}
\message{\string\ifx}
{\let\ifx\relax \message{\ifx}}
```

all write out '\ifx'.

Note, however, that spaces after expandable control sequences are removed in the input processor, which goes into state S after a control sequence. Therefore

```
\def\a{b}\def\c{d}
\message{\a \c}
```

writes out 'bd'. Inserting a space can be done as follows:

```
\def\space{ } % in plain TeX
\message{\a\space\c}
```

displays 'b d'. Note that

```
\message{\a{ }\c}
```

does not work: it displays 'b{ }d' since braces are unexpandable character tokens.

CHAPTER 31

Allocation

TeX has registers of a number of types. For some of these, explicit commands exist to define a synonym for a certain register; for all of them macros exist in the plain format to allocate an unused register. This chapter treats the synonym and allocation commands, and discusses some guidelines for macro writers regarding allocation.

\countdef   Define a synonym for a \count register.
\dimendef   Define a synonym for a \dimen register.
\muskipdef   Define a synonym for a \muskip register.
\skipdef   Define a synonym for a \skip register.
\toksdef   Define a synonym for a \toks register.
\newbox   Allocate an unused \box register.
\newcount   Allocate an unused \count register.
\newdimen   Allocate an unused \dimen register.
\newfam   Allocate an unused math family.
\newinsert   Allocate an unused insertion class.
\newlanguage   (TeX3 only) Allocate a new language number.
\newmuskip   Allocate an unused \muskip register.
\newskip   Allocate an unused \skip register.
\newtoks   Allocate an unused \toks register.
\newread   Allocate an unused input stream.
\newwrite   Allocate an unused output stream.

31.1   ALLOCATION COMMANDS

In plain TeX, \new... macros are defined for allocation of registers. The registers of TeX fall into two classes that are allocated in different ways. This is treated below.

The \newlanguage macro of plain TeX does not allocate any register. Instead it merely assigns a number, starting from 0. TeX (version 3) can have at most 256 different sets of hyphenation patterns.

The \new... macros of plain TeX are defined to be \outer (see Chapter 11 for a precise explanation), which precludes use of the allocation macros in other macros. Therefore the LaTeX format redefines these macros without the \outer prefix.

31.1.1 \count, \dimen, \skip, \muskip, \toks

For these registers there exists a ⟨registerdef⟩ command, for instance \countdef, to couple a specific register to a control sequence:

⟨registerdef⟩⟨control sequence⟩⟨equals⟩⟨8-bit number⟩

After the definition

`\countdef\MyCount=42`

the allocated register can be used as

`\MyCount=314`

or

`\vskip\MyCount\baselineskip`

The ⟨registerdef⟩ commands are used in plain TeX macros \newcount et cetera that allocate an unused register; after

`\newcount\MyCount`

\MyCount can be used exactly as in the above two examples.

31.1.2 \box, \fam, \write, \read, \insert

For these registers there exists no ⟨registerdef⟩ command in TeX, so \chardef is used to allocate box registers in the corresponding plain TeX macros \newbox, for instance.

The fact that \chardef is used implies that the defined control sequence does not stand for the register itself, but only for its number. Thus after

`\newbox\MyBox`

it is necessary to write

`\box\MyBox`

Leaving out the \box means that the character in the current font with number \MyBox is typeset. The \chardef command is treated further in Chapter 3.

31.2 GROUND RULES FOR MACRO WRITERS

The \new... macros of plain TeX have been designed to form a foundation for macro packages, such that several of such packages can operate without collisions in the same run of TeX. In appendix B of *The TeXbook* Knuth formulates some ground rules that macro writers should adhere to.

1. The \new... macros do not allocate registers with numbers 0–9. These can therefore be used as 'scratch' registers. However, as any macro family can use

them, no assumption can be made about the permanency of their contents. Results that are to be passed from one call to another should reside in specifically allocated registers.

Note that count registers 0–9 are used for page identification in the `dvi` file (see Chapter 33), so no global assignments to these should be made.

2. `\count255`, `\dimen255`, and `\skip255` are also available. This is because inserts are allocated from 254 downward and, together with an insertion box, a count, dimen, and skip register, all with the same number, are allocated. Since `\box255` is used by the output routine (see Chapter 28), the count, dimen, and skip with number 255 are freely available.

3. Assignments to scratch registers 0, 2, 4, 6, 8, and 255 should be local; assignments to registers 1, 3, 5, 7, 9 should be `\global` (with the exception of the `\count` registers). This guideline prevents 'save stack build-up' (see Chapter 35).

4. Any register can be used inside a group, as TeX's grouping mechanism will restore its value outside the group. There are two conditions on this use of a register: no global assignments should be made to it, and it must not be possible that other macros may be activated in that group that perform global assignments to that register.

5. Registers that are used over longer periods of time, or that have to survive in between calls of different macros, should be allocated by `\new`....

CHAPTER

32

Running TEX

This chapter treats the run modes of TEX, and some other commands associated with the job being processed.

\everyjob   Token list that is inserted at the start of each new job.
\jobname   Name of the main TEX file being processed.
\end   Command to finish off a run of TEX.
\bye   Plain TEX macro to force the final output.
\pausing   Specify that TEX should pause after each line that is read from a file.
\errorstopmode   TEX will ask for user input on the occurrence of an error.
\scrollmode   TEX fixes errors itself, but will ask the user for missing files.
\nonstopmode   TEX fixes errors itself, and performs an emergency stop on serious errors such as missing input files.
\batchmode   TEX fixes errors itself and performs an emergency stop on serious errors such as missing input files, but no terminal output is generated.

32.1   JOBS

TEX associates with each run a name for the file being processed: the \jobname. If TEX is run interactively – meaning that it has been invoked without a file argument, and the user types commands – the jobname is `texput`.

The \jobname can be used to generate the names of auxiliary files to be read or written during the run. For instance, for a file `story.tex` the \jobname is `story`, and writing

```
\openout\Auxiliary=\jobname.aux
\openout\TableOfContents=\jobname.toc
```

will create the files `story.aux` and `story.toc`.

32.1.1   Start of the job

TEX starts each job by inserting the \everyjob token list into the command stream. Setting this variable during a run of TEX has no use, but a format can use it to identify itself to the user. If a format fills the token list, the commands therein are automatically executed when TEX is run using that format.

32.1.2 End of the job

A TeX job is terminated by the \end command. This may involve first forcing the output routine to process any remaining material (see Chapter 27). If the end of job occurs inside a group TeX will give a diagnostic message. The \end command is not allowed in internal vertical mode, because this would be inside a vertical box.

Usually some sugar coating of the \end command is necessary. For instance the plain TeX macro \bye is defined as

```
\def\bye{\par\vfill\supereject\end}
```

where the \supereject takes care of any leftover insertions.

32.1.3 The log file

For each run TeX creates a log file. Usually this will be a file with as name the value of \jobname, and the extension .log. Other extensions such as .lis are used by some implementations. This log file contains all information that is displayed on the screen during the run of TeX, but it will display some information more elaborately, and it can contain statistics that are usually not displayed on the screen. If the parameter \tracingonline has a positive value, all the log file information will be shown on the screen.

Overfull and underfull boxes are reported on the terminal screen, and they are dumped using the parameters \showboxdepth and \showboxbreadth in the log file (see Chapter 34). These parameters are also used for box dumps caused by the \showbox command, and for the dump of boxes written by \shipout if \tracingoutput is set to a positive value.

Statistics generated by commands such as \tracingparagraphs will be written to the log file; if \tracingonline is positive they will also be shown on the screen.

Output operations to a stream that is not open, or to a stream with a number that is not in the range 0–15, go to the log file. If the stream number is positive, they also go to the terminal.

32.2 RUN MODES

By default, TeX goes into \errorstopmode if an error occurs: it stops and asks for input from the user. Some implementations have a way of forcing TeX into errorstopmode when the user interrupts TeX, so that the internal state of TeX can be inspected (and altered). See page 264 for ways to switch the run mode when TeX has been interrupted.

Often, TeX can fix an error itself if the user asks TeX just to continue (usually by hitting the return key), but sometimes (for instance in alignments) it may take a while before TeX is on the right track again (and sometimes it never is). In such cases the user may want to turn on \scrollmode, which instructs TeX to fix as best it can any occurring error without confirmation from the user. This is usually done by typing 's' when TeX asks for input.

In \scrollmode, TeX also does not ask for input after \show... commands. However, some errors, such as a file that could not be found for \input, are not so easily remedied, so the user will still be asked for input.

With \nonstopmode TeX will scroll through errors and, in the case of the kind of error that cannot be recovered from, it will make an emergency stop, aborting the run. Also TeX will abort the run if a \read is attempted from the terminal. The \batchmode differs only from nonstopmode in that it gives messages only to the log file, not to the terminal.

CHAPTER 33

TeX and the Outside World

This chapter treats those commands that bear relevance to `dvi` files and formats. It gives some global information about IniTeX, font and format files, Computer Modern typefaces, and WEB.

`\dump`   Dump a format file; possible only in IniTeX, not allowed inside a group.
`\special`   Write a ⟨balanced text⟩ to the `dvi` file.
`\mag`   1000 times the magnification of the document.
`\year`   The year of the current job.
`\month`   The month of the current job.
`\day`   The day of the current job.
`\time`   Number of minutes after midnight that the current job started.
`\fmtname`   Macro containing the name of the format dumped.
`\fmtversion`   Macro containing the version of the format dumped.

33.1   TeX, IniTeX, VirTeX

In the terminology established in *TeX: the Program*, Knuth (1986a), TeX programs come in three flavours. IniTeX is a version of TeX that can generate formats; VirTeX is a production version without preloaded format, and TeX is a production version with preloaded (plain) format. Unfortunately, this terminology is not adhered to in general. A lot of systems do not use preloaded formats (the procedure for making them may be impossible on some operating systems), and call the 'virgin TeX' simply TeX. This manual also follows that convention.

33.1.1   Formats: loading

A format file (usually with extension `.fmt`) is a compact dump of TeX's internal structures. Loading a format file takes a considerably shorter time than would be needed for loading the font information and the macros that constitute the format.

Both TeX and IniTeX can load a format; the user specifies this by putting the name on the command line

```
% tex &plain
```

or at the ** prompt

```
% tex
This is TeX. Version ....
** &plain
```

preceded by an ampersand (for Unix, this should be \& on the command line). An input file name can follow the format name in both places.

IniTeX does not need a format, but if no format is specified for (Vir)TeX, it will try to load the plain format, and halt if that cannot be found.

33.1.2 Formats: dumping

IniTeX is the only version of TeX that can dump a format, since it is the only version of TeX that has the command \dump, which causes the internal structures to be dumped as a format. It is also the only version of TeX that has the command \patterns, which is needed to specify a list of hyphenation patterns.

Dumping is not allowed inside a group, that is

```
{ ... \dump }
```

is not allowed. This restriction prevents difficulties with TeX's save stack. After the \dump command TeX gives an elaborate listing of its internal state, and of the font names associated with fonts that have been loaded and ends the job.

An interesting possibility arises from the fact that IniTeX can both load and dump a format. Suppose you have written a set of macros that build on top of plain TeX, superplain.tex. You could then call

```
% initex &plain superplain
*\dump
```

and get a format file superplain.fmt that has all of plain, and all of your macros.

33.1.3 Formats: preloading

On some systems it is possible to interrupt a running program, and save its 'core image' such that this can be started as an independent program. The executable made from the core image of a TeX program interrupted after it has loaded a format is called a TeX program with preloaded format. The idea behind preloaded formats is that interrupting TeX after it has loaded a format, and making this program available to the user, saves in each run the time for loading the format. In the good old days when computers were quite a bit slower this procedure made sense. Nowadays, it does not seem so necessary. Besides, dumping a core image may not always be possible.

33.1.4 The knowledge of IniTeX

If no format has been loaded, IniTeX knows very little. For instance, it has no open/close group characters. However, it can not be completely devoid of knowledge lest there be no way to define anything.

Here is the extent of its knowledge.

- \catcode`\\=0, \escapechar=`\\ (see page 9).
- \catcode`\^^M=5, \endlinechar=`\^^M (see page 9).
- \catcode`\ =10 (see page 10).
- \catcode`\%=14 (see page 10).
- \catcode`\^^?=15 (see page 10).
- \catcode$x$=11 for $x =$ `a..`z, `A..`Z (see page 10).
- \catcode$x$=12 for all other character codes (see page 10).
- \sfcode$x$=999 for $x =$ `A..`Z, \sfcode$x$=1000 for all other characters (see page 177).
- \lccode`a..`z, `A..`Z=`a..`z, \uccode`a..`z, `A..`Z=`A..`Z, \lccode$x$=0, \uccode$x$=0 for all other characters (see page 29).
- \delcode`.=0, \delcode$x$=-1 for all other characters (see page 182).
- \mathcode$x$="7100 + x for all lowercase and uppercase letters, \mathcode$x$="7000 + x for all digits, \mathcode$x$=x for all other characters (see page 187).
- \tolerance=10000, \mag=1000, \maxdeadcycles=25.

33.1.5 Memory sizes of TeX and IniTeX

The main memory size of TeX and IniTeX is controlled by four constants in the source code: `mem_bot`, `mem_top`, `mem_min`, and `mem_max`. For IniTeX's memory `mem_bot = mem_min` and `mem_top = mem_max`; for TeX `mem_bot` and `mem_top` record the main memory size of the IniTeX used to dump the format. Thus versions of TeX and IniTeX have to be adapted to each other in this respect.

TeX's own main memory can be bigger than that of the corresponding IniTeX: in general `mem_min` ≤ `mem_bot` and `mem_top` ≤ `mem_max`.

For IniTeX a smaller main memory can suffice, as this program is typically not meant to do real typesetting. There may even be a real need for the main memory to be smaller, because IniTeX needs a lot of auxiliary storage for initialization and for building the hyphenation table.

33.2 MORE ABOUT FORMATS

33.2.1 Compatibility

TeX has a curious error message: 'Fatal format error: I'm stymied', which is given if TeX tries to load a format that was made with an incompatible version of IniTeX. See the point above about memory sizes, and Chapter 35 for the hash size (parameters `hash_size` and `hash_prime`) and the hyphenation exception dictionary (parameter `hyph_size`).

33.2.2 Preloaded fonts

During a run of TeX the only information needed about fonts is the data that is found in the `tfm` files (see below). Since a run of TeX, especially if the input contains math material, can easily access 30–40 fonts, the disk access for all the `tfm` files can become significant. Therefore the plain format and LaTeX load these metrics files in IniTeX. A TeX version using such a format does not need to load any `tfm` files.

On the other hand, if a format has the possibility of accessing a range of typefaces, it may be advantageous to have metrics files loaded on demand during the actual run of TeX.

33.2.3 The plain format

The first format written for TeX, and the basis for all later ones, is the plain format, described in *The TeXbook*. It is a mixture of

- definitions and macros one simply cannot live without such as the initial `\catcode` assignments, all of the math delimiter definitions, and the `\new...` macros;
- constructs that are useful, but for which LaTeX and other packages use a different implementation, such as the tabbing environment; and
- some macros that are insufficient for any but the simplest applications: `\item` and `\beginsection` are in this category.

It is the first category which Knuth meant to serve as a foundation for future macro packages, so that they can live peacefully together (see Chapter 31). This idea is reflected in the fact that the name 'plain' is not capitalized: it is the basic set of macros.

33.2.4 The LaTeX format

The LaTeX format, written by Leslie Lamport of Digital Equipment Corporation and described in Lamport (1986), was released around 1985. The LaTeX format, using its own version of `plain.tex` (called `lplain.tex`), is not compatible with plain TeX; a number of plain macros are not available. Still, it contains large parts of the plain format (even when they overlap with its own constructs).

LaTeX is a powerful format with facilities such as marginal notes, floating objects, cross referencing, and automatic table of contents generation. Its main drawback is that the 'style files' which define the actual layout are quite hard to write (although LaTeX is in the process of a major revision, in which this problem will be tackled; see Mittelbach and Schöpf (1989) and Mittelbach and Schöpf (1991)). As a result, people have had at their disposal mostly the styles written by Leslie Lamport, the layout of which is rather idiosyncratic. See Braams *et al.* (1989) for a successful attempt to replace these styles.

33.2.5 Mathematical formats

There are two formats with extensive facilities for mathematics typesetting: $\mathcal{A}_\mathcal{M}\mathcal{S}$-TeX (Spivak 1986) (which originated at the American Mathematical Society) and $\mathcal{L}\mathcal{A}_\mathcal{M}\mathcal{S}$-TeX (Spivak 1989). The first of these includes more facilities than plain TeX or LaTeX for typesetting mathematics, but it lacks features such as automatic numbering and cross-referencing, available in LaTeX, for instance. $\mathcal{L}\mathcal{A}_\mathcal{M}\mathcal{S}$-TeX, then, is the synthesis of $\mathcal{A}_\mathcal{M}\mathcal{S}$-TeX and LaTeX. Also it includes still more features for mathematics, such as complicated tables and commutative diagrams.

33.2.6 Other formats

Other formats than the above exist: for instance, Phyzzx (Weinstein 1984), TeX-sis (Myers and Paige), Macro TeX (Hendrikson 1991), eplain (Berry 1990), and TeXT1 (Guenther 1990). Typically, such formats provide the facilities of LaTeX, but try to be more easily adaptable by the user. Also, in general they have been written with the intention of being an add-on product to the plain format.

This book is also written in an 'other format': the lollipop format. This format does not contain user macros, but the tools with which a style designer can program them; see Eijkhout and Lenstra (1991).

33.3 THE DVI FILE

The dvi file (this term stands for 'device independent') contains the output of a TeX run: it contains compactly dumped representations of boxes that have been sent there by \shipout⟨box⟩. The act of shipping out usually occurs inside the output routine, but this is not necessarily so.

33.3.1 The dvi file format

A dvi file is a byte-oriented file, consisting of a preamble, a postamble, and a list of pages.

Access for subsequent software to a completed dvi file is strictly sequential in nature: the pages are stored as a backwards linked list. This means that only two ways of accessing are possible:

- given the start of a page, the next can be found by reading until an end-of-page code is encountered, and
- starting at the end of the file pages can be read backwards at higher speed, as each beginning-of-page code contains the byte position of the previous one.

The preamble and postamble contain

- the magnification of the document (see below),
- the unit of measurement used for the document, and

- possibly a comment string.

The postamble contains in addition a list of the font definitions that appear on the pages of the file.

Neither the preamble nor the postamble of the file contains a table of byte positions of pages. The full definition of the dvi file format can be found in Knuth (1986a).

33.3.2 Page identification

Whenever a \shipout occurs, TEX also writes the values of counters 0–9 to the dvi file and the terminal. Ordinarily, only counter 0, the page number, is used, and the other counters are zero. Those zeros are not output to the terminal. The other counters can be used to indicate further structure in the document. Log output shows the non-zero counters and the zero counters in between.

33.3.3 Magnification

Magnification of a document can be indicated by the ⟨integer parameter⟩ \mag, which specifies 1000 times the magnification ratio.

The dvi file contains the value of \mag for the document in its preamble and postamble. If no true dimensions are used the dvi file will look the same as when no magnification would have been used, except for the \mag value in the preamble and the postamble.

Whenever a true dimension is used it is divided by the value of \mag, so that the final output will have the dimension as prescribed by the user. The \mag parameter cannot be changed after a true dimension has been used, or after the first page has been shipped to the dvi file.

Plain TEX has the \magnification macro for globally sizing the document, without changing the physical size of the page:

```
\def\magnification{\afterassignment\m@g\count@}
\def\m@g{\mag\count@
   \hsize6.5truein\vsize8.9truein\dimen\footins8truein}
```

The explanation for this is as follows: the command \m@g is saved with an \afterassignment command, and the magnification value (which is 1000 times the actual magnification factor) is assigned to \count@. After this assignment, the macro \m@g assigns the magnification value to \mag, and the horizontal and vertical size are reset to their original values 6.5truein and 8.9truein. The \footins is also reset.

33.4 SPECIALS

TEX is to a large degree machine-independent, but it still needs a hook for machine-dependent extensions. This is the \special command, which writes a

⟨balanced text⟩ to the `dvi` file. TeX does not interpret this token list: it assumes that the printer driver knows what to do with it. `\special` commands are supposed not to change the *x* and *y* position on the page, so that the implementation of TeX remains independent of the actual device driver that handles the `\special`.

The most popular application of specials is probably the inclusion of graphic material, written in some page description language, such as PostScript. The size of the graphics can usually be determined from the file containing it (in the case of encapsulated PostScript through the 'bounding box' data), so TeX can leave space for such material.

33.5 TIME

TeX has four parameters, `\year`, `\month`, `\day`, and `\time`, that tell the time when the current job started. After this, the parameters are not updated. The user can change them at any time.

All four parameters are integers; the `\time` parameter gives the number of minutes since midnight that the current job started.

33.6 FONTS

Font information is split in the TeX system into the metric information (how high, wide, and deep is a character), and the actual description of the characters in a font. TeX, the formatter, needs only the metric information; printer drivers and screen previewers need the character descriptions. With this approach it is for instance possible for TeX to use with relative ease the resident fonts of a printer.

33.6.1 Font metrics

The metric information of TeX's fonts is stored in `tfm` files, which stands for 'TeX font metric' files. Metrics files contain the following information (see Knuth (1986a) for the full definition):

- the design size of a font;
- the values for the `\fontdimen` parameters (see Chapter 4);
- the height, depth, width, and italic correction of individual characters;
- kerning tables;
- ligature tables;
- information regarding successors and extensions of math characters (see Chapter 21).

Metrics files use a packed format, but they can be converted to and from a readable format by the auxiliary programs `tftopl` and `pltotf` (see Knuth and Fuchs (1986)). Here `pl` stands for 'property list', a term deriving from the programming language Lisp. Files in `pl` format are just text, so they can easily be edited; after conversion they can then again be used as `tfm` files.

33.6.2 Virtual fonts

With 'virtual fonts' (see Knuth (1990)) it is possible that what looks like one font to TeX resides in more than one physical font file. Also, virtual fonts can be used to change in effect the internal organization of font files.

For TeX itself, the presence of virtual fonts makes no difference: everything is still based on `tfm` files containing metric information. However, the screen or printer driver that displays the resulting `dvi` file on the screen or on a printer will search for files with extension `.vf` to determine how characters are to be interpreted. The `vf` file can, for instance, instruct the driver to interpret a character as a certain position in a certain font file, to interpret a character as more than one position (a way of forming accented characters), or to include `\special` information (for instance to set gray levels).

Readable variants of `vf` files have extension `vpl`, analogous to the `pl` files for the `tfm` files; see above. Conversion between `vf` and `vpl` files can be performed with the `vftovp` and `vptovf` programs.

However, because virtual fonts are a matter for device drivers, no more details will be given in this book.

33.6.3 Font files

Character descriptions are stored in three types of files.

gf Generic Font files. This is the file type that the Metafont program generates. There are not many previewers or printer drivers that use this type of file directly.

pxl Pixel files. The `pxl` format is a pure bitmap format. Thus it is easy to generate `pxl` files from, for instance, scanner images.

This format should be superseded by the `pk` format. Pixel files can become rather big, as their size grows quadratically in the size of the characters.

pk Packed files. Pixel files can be packed by a form of run-length encoding: instead of storing the complete bitmap only the starting positions and lengths of 'runs' of black and white pixels are stored. This makes the size of `pk` files approximately linear in the size of the characters. However, a previewer or printer driver using a packed font file has to unpack it before it is able to use it.

The following conversion programs exist: `gftopxl`, `gftopk`, `pktopxl`, `pxltopk`.

33.6.4 Computer Modern

The only family of typefaces that comes with TeX in the standard distribution is the 'Computer Modern' family. This is an adaptation (using the terminology of Southall (1984)) by Donald Knuth of the Monotype Modern 8A typeface that was used for the first volume of his *Art of Computer Programming* series. The 'modern faces' all derive from the types that were cut between 1780 and 1800 by Firmin

Didot in France, Giambattista Bodoni in Italy, and Justus Erich Walbaum in Germany. After the first two, these types are also called 'Didone' types. This name was coined in the Vox classification of types (Vox 1955). Ultimately, the inspiration for the Didone types is the 'Romain du Roi', the type that was designed by Nicolas Jaugeon around 1692 for the French Imprimerie Royale.

Didone types are characterized by a strong vertical orientation, and thin hairlines. The vertical accent is strengthened by the fact that the insides of curves are flattened. The result is a clear and brilliant page, provided that the printing is done carefully and on good quality paper. However, they are quite vulnerable; Updike (1937) compares them to the distinguished but fragile furniture from the same period, saying one is afraid to use either, 'for both seem in danger of breaking in pieces'. With the current proliferation of low resolution (around 300 dot per inch) printers, the Computer Modern is a somewhat unfortunate choice.

Recently, Donald Knuth has developed a new typeface (or rather, a subfamily of typefaces) by changing parameters in the Computer Modern family. The result is a so-called 'Egyptian' typeface: Computer Concrete (Knuth 1989a). The name derives from the fact that it was intended primarily for the book *Concrete Mathematics*. Egyptian typefaces (they fall under the 'Mécanes' in the Vox classification, meaning constructed, not derived from written letters) have a very uniform line width and square serifs. They do not have anything to do with Egypt; such types happened to be popular in the first half of the nineteenth century when Egyptology was developing and popular.

33.7 TeX AND WEB

The TeX program is written in WEB, a programming language that can be considered as a subset of Pascal, augmented with a preprocessor.

TeX makes no use of some features of Pascal, in order to facilitate porting to Pascal systems other than the one it was originally designed for, and even to enable automatic translation to other programming languages such as C. For instance, it does not use the Pascal With construct. Also, procedures do not have output parameters; apart from writing to global variables, the only way values are returned is through Function values.

Actually, WEB is more than a superset of a subset of Pascal (and to be more precise, it can also be used with other programming languages); it is a 'system of structured documentation'. This means that the WEB programmer writes pieces of program code, interspersed with their documentation, in one file. This idea of 'literate programming' was introduced in Knuth (1984b); for more information, see Sewell (1989).

Two auxiliary programs, Tangle and Weave, can then be used to strip the documentation and convert WEB into regular Pascal, or to convert the WEB file into a TeX file that will typeset the program and documentation.

Portability of WEB programs is achieved by the 'change file' mechanism. A change file is a list of changes to be made to the WEB file; a bit like a stream editor script. These changes can comprise both adaptations of the WEB file to the particular Pascal compiler that will be used, and bug fixes to TeX. Thus the `TeX.web` file need never be edited.

33.8 THE TeX USERS GROUP

TeX users have joined into several users groups over the last decade. Many national or language users groups exist, and a lot of them publish newsletters. The oldest of all TeX users groups is simply called that: the TeX Users Group, or TUG, and its journal is called *TUGboat*. You can reach them at

> TeX Users Group
> P.O. Box 9506
> Providence, RI 02940-9506, USA

or electronically at `tug@math.ams.com` on the Internet.

CHAPTER

34

Tracing

TeX's workings are often quite different from what the programmer expected, so there are ways to discover how TeX arrived at the result it did. The \tracing... commands write all information of a certain kind to the log file (and to the terminal if \tracingonline is positive), and a number of \show... commands can be used to ask the current status or value of various items of TeX.

In the following list, only \show and \showthe display their output on the terminal by default, other \show... and \tracing... commands write to the log file. They will write in addition to the terminal if \tracingonline is positive.

\meaning   Give the meaning of a control sequence as a string of characters.

\show   Display the meaning of a control sequence.

\showthe   Display the result of prefixing a token with \the.

\showbox   Display the contents of a box.

\showlists   Display the contents of the partial lists currently built in all modes. This is treated on page 60.

\tracingcommands   If this is 1 TeX displays primitive commands executed; if this is 2 or more the outcome of conditionals is also recorded.

\tracingmacros   If this is 1, TeX shows expansion of macros that are performed and the actual values of the arguments; if this is 2 or more ⟨token parameter⟩s such as \output and \everypar are also traced.

\tracingoutput   If this is positive, the log file shows a dump of boxes that are shipped to the dvi file.

\showboxdepth   The number of levels of box dump that are shown when boxes are displayed.

\showboxbreadth   Number of successive elements on each level that are shown when boxes are displayed.

\tracingonline   If this parameter is positive, TeX will write trace information to the terminal in addition to the log file.

\tracingparagraphs   If this parameter is positive, TeX generates a trace of the line breaking algorithm.

\tracingpages   If this parameter is positive, TeX generates a trace of the page breaking algorithm.

\tracinglostchars   If this parameter is positive, TeX gives diagnostic messages whenever a character is accessed that is not present in a font. Plain default: 1.

\tracingrestores   If this parameter is positive, TeX will report all values that are restored when a group ends.

\tracingstats   If this parameter is 1, TeX reports at the end of the job the usage of various internal arrays; if it is 2, the memory demands are given whenever a page is shipped out.

34.1 MEANING AND CONTENT: \show, \showthe, \meaning

The meaning of control sequences, and the contents of those that represent internal quantities, can be obtained by the primitive commands \show, \showthe, and \meaning.

The control sequences \show and \meaning are similar: the former will give output to the log file and the terminal, whereas the latter will produce the same tokens, but they are placed in TeX's input stream.

The meaning of a primitive command of TeX is that command itself:

```
\show\baselineskip
```

gives

```
\baselineskip=\baselineskip
```

The meaning of a defined quantity is its definition:

```
\show\pageno
```

gives

```
\pageno=\count0
```

The meaning of a macro is its parameter text and replacement text:

```
\def\foo#1?#2\par{\set{#1!}\set{#2?}}
\show\foo
```

gives

```
\foo=macro:
#1?#2\par ->\set {#1!}\set {#2?}
```

For macros without parameters the part before the arrow (the parameter text) is empty.

The \showthe command will display on the log file and terminal the tokens that \the produces. After \show, \showthe, \showbox, and \showlists TeX asks the user for input; this can be prevented by specifying \scrollmode. Characters generated by \meaning and \the have category 12, except for spaces (see page 15); the value of \escapechar is used when control sequences are represented.

34.2 SHOW BOXES: \showbox, \tracingoutput

If \tracingoutput is positive the log file will receive a dumped representation of all boxes that are written to the dvi file with \shipout. The same representation is used by the command \showbox⟨8-bit number⟩.

In the first case TeX will report 'Completed box being shipped out'; in the second case it will enter \errorstopmode, and tell the user 'OK. (see the transcript file)'. If \tracingonline is positive, the box is also displayed on the terminal; if \scrollmode has been specified, TeX does not stop for input.

The upper bound on the number of nested boxes that is dumped is \showboxdepth; each time a level is visited at most \showboxbreadth items are shown, the remainder of the list is summarized with etc. For each box its height, depth, and width are indicated in that order, and for characters it is stated from what font they were taken.

Example
After
```
\font\tenroman=cmr10 \tenroman
\setbox0=\hbox{g}
\showbox0
```
the log file will show
```
\hbox(4.30554+1.94444)x5.00002
.\tenroman g
```
indicating that the box was 4.30554pt high, 1.94444pt deep, and 5.00002pt wide, and that it contained a character 'g' from the font \tenroman. Note that the fifth decimal of all sizes may be rounded because TeX works with multiples of 2^{-16}pt.

The next example has nested boxes,
```
\vbox{\hbox{g}\hbox{o}}
```
and it contains \baselineskip glue between the boxes. After a \showbox command the log file output is:
```
\vbox(16.30554+0.0)x5.00002
.\hbox(4.30554+1.94444)x5.00002
..\tenroman g
.\glue(\baselineskip) 5.75002
.\hbox(4.30554+0.0)x5.00002
..\tenroman o
```
Each time a new level is entered an extra dot is added to the front of the line. Note that TeX tells explicitly that the glue is \baselineskip glue; it inserts names like this for all automatically inserted glue. The value of the baselineskip glue here is such that the baselines of the boxes are at 12 point distance.

Now let us look at explicit (user) glue. TeX indicates the ratio by which it is stretched or shrunk.

Examples
```
\hbox to 20pt {\kern10pt \hskip0pt plus 5pt}
```
gives (indicating that the available stretch has been multiplied by 2.0):
```
\hbox(0.0+0.0)x20.0, glue set 2.0
```

```
.\kern 10.0
.\glue 0.0 plus 5.0
```
and
```
\hbox to 0pt {\kern10pt \hskip0pt minus 20pt}
```
gives (the shrink has been multiplied by 0.5)
```
\hbox(0.0+0.0)x0.0, glue set - 0.5
.\kern 10.0
.\glue 0.0 minus 20.0
```
respectively.

This is an example with infinitely stretchable or shrinkable glue:
```
\hbox(4.00000+0.14000)x15.0, glue set 9.00000fil
```
This means that the horizontal box contained `fil` glue, and it was set such that its resulting width was 9pt.

Underfull boxes are dumped like all other boxes, but the usual 'Underfull hbox detected at line...' is given. Overfull horizontal boxes contain a vertical rule of width \overfullrule:
```
\hbox to 5pt {\kern10pt}
```
gives
```
\hbox(0.0+0.0)x5.0
.\kern 10.0
.\rule(*+*)x5.0
```
Box leaders are not dumped completely:
```
.\leaders 40.0
..\hbox(4.77313+0.14581)x15.0, glue set 9.76852fil
...\tenrm a
...\glue 0.0 plus 1.0fil
```
is the dump for
```
\leaders\hbox to 15pt{\tenrm a\hfil}\hskip 40pt
```
Preceding or trailing glue around the leader boxes is also not indicated.

34.3 GLOBAL STATISTICS

The parameter \tracingstats can be used to force TEX to report at the end of the job the global use of resources. Some production versions of TEX may not have this option.

As an example, here are the statistics for this book:
```
Here is how much of TeX's memory you used:
```

String memory (bounded by 'pool size'):

```
877 strings out of 4649
9928 string characters out of 61781
```

Main memory, control sequences, font memory:

```
53071 words of memory out of 262141
2528 multiletter control sequences out of 9500
20137 words of font info for 70 fonts,
    out of 72000 for 255
```

Hyphenation:

```
14 hyphenation exceptions out of 607
```

Stacks: input, nest, parameter, buffer, and save stack respectively,

```
17i,6n,19p,245b,422s stack positions out of
300i,40n,60p,3000b,4000s
```

CHAPTER

35

Errors, Catastrophes, and Help

When TeX is running, various errors can occur. This chapter treats how errors in the input are displayed, and what sort of overflow of internal data structures of TeX can occur.

\errorcontextlines   (TeX3 only) Number of additional context lines shown in error messages.

\errmessage   Report an error, giving the parameter of this command as message.

\errhelp   Tokens that will be displayed if the user asks further help after an \errmessage.

35.1   ERROR MESSAGES

When TeX is running in \errorstopmode (which it usually is; see Chapter 32 for the other running modes), errors occurring are reported on the user terminal, and TeX asks the user for further instructions. Errors can occur either because of some internal condition of TeX, or because a macro has issued an \errmessage command.

If an error occurs TeX shows the input line on which the error occurred. If the offending command was not on that line but, for instance, in a macro that was called – possibly indirectly – from that line, the line of that command is also shown. If the offending command was indirectly called, an additional \errorcontextlines number of lines is shown with the preceding macro calls.

A value of \errorcontextlines = 0 causes ... to be printed as the sole indication that there is a context. Negative values inhibit even this.

For each macro in the sequence that leads to the offending command, TeX attempts to display some preceding and some following tokens. First one line is displayed ending with the – indirectly – offending command; then, one line lower some following tokens are given.

Example

```
This paragraph ends \vship1cm with a skip.
```

gives

```
! Undefined control sequence.
```

```
    1.1 This paragraph ends \vship
                        1cm with a skip.
```

If TeX is not running in some non-stop mode, the user is given the chance to patch errors or to ask for further information. In general the following options are available:

⟨return⟩ TeX will continue processing. If the error was something innocent that TeX could either ignore or patch itself, this is the easy way out.
h Give further details about the error. If the error was caused by an \errmessage command, the \errhelp tokens will be displayed here.
i Insert. The user can insert some material. For example, if a control sequence is misspelled, the correct command can sometimes be inserted, as

```
    i\vskip
```

for the above example. Also, this is an opportunity for inserting \show commands to inspect TeX's internal state. However, if TeX is in the middle of scanning something complicated, such commands will not be executed, or will even add to the confusion.
s (\scrollmode) Scroll further errors, but display the messages. TeX will patch any further errors. This is a handy option, for instance if the error occurs in an alignment, because the number of subsequent errors tends to be rather large.
r (\nonstopmode) Run without stopping. TeX will never stop for user interaction.
q (\batchmode) Quiet running. TeX will never stop for user interaction, and does not give any more terminal output.
x Exit. Abort this run of TeX.
e Edit. This option is not available on all TeX system. If it is, the run of TeX is aborted, and an editor is started, opening with the input file, maybe even on the offending line.

35.2 OVERFLOW ERRORS

Harsh reality imposes some restrictions on how elaborate TeX's workings can get. Some restrictions are imposed by compile-time constants, and are therefore fairly loose, but some depend strongly on the actual computer implementation.

Here follows the list of all categories of overflow that prompt TeX to report 'Capacity exceeded'. Most bounds involved are (determined by) compile-time constants; their values given here in parentheses are those used in the source listing of TeX in Knuth (1984a). Actual values may differ, and probably will. Remember that TeX was developed in the good old days when even big computers were fairly small.

35.2.1 Buffer size (500)

Current lines of all files that are open are kept in TeX's input buffer, as are control sequence names that are being built with \csname...\endcsname.

35.2.2 Exception dictionary (307)

The maximum number of hyphenation exceptions specified by \hyphenation must be a prime number. Two arrays with this many halfwords are allocated.
   Changing this number makes formats incompatible; that is, TeX can only use a format that was made by an IniTeX with the same value for this constant.

35.2.3 Font memory (20 000)

Information about fonts is stored in an array of memory words. This is easily overflowed by preloading too many fonts in IniTeX.

35.2.4 Grouping levels

The number of open groups should be recordable in a quarter word. There is no compile-time constant corresponding to this.

35.2.5 Hash size (2100)

Maximum number of control sequences. It is suggested that this number should not exceed 10% of the main memory size. The values in TeX and IniTeX should agree; also the hash_prime values should agree.
   This value is rather low; for macro packages that are more elaborate than plain TeX a value of about 3000 is more realistic.

35.2.6 Number of strings (3000)

The maximum number of strings must be recordable in a half word.

35.2.7 Input stack size (200)

For each input source an item is allocated on the input stack. Typical input sources are input files (but their simultaneous number is more limited; see below), and token lists such as token variables, macro replacement texts, and alignment templates. A macro with 'runaway recursion' (for example, \def\mac{\mac}) will overflow this stack.
   TeX performs some optimization here: before the last call in a token list all token lists ending with this call are cleared. This process is similar to 'resolving tail recursion' (see Chapter 11).

35.2.8 Main memory size (30 000)

Almost all 'dynamic' objects of TeX, such as macro definition texts and all material on the current page, are stored in the main memory array. Formats may already take 20 000 words of main memory for macro definitions, and complicated pages containing for instance the LaTeX picture environment may easily overflow this array.

TeX's main memory is divided in words, and a half word is supposed to be able to address the whole of the memory. Thus on current 32-bit computers the most common choice is to let the main memory size be at most 64K bytes. A half word address can then be stored in 16 bits, half a machine word.

However, so-called 'Big TeX' implementations exist that have a main memory larger than 64K words. Most compilers will then allocate 32-bit words for addressing this memory, even if (say) 18 bits would suffice. Big TeXs therefore become immediately a lot bigger when they cross the 64K threshold. Thus they are usually not found on microcomputers, although virtual memory schemes for these are possible; see for instance Thull (1989).

TeX can have a bigger main memory than IniTeX; see Chapter 33 for further details.

35.2.9 Parameter stack size (60)

Macro parameters may contain macro calls with further parameters. The number of parameters that may occur nested is bounded by the parameter stack size.

35.2.10 Pattern memory (8000)

Hyphenation patterns are stored in a trie array. The default size of 8000 hyphenation patterns seems sufficient for English or Italian, for example, but it is not for Dutch or German.

35.2.11 Pattern memory ops per language

The number of hyphenation ops (see the literature about hyphenation: Liang (1983) and appendix H of Knuth (1984a)) should be recordable in a quarter word. There is no compile-time constant corresponding to this. TeX version 2 had the same upper bound, but gave no error message in case of overflow. Again, for languages such as Dutch and German this bound is too low. There are versions of TeX that have a higher bound here.

35.2.12 Pool size (32 000)

Strings are error messages and control sequence names. They are stored using one byte per character. TeX has initially about 23 000 characters worth of strings.

The pool will overflow if a user defines a large number of control sequences on top of a substantial macro package. However, even if the user does not define any new commands overflow may occur: cross-referencing schemes also work by defining control sequences. For large documents a pool size of 40 000 or 60 000 is probably sufficient.

35.2.13 Save size (600)

Quantities that are assigned to inside a group must be restored after the end of that group. The save stack is were the values to be restored are kept; the size of the save stack limits the number of values that can be restored.

Alternating global and local assignments to a value will lead to 'save stack build-up': for each local assignment following a global assignment the previous value of the variable is saved. Thus an alternation of such assignments will lead to an unnecessary proliferation of items on the save stack.

35.2.14 Semantic nest size (40)

Each time TeX switches to a mode nested inside another mode (for instance when processing an \hbox inside a \vbox) the current state is pushed on the semantic nest stack. The semantic nest size is the maximum number of levels that can be pushed.

35.2.15 Text input levels (6)

The number of nested \input files has to be very limited, as the current lines are all kept in the input buffer.

CHAPTER 36

The Grammar of TeX

Many chapters in this book contain pieces of the grammar that defines the formal syntax of TeX. In this chapter the structure of the rewriting rules of the grammar is explained, and some key notions are presented.

In *The TeXbook* a grammar appears in Chapters 24–27. An even more rigorous grammar of TeX can be found in Appelt (1988). The grammar presented in this book is virtually identical to that of *The TeXbook*.

36.1 NOTATIONS

Basic to the grammar are

grammatical terms   These are enclosed in angle brackets:

⟨term⟩

control sequences   These are given in typewriter type with a backslash for the escape character:

`\command`

Lastly there are

keywords   Also given in typewriter type

`keyword`

This is a limited collection of words that have a special meaning for TeX in certain contexts; see below.

The three elements of the grammar are used in syntax rules:

⟨snark⟩ ⟶ `boojum` | ⟨empty⟩

This rule says that the grammatical entity ⟨snark⟩ is either the keyword `boojum`, or the grammatical entity ⟨empty⟩.

There are two other notational conventions. The first is that the double quote is used to indicate hexadecimal (base 16) notation. For instance `"ab56` stands for $10 \times 16^3 + 11 \times 16^2 + 5 \times 16^1 + 6 \times 16^0$. The second convention is that subscripts are used to denote category codes. Thus a_{12} denotes an 'a' of category 12.

36.2 KEYWORDS

A keyword is sequence of characters (or character tokens) of any category code but 13 (active). Unlike the situation in control sequences, TeX does not distinguish between lowercase and uppercase characters in keywords. Uppercase characters in keywords are converted to lowercase by adding 32 to them; the \lccode and \uccode are not used here. Furthermore, any keyword can be preceded by optional spaces.

Thus both `true cm` and `truecm` are legal. By far the strangest example, however, is provided by the grammar rule

⟨fil unit⟩ ⟶ `fil` | ⟨fil unit⟩`l`

which implies that `fil L l` is also a legal ⟨fil dimen⟩. Strange errors can ensue from this; see page 117 for an example.

Here is the full list of all keywords: `at`, `bp`, `by`, `cc`, `cm`, `dd`, `depth`, `em`, `ex`, `fil`, `height`, `in`, `l`, `minus`, `mm`, `mu`, `pc`, `plus`, `pt`, `scaled`, `sp`, `spread`, `to`, `true`, `width`.

36.3 SPECIFIC GRAMMATICAL TERMS

Some grammatical terms appear in a lot of rules. One such term is ⟨optional spaces⟩. It is probably clear what is meant, but here is the formal definition:

⟨optional spaces⟩ ⟶ ⟨empty⟩ | ⟨space token⟩⟨optional spaces⟩

which amounts to saying that ⟨optional spaces⟩ is zero or more space tokens.

Other terms may not be so immediately obvious. Below are some of them.

36.3.1 ⟨equals⟩

In assignments the equals sign is optional; therefore there is a term

⟨equals⟩ ⟶ ⟨optional spaces⟩ | ⟨optional spaces⟩$=_{12}$

in TeX's grammar. One assignment exists where the equals sign cannot be left out:

`\let\spacetoken= %assign a space`

Here the space would have been skipped in TeX's input processor if the equals sign had been left out.

36.3.2 ⟨filler⟩, ⟨general text⟩

More obscure than the ⟨optional spaces⟩ is the combination of spaces and \relax tokens that is allowed in some places, for instance

`\setbox0= \relax\box1`

The quantity involved is

⟨filler⟩ ⟶ ⟨optional spaces⟩ | ⟨filler⟩\relax⟨optional spaces⟩

One important occurrence of ⟨filler⟩ is in

⟨general text⟩ ⟶ ⟨filler⟩{⟨balanced text⟩⟨right brace⟩

A ⟨general text⟩ follows such control sequences as \message, \uppercase, or \mark. The braces around the ⟨balanced text⟩ are explained in the next point.

36.3.3 {} and ⟨left brace⟩⟨right brace⟩

The TeX grammar uses a perhaps somewhat unfortunate convention for braces. First of all

{ and }

stand for braces that are either explicit open/close group characters, or control sequences defined by \let, such as

\let\bgroup={ \let\egroup=}

The grammatical terms

⟨left brace⟩ and ⟨right brace⟩

stand for explicit open/close group characters, that is, characters of categories 1 and 2 respectively.

Various combinations of these two kinds of braces exist. Braces around boxes can be implicit:

\hbox⟨box specification⟩{⟨horizontal mode material⟩}

Around a macro definition there must be explicit braces:

⟨definition text⟩ ⟶ ⟨parameter text⟩⟨left brace⟩⟨balanced text⟩⟨right brace⟩

Finally, the ⟨general text⟩ that was mentioned above has to be explicitly closed, but it can be implicitly opened:

⟨general text⟩ ⟶ ⟨filler⟩{⟨balanced text⟩⟨right brace⟩

The closing brace of a ⟨general text⟩ has to be explicit, since a general text is a token list, which may contain \egroup tokens. TeX performs expansion to find the opening brace of a ⟨general text⟩.

36.3.4 ⟨math field⟩

In math mode various operations such as subscripting or applying \underline take an argument that is a ⟨math field⟩: either a single symbol, or a group. Here is the exact definition.

⟨math field⟩ ⟶ ⟨math symbol⟩ | ⟨filler⟩{⟨math mode material⟩}
⟨math symbol⟩ ⟶ ⟨character⟩ | ⟨math character⟩

See page 28 for ⟨character⟩, and page 181 for ⟨math character⟩.

36.4 DIFFERENCES BETWEEN TEX VERSIONS 2 AND 3

In 1989 Knuth released TEX version 3.0, which is the first real change in TEX since version 2.0, which was released in 1986 (version 0 of TEX was released in 1982; see Knuth (1989c) for more about the history of TEX). All intermediate versions were merely bug fixes.

The main difference between versions 2 and 3 lies in the fact that 8-bit input has become possible. Associated with this, various quantities that used to be 127 or 128 have been raised to 255 or 256 respectively. Here is a short list. The full description is in Knuth (1989b).

- All 'codes' (\catcode, \sfcode, et cetera; see page 31) now apply to 256 character codes instead of 128.
- A character with code \endlinechar is appended to the line unless this parameter is negative or more than 255 (this was 127) (see page 9).
- No escape character is output by \write and other commands if \escapechar is negative or more than 255 (this was 127) (see page 15).
- The ^^ replacement mechanism has been extended (see page 12).
- Parameters \language, \inputlineno, \errorcontextlines, \lefthyphenmin, \righthyphenmin, \badness, \holdinginserts, \emergencystretch, and commands \noboundary, \setlanguage have been added.
- The value of \outputpenalty is no longer zero if the page break was not at a penalty item; instead it is 10 000 (see page 218).

The plain format has also been updated, mostly with default settings for parameters such as \lefthyphenmin, but also a few macros have been added.

CHAPTER 37

Glossary of TeX Primitives

This chapter gives the list of all primitives of TeX. After each control sequence the grammatical category of the command or parameter is given, plus a short description. For some commands the syntax of their use is given.

For parameters the class to which they belong is given. Commands that have no grammatical category in *The TeXbook* are denoted either '⟨expandable command⟩' or '⟨primitive command⟩' in this list.

Grammatical terms such as ⟨equals⟩ and ⟨optional space⟩ are explained in Chapter 36.

\- ⟨horizontal command⟩ Discretionary hyphen; this is equivalent to `\discretionary{-}{}{}`. Can be used to indicate hyphenatable points in a word.

\␣ ⟨horizontal command⟩ Control space. Insert the same amount of space as a space token would if `\spacefactor = 1000`.

\/ ⟨primitive command⟩ Italic correction: insert a kern specified by the preceding character. Each character has an italic correction, possibly zero, specified in the `tfm` file. For slanted fonts this compensates for overhang.

\above⟨dimen⟩ ⟨generalized fraction command⟩ Fraction with specified bar width.

\abovedisplayshortskip ⟨glue parameter⟩ Glue above a display if the line preceding the display was short.

\abovedisplayskip ⟨glue parameter⟩ Glue above a display.

\abovewithdelims⟨delim$_1$⟩⟨delim$_2$⟩⟨dimen⟩ ⟨generalized fraction command⟩ Generalized fraction with delimiters.

\accent⟨8-bit number⟩⟨optional assignments⟩⟨character⟩ ⟨horizontal command⟩ Command to place accents on characters.

\adjdemerits ⟨integer parameter⟩ Penalty for adjacent not visually compatible lines. Default 10 000 in plain TeX.

\advance⟨numeric variable⟩⟨optional by⟩⟨number⟩ ⟨arithmetic assignment⟩ Arithmetic command to increase or decrease a ⟨numeric variable⟩, that is, a ⟨count variable⟩, ⟨dimen variable⟩, ⟨glue variable⟩, or ⟨muglue variable⟩.

\afterassignment⟨token⟩ ⟨primitive command⟩ Save the next token for execution after the next assignment. Only one token can be saved this way.

\aftergroup⟨token⟩ ⟨primitive command⟩ Save the next token for insertion after the current group. Several tokens can be saved this way.

\atop⟨dimen⟩ ⟨generalized fraction command⟩ Place objects over one another.

\atopwithdelims⟨delim₁⟩⟨delim₂⟩ ⟨generalized fraction command⟩ Place objects over one another with delimiters.

\badness ⟨internal integer⟩ (TEX3 only) Badness of the most recently constructed box.

\baselineskip ⟨glue parameter⟩ The 'ideal' baseline distance between neighbouring boxes on a vertical list; 12pt in plain TEX.

\batchmode ⟨interaction mode assignment⟩ TEX patches errors itself and performs an emergency stop on serious errors such as missing input files, but no terminal output is generated.

\begingroup ⟨primitive command⟩ Open a group that must be closed with \endgroup.

\belowdisplayshortskip ⟨glue parameter⟩ Glue below a display if the line preceding the display was short.

\belowdisplayskip ⟨glue parameter⟩ Glue below a display.

\binoppenalty ⟨integer parameter⟩ Penalty for breaking after a binary operator not enclosed in a subformula. Plain TEX default: 700.

\botmark ⟨expandable command⟩ The last mark on the current page.

\box⟨8-bit number⟩ ⟨box⟩ Use a box register, emptying it.

\boxmaxdepth ⟨dimen parameter⟩ Maximum allowed depth of boxes. Default \maxdimen in plain TEX.

\brokenpenalty ⟨integer parameter⟩ Additional penalty for breaking a page after a hyphenated line. Default 100 in plain TEX.

\catcode⟨8-bit number⟩ ⟨internal integer⟩; the control sequence itself is a ⟨codename⟩. Access category codes.

\char⟨number⟩ ⟨character⟩ Explicit denotation of a character to be typeset.

\chardef⟨control sequence⟩⟨equals⟩⟨number⟩ ⟨shorthand definition⟩ Define a control sequence to be a synonym for a character code.

\cleaders ⟨leaders⟩ As \leaders, but with box leaders any excess space is split into equal glue items before and after the leaders.

\closein⟨4-bit number⟩ ⟨primitive command⟩ Close an input stream.

\closeout⟨4-bit number⟩ ⟨primitive command⟩ Close an output stream.

\clubpenalty ⟨integer parameter⟩ Additional penalty for breaking a page after the first line of a paragraph. Default 150 in plain TEX.

\copy⟨8-bit number⟩ ⟨box⟩ Use a box register and retain the contents.

\count⟨8-bit number⟩ ⟨internal integer⟩; the control sequence itself is a ⟨register prefix⟩. Access count registers.

\countdef⟨control sequence⟩⟨equals⟩⟨8-bit number⟩ ⟨shorthand definition⟩; the control sequence itself is a ⟨registerdef⟩. Define a control sequence to be a synonym for a \count register.

\cr ⟨primitive command⟩ Terminate an alignment line.

\crcr ⟨primitive command⟩ Terminate an alignment line if it has not already been terminated by \cr.

\csname ⟨expandable command⟩ Start forming the name of a control sequence. Has to be balanced with \endcsname.

\day ⟨integer parameter⟩ The day of the current job.

\deadcycles ⟨special integer⟩ Counter that keeps track of how many times the output routine has been called without a \shipout taking place. If this number reaches \maxdeadcycles TeX gives an error message. Plain TeX default: 25.

\def ⟨def⟩ Start a macro definition.

\defaulthyphenchar ⟨integer parameter⟩ Value of \hyphenchar when a font is loaded. Default value in plain TeX is '\-.

\defaultskewchar ⟨integer parameter⟩ Value of \skewchar when a font is loaded. Default value in plain TeX is -1.

\delcode⟨8-bit number⟩ ⟨internal integer⟩; the control sequence itself is a ⟨codename⟩. Access the code specifying how a character should be used as delimiter after \left or \right.

\delimiter⟨27-bit number⟩ ⟨math character⟩ Explicit denotation of a delimiter.

\delimiterfactor ⟨integer parameter⟩ 1000 times the part of a delimited formula that should be covered by a delimiter. Plain TeX default: 901.

\delimitershortfall ⟨integer parameter⟩ Size of the part of a delimited formula that is allowed to go uncovered by a delimiter. Plain TeX default: 5pt.

\dimen⟨8-bit number⟩ ⟨internal dimen⟩; the control sequence itself is a ⟨register prefix⟩. Access dimen registers.

\dimendef⟨control sequence⟩⟨equals⟩⟨8-bit number⟩ ⟨shorthand definition⟩; the control sequence itself is a ⟨registerdef⟩. Define a control sequence to be a synonym for a \dimen register.

\discretionary{*pre-break*}{*post-break*}{*no-break*} ⟨horizontal command⟩ Specify the way a character sequence is split up at a line break.

\displayindent ⟨dimen parameter⟩ Distance by which the box, in which the display is centred, is indented owing to hanging indentation. This value is set automatically for each display.

\displaylimits ⟨primitive command⟩ Restore default placement for limits.

\displaystyle ⟨primitive command⟩ Select the display style of math typesetting.

\displaywidowpenalty ⟨integer parameter⟩ Additional penalty for breaking a page before the last line above a display formula. Default 50 in plain TeX.

\displaywidth ⟨dimen parameter⟩ Width of the box in which the display is centred. This value is set automatically for each display.

\divide⟨numeric variable⟩⟨optional by⟩⟨number⟩ ⟨arithmetic assignment⟩ Arithmetic command to divide a ⟨numeric variable⟩ (see \advance).

\doublehyphendemerits ⟨integer parameter⟩ Penalty for consecutive lines ending with a hyphen. Default 10 000 in plain TeX.

\dp⟨8-bit number⟩ ⟨internal dimen⟩; the control sequence itself is a ⟨box dimension⟩. Depth of the box in a box register.

\dump ⟨vertical command⟩ Dump a format file; possible only in IniTeX, not allowed inside a group.

\edef ⟨def⟩ Start a macro definition; the replacement text is expanded at definition time.

\else ⟨expandable command⟩ Select ⟨false text⟩ of a conditional or default case of \ifcase.

\emergencystretch ⟨dimen parameter⟩ (TEX3 only) Assumed extra stretchability in lines of a paragraph in third pass of the line-breaking algorithm.
\end ⟨vertical command⟩ End this run.
\endcsname ⟨expandable command⟩ Delimit the name of a control sequence that was begun with \csname.
\endgroup ⟨primitive command⟩ End a group that was opened with \begingroup.
\endinput ⟨expandable command⟩ Terminate inputting the current file after the current line.
\endlinechar ⟨integer parameter⟩ The character code of the end-of-line character appended to input lines. IniTEX default: 13.
\eqno⟨math mode material⟩$$ ⟨eqno⟩ Place a right equation number in a display formula.
\errhelp ⟨token parameter⟩ Tokens that will be displayed if the user asks for help after an \errmessage.
\errmessage⟨general text⟩ ⟨primitive command⟩ Report an error and give the user opportunity to act.
\errorcontextlines ⟨integer parameter⟩ (TEX3 only) Number of additional context lines shown in error messages.
\errorstopmode ⟨interaction mode assignment⟩ Ask for user input on the occurrence of an error.
\escapechar ⟨integer parameter⟩ Number of the character that is used when control sequences are being converted into character tokens. IniTEX default: 92.
\everycr ⟨token parameter⟩ Token list inserted after every \cr or non-redundant \crcr.
\everydisplay ⟨token parameter⟩ Token list inserted at the start of a display.
\everyhbox ⟨token parameter⟩ Token list inserted at the start of a horizontal box.
\everyjob ⟨token parameter⟩ Token list inserted at the start of each job.
\everymath ⟨token parameter⟩ Token list inserted at the start of non-display math.
\everypar ⟨token parameter⟩ Token list inserted in front of paragraph text.
\everyvbox ⟨token parameter⟩ Token list inserted at the start of a vertical box.
\exhyphenpenalty ⟨integer parameter⟩ Penalty for breaking a horizontal line at a discretionary in the special case where the prebreak text is empty. Default 50 in plain TEX.
\expandafter ⟨expandable command⟩ Take the next two tokens and place the expansion of the second after the first.
\fam ⟨integer parameter⟩ The number of the current font family.
\fi ⟨expandable command⟩ Closing delimiter for all conditionals.
\finalhyphendemerits ⟨integer parameter⟩ Penalty added when the penultimate line of a paragraph ends with a hyphen. Plain TEX default 5000.
\firstmark ⟨expandable command⟩ The first mark on the current page.
\floatingpenalty ⟨integer parameter⟩ Penalty amount added to \insertpenalties when an insertion is split.

\font⟨control sequence⟩⟨equals⟩⟨file name⟩⟨at clause⟩   ⟨simple assignment⟩ Associate a control sequence with a tfm file. When used on its own, this control sequence is a ⟨font⟩, denoting the current font.

\fontdimen⟨number⟩⟨font⟩   ⟨internal dimen⟩ Access various parameters of fonts.

\fontname⟨font⟩   ⟨primitive command⟩ The external name of a font.

\futurelet⟨control sequence⟩⟨token$_1$⟩⟨token$_2$⟩   ⟨let assignment⟩ Assign the meaning of ⟨token$_2$⟩ to the ⟨control sequence⟩.

\gdef   ⟨def⟩ Synonym for \global\def.

\global   ⟨prefix⟩ Make the next definition, arithmetic statement, or assignment global.

\globaldefs   ⟨integer parameter⟩ Override \global specifications: a positive value of this parameter makes all assignments global, a negative value makes them local.

\halign⟨box specification⟩{⟨alignment material⟩}   ⟨vertical command⟩ Horizontal alignment. Display alignment:

$$\$\$\halign \langle\text{box specification}\rangle\{\ldots\}\langle\text{optional assignments}\rangle\$\$$$

\hangafter   ⟨integer parameter⟩ If positive, this denotes the number of lines before indenting starts; if negative, its absolute value is the number of indented lines starting with the first line of the paragraph. The default value of 1 is restored after every paragraph.

\hangindent   ⟨dimen parameter⟩ If positive, this indicates indentation from the left margin; if negative, this is the negative of the indentation from the right margin. The default value of 0pt is restored after every paragraph.

\hbadness   ⟨integer parameter⟩ Threshold below which TeX does not report an underfull or overfull horizontal box. Plain TeX default: 1000.

\hbox⟨box specification⟩{⟨horizontal material⟩}   ⟨box⟩ Construct a horizontal box.

\hfil   ⟨horizontal command⟩ Horizontal skip equivalent to \hskip 0cm plus 1fil.

\hfill   ⟨horizontal command⟩ Horizontal skip equivalent to \hskip 0cm plus 1fill.

\hfilneg   ⟨horizontal command⟩ Horizontal skip equivalent to \hskip 0cm minus 1fil.

\hfuzz   ⟨dimen parameter⟩ Excess size that TeX tolerates before it considers a horizontal box overfull. Plain TeX default: 0.1pt.

\hoffset   ⟨dimen parameter⟩ Distance by which the page is shifted to the right of the reference point which is at one inch from the left margin.

\holdinginserts   ⟨integer parameter⟩ (only TeX3) If this is positive, insertions are not placed in their boxes when the \output tokens are inserted.

\hrule   ⟨vertical command⟩ Rule that spreads in horizontal direction.

\hsize   ⟨dimen parameter⟩ Line width used for text typesetting inside a vertical box.

\hskip⟨glue⟩   ⟨horizontal command⟩ Insert in horizontal mode a glue item.

\hss ⟨horizontal command⟩ Horizontal skip equivalent to \hskip 0cm plus 1fil minus 1fil.

\ht⟨8-bit number⟩ ⟨internal dimen⟩; the control sequence itself is a ⟨box dimension⟩. Height of the box in a box register.

\hyphenation⟨general text⟩ ⟨hyphenation assignment⟩ Define hyphenation exceptions for the current value of \language.

\hyphenchar⟨font⟩ ⟨internal integer⟩ Number of the character behind which a \discretionary{}{}{} is inserted.

\hyphenpenalty ⟨integer parameter⟩ Penalty associated with break at a discretionary in the general case. Default 50 in plain TeX.

\if⟨token$_1$⟩⟨token$_2$⟩ ⟨expandable command⟩ Test equality of character codes.

\ifcase⟨number⟩⟨case$_0$⟩\or...\or⟨case$_n$⟩\else⟨other cases⟩\fi ⟨expandable command⟩ Enumerated case statement.

\ifcat⟨token$_1$⟩⟨token$_2$⟩ ⟨expandable command⟩ Test whether two characters have the same category code.

\ifdim⟨dimen$_1$⟩⟨relation⟩⟨dimen$_2$⟩ ⟨expandable command⟩ Compare two dimensions.

\ifeof⟨4-bit number⟩ ⟨expandable command⟩ Test whether a file has been fully read, or does not exist.

\iffalse ⟨expandable command⟩ This test is always false.

\ifhbox⟨8-bit number⟩ ⟨expandable command⟩ Test whether a box register contains a horizontal box.

\ifhmode ⟨expandable command⟩ Test whether the current mode is (possibly restricted) horizontal mode.

\ifinner ⟨expandable command⟩ Test whether the current mode is an internal mode.

\ifmmode ⟨expandable command⟩ Test whether the current mode is (possibly display) math mode.

\ifnum⟨number$_1$⟩⟨relation⟩⟨number$_2$⟩ ⟨expandable command⟩ Test relations between numbers.

\ifodd⟨number⟩ ⟨expandable command⟩ Test whether a number is odd.

\iftrue ⟨expandable command⟩ This test is always true.

\ifvbox⟨8-bit number⟩ ⟨expandable command⟩ Test whether a box register contains a vertical box.

\ifvmode ⟨expandable command⟩ Test whether the current mode is (possibly internal) vertical mode.

\ifvoid⟨8-bit number⟩ ⟨expandable command⟩ Test whether a box register is empty.

\ifx⟨token$_1$⟩⟨token$_2$⟩ ⟨expandable command⟩ Test equality of macro expansion, or equality of character code and category code.

\ignorespaces ⟨primitive command⟩ Expands following tokens until something other than a ⟨space token⟩ is found.

\immediate ⟨primitive command⟩ Prefix to have output operations executed right away.

\indent ⟨primitive command⟩ Switch to horizontal mode and insert box with width \parindent. This command is automatically inserted before a ⟨horizontal command⟩ in vertical mode.

\input⟨file name⟩ ⟨expandable command⟩ Read a specified file as TeX input.

\inputlineno ⟨internal integer⟩ (TeX3 only) Number of the current input line.

\insert⟨8-bit number⟩{⟨vertical mode material⟩} ⟨primitive command⟩ Start an insertion item.

\insertpenalties ⟨special integer⟩ Total of penalties for split insertions. Inside the output routine the number of held-over insertions.

\interlinepenalty ⟨integer parameter⟩ Penalty for breaking a page between lines of a paragraph. Default 0 in plain TeX.

\jobname ⟨expandable command⟩ Name of the main TeX file being processed.

\kern⟨dimen⟩ ⟨kern⟩ Add a kern item of the specified ⟨dimen⟩ to the list; this can be used both in horizontal and vertical mode.

\language ⟨integer parameter⟩ (TeX3 only) Choose a set of hyphenation patterns and exceptions.

\lastbox ⟨box⟩ Register containing the last element added to the current list, if this was a box.

\lastkern ⟨internal dimen⟩ If the last item on the list was a kern, the size of this.

\lastpenalty ⟨internal integer⟩ If the last item on the list was a penalty, the value of this.

\lastskip ⟨internal glue⟩ or ⟨internal muglue⟩. If the last item on the list was a skip, the size of this.

\lccode⟨8-bit number⟩ ⟨internal integer⟩; the control sequence itself is a ⟨codename⟩. Access the character code that is the lowercase variant of a given code.

\leaders⟨box or rule⟩⟨vertical/horizontal/mathematical skip⟩ ⟨leaders⟩ Fill a specified amount of space with a rule or copies of box.

\left ⟨primitive command⟩ Use the following character as an open delimiter.

\lefthyphenmin ⟨integer parameter⟩ (TeX3 only) Minimum number of characters before a hyphenation.

\leftskip ⟨glue parameter⟩ Glue that is placed to the left of all lines.

\leqno⟨math mode material⟩$$ ⟨eqno⟩ Place a left equation number in a display formula.

\let⟨control sequence⟩⟨equals⟩⟨token⟩ ⟨let assignment⟩ Define a control sequence to a token, assign its meaning if the token is a command or macro.

\limits ⟨primitive command⟩ Place limits over and under a large operator. This is the default position in display style.

\linepenalty ⟨integer parameter⟩ Penalty value associated with each line break. Default 10 in plain TeX.

\lineskip ⟨glue parameter⟩ Glue added if distance between bottom and top of neighbouring boxes is less than \lineskiplimit. Default 1pt in plain TeX.

\lineskiplimit ⟨dimen parameter⟩ Distance to be maintained between the bottom and top of neighbouring boxes on a vertical list. Default 0pt in plain TeX.

\long ⟨prefix⟩ Indicate that the arguments of the macro to be defined are allowed to contain \par tokens.

\looseness ⟨integer parameter⟩ Number of lines by which this paragraph has to be made longer (or, if negative, shorter) than it would be ideally.

\lower⟨dimen⟩⟨box⟩ ⟨primitive command⟩ Adjust vertical positioning of a box in horizontal mode.

\lowercase⟨general text⟩ ⟨primitive command⟩ Convert the argument to its lowercase form.

\mag ⟨integer parameter⟩ 1000 times the magnification of the document. Default 1000 in IniTeX.

\mark⟨general text⟩ ⟨primitive command⟩ Specify a mark text.

\mathaccent⟨15-bit number⟩⟨math field⟩ ⟨primitive command⟩ Place an accent in math mode.

\mathbin⟨math field⟩ ⟨math atom⟩ Let the following ⟨math field⟩ function as a binary operation.

\mathchar⟨15-bit number⟩ ⟨primitive command⟩ Explicit denotation of a mathematical character.

\mathchardef⟨control sequence⟩⟨equals⟩⟨15-bit number⟩ ⟨shorthand definition⟩ Define a control sequence to be a synonym for a math character code.

\mathchoice{D}{T}{S}{SS} ⟨primitive command⟩ Give four variants of a formula for the four styles of math typesetting.

\mathclose⟨math field⟩ ⟨math atom⟩ Let the following ⟨math field⟩ function as a closing symbol.

\mathcode⟨8-bit number⟩ ⟨internal integer⟩; the control sequence itself is a ⟨codename⟩. Code of a character determining its treatment in math mode.

\mathinner⟨math field⟩ ⟨math atom⟩ Let the following ⟨math field⟩ function as an inner formula.

\mathop⟨math field⟩ ⟨math atom⟩ Let the following ⟨math field⟩ function as a large operator.

\mathopen⟨math field⟩ ⟨math atom⟩ Let the following ⟨math field⟩ function as an opening symbol.

\mathord⟨math field⟩ ⟨math atom⟩ Let the following ⟨math field⟩ function as an ordinary object.

\mathpunct⟨math field⟩ ⟨math atom⟩ Let the following ⟨math field⟩ function as a punctuation symbol.

\mathrel⟨math field⟩ ⟨math atom⟩ Let the following ⟨math field⟩ function as a relation.

\mathsurround ⟨dimen parameter⟩ Kern amount placed before and after in-line formulas.

\maxdeadcycles ⟨integer parameter⟩ The maximum number of times that the output routine is allowed to be called without a \shipout occurring. IniTeX default: 25.

\maxdepth ⟨dimen parameter⟩ Maximum depth of the page box. Default 4pt in plain TeX.

\meaning ⟨expandable command⟩ Give the meaning of a control sequence as a string of characters.

\medmuskip ⟨muglue parameter⟩ Medium amount of mu glue. Default value in plain TeX: 4mu plus 2mu minus 4mu

\message⟨general text⟩ ⟨primitive command⟩ Write a message to the terminal.

\mkern ⟨primitive command⟩ Insert a kern measured in mu units.

\month ⟨integer parameter⟩ The month of the current job.

\moveleft⟨dimen⟩⟨box⟩ ⟨primitive command⟩ Adjust horizontal positioning of a box in vertical mode.

\moveright⟨dimen⟩⟨box⟩ ⟨primitive command⟩ Adjust horizontal positioning of a box in vertical mode.

\mskip ⟨mathematical skip⟩ Insert glue measured in mu units.

\multiply⟨numeric variable⟩⟨optional by⟩⟨number⟩ ⟨arithmetic assignment⟩ Arithmetic command to multiply a ⟨numeric variable⟩ (see \advance).

\muskip⟨8-bit number⟩ ⟨internal muglue⟩; the control sequence itself is a ⟨register prefix⟩. Access skips measured in mu units.

\muskipdef⟨control sequence⟩⟨equals⟩⟨8-bit number⟩ ⟨shorthand definition⟩; the control sequence itself is a ⟨registerdef⟩. Define a control sequence to be a synonym for a \muskip register.

\newlinechar ⟨integer parameter⟩ Number of the character that triggers a new line in \write statements. Plain TeX default −1.

\noalign⟨filler⟩{⟨vertical (horizontal) mode material⟩} ⟨primitive command⟩ Specify vertical (horizontal) material to be placed in between rows (columns) of an \halign (\valign).

\noboundary ⟨horizontal command⟩ (TeX3 only) Omit implicit boundary character.

\noexpand⟨token⟩ ⟨expandable command⟩ Do not expand the next token.

\noindent ⟨primitive command⟩ Switch to horizontal mode with an empty horizontal list.

\nolimits ⟨primitive command⟩ Place limits of a large operator as subscript and superscript expressions. This is the default position in text style.

\nonscript ⟨primitive command⟩ Cancel the next glue item if it occurs in scriptstyle or scriptscriptstyle.

\nonstopmode ⟨interaction mode assignment⟩ TeX fixes errors as best it can, and performs an emergency stop when user interaction is needed.

\nulldelimiterspace ⟨dimen parameter⟩ Width taken for empty delimiters. Default 1.2pt in plain TeX.

\nullfont ⟨fontdef token⟩ Name of an empty font that TeX uses in emergencies.

\number⟨number⟩ ⟨expandable command⟩ Convert a ⟨number⟩ to decimal representation.

\omit ⟨primitive command⟩ Omit the template for one alignment entry.

\openin⟨4-bit number⟩⟨equals⟩⟨filename⟩ ⟨primitive command⟩ Open a stream for input.

\openout⟨4-bit number⟩⟨equals⟩⟨filename⟩ ⟨primitive command⟩ Open a stream for output.

\or ⟨primitive command⟩ Separator for entries of an \ifcase.

`\outer` ⟨prefix⟩ Indicate that the macro being defined should occur on the outer level only.

`\output` ⟨token parameter⟩ Token list with instructions for shipping out pages.

`\outputpenalty` ⟨integer parameter⟩ Value of the penalty at the current page break, or 10 000 if the break was not at a penalty.

`\over` ⟨generalized fraction command⟩ Fraction.

`\overfullrule` ⟨dimen parameter⟩ Width of the rule that is printed to indicate overfull horizontal boxes. Plain TeX default: 5pt.

`\overline`⟨math field⟩ ⟨math atom⟩ Overline the following ⟨math field⟩.

`\overwithdelims`⟨delim$_1$⟩⟨delim$_2$⟩ ⟨generalized fraction command⟩ Fraction with delimiters.

`\pagedepth` ⟨special dimen⟩ Depth of the current page.

`\pagefilllstretch` ⟨special dimen⟩ Accumulated third-order stretch of the current page.

`\pagefillstretch` ⟨special dimen⟩ Accumulated second-order stretch of the current page.

`\pagefilstretch` ⟨special dimen⟩ Accumulated first-order stretch of the current page.

`\pagegoal` ⟨special dimen⟩ Goal height of the page box. This starts at `\vsize`, and is diminished by heights of insertion items.

`\pageshrink` ⟨special dimen⟩ Accumulated shrink of the current page.

`\pagestretch` ⟨special dimen⟩ Accumulated zeroth-order stretch of the current page.

`\pagetotal` ⟨special dimen⟩ Accumulated natural height of the current page.

`\par` ⟨primitive command⟩ Close off a paragraph and go into vertical mode.

`\parfillskip` ⟨glue parameter⟩ Glue that is placed between the last element of the paragraph and the line end. Plain TeX default: 0pt plus 1fil.

`\parindent` ⟨dimen parameter⟩ Size of the indentation box added in front of a paragraph.

`\parshape` ⟨internal integer⟩ Command for general paragraph shapes:

$$\text{\texttt{\textbackslash parshape}}\langle\text{equals}\rangle n \ i_1 \ \ell_1 \ \ldots \ i_n \ \ell_n$$

specifies a number of lines n, and n pairs of an indentation and line length.

`\parskip` ⟨glue parameter⟩ Amount of glue added to vertical list when a paragraph starts; default value 0pt plus 1pt in plain TeX.

`\patterns`⟨general text⟩ ⟨hyphenation assignment⟩ Define a list of hyphenation patterns for the current value of `\language`; allowed only in IniTeX.

`\pausing` ⟨integer parameter⟩ Specify that TeX should pause after each line that is read from a file.

`\penalty` ⟨primitive command⟩ Specify desirability of not breaking at this point.

`\postdisplaypenalty` ⟨integer parameter⟩ Penalty placed in the vertical list below a display.

`\predisplaypenalty` ⟨integer parameter⟩ Penalty placed in the vertical list above a display. Plain TeX default: 10 000.

`\predisplaysize` ⟨dimen parameter⟩ Effective width of the line preceding the display.

\pretolerance ⟨integer parameter⟩ Tolerance value for a paragraph that uses no hyphenation. Default 100 in plain TeX.

\prevdepth ⟨special dimen⟩ Depth of the last box added to a vertical list as it is perceived by TeX.

\prevgraf ⟨special integer⟩ The number of lines in the paragraph last added to the vertical list.

\radical⟨24-bit number⟩ ⟨primitive command⟩ Command for setting things such as root signs.

\raise⟨dimen⟩⟨box⟩ ⟨primitive command⟩ Adjust vertical positioning of a box in horizontal mode.

\read⟨number⟩to⟨control sequence⟩ ⟨simple assignment⟩ Read a line from a stream into a control sequence.

\relax ⟨primitive command⟩ Do nothing.

\relpenalty ⟨integer parameter⟩ Penalty for breaking after a binary relation, not enclosed in a subformula. Plain TeX default: 500.

\right ⟨primitive command⟩ Use the following character as a closing delimiter.

\righthyphenmin ⟨integer parameter⟩ (TeX3 only) Minimum number of characters after a hyphenation.

\rightskip ⟨glue parameter⟩ Glue that is placed to the right of all lines.

\romannumeral⟨number⟩ ⟨expandable command⟩ Convert a positive ⟨number⟩ to lowercase roman representation.

\scriptfont⟨4-bit number⟩ ⟨family member⟩; the control sequence itself is a ⟨font range⟩. Access the scriptfont of a family.

\scriptscriptfont⟨4-bit number⟩ ⟨family member⟩; the control sequence itself is a ⟨font range⟩. Access the scriptscriptfont of a family.

\scriptscriptstyle ⟨primitive command⟩ Select the scriptscript style of math typesetting.

\scriptspace ⟨dimen parameter⟩ Extra space after subscripts and superscripts. Default .5pt in plain TeX.

\scriptstyle ⟨primitive command⟩ Select the script style of math typesetting.

\scrollmode ⟨interaction mode assignment⟩ TeX patches errors itself, but will ask the user for missing files.

\setbox⟨8-bit number⟩⟨equals⟩⟨box⟩ ⟨simple assignment⟩ Assign a box to a box register.

\setlanguage⟨number⟩ ⟨primitive command⟩ (TeX3 only) Insert a whatsit resetting the current language to the ⟨number⟩ specified.

\sfcode⟨8-bit number⟩ ⟨internal integer⟩; the control sequence itself is a ⟨code-name⟩. Access the value of the \spacefactor associated with a character.

\shipout⟨box⟩ ⟨primitive command⟩ Ship a box to the dvi file.

\show⟨token⟩ ⟨primitive command⟩ Display the meaning of a token on the screen.

\showbox⟨8-bit number⟩ ⟨primitive command⟩ Write the contents of a box to the log file.

\showboxbreadth ⟨integer parameter⟩ Number of successive elements that are shown when \tracingoutput is positive, each time a level is visited. Plain TeX default: 5.

\showboxdepth ⟨integer parameter⟩ The number of levels that are shown when \tracingoutput is positive. Plain TeX default: 3.

\showlists ⟨primitive command⟩ Write to the log file the contents of the partial lists currently built in all modes.

\showthe⟨internal quantity⟩ ⟨primitive command⟩ Display on the terminal the result of prefixing a token with \the.

\skewchar⟨font⟩ ⟨internal integer⟩ Font position of an after-placed accent.

\skip⟨8-bit number⟩ ⟨internal glue⟩; the control sequence itself is a ⟨register prefix⟩. Access skip registers

\skipdef⟨control sequence⟩⟨equals⟩⟨8-bit number⟩ ⟨shorthand definition⟩; the control sequence itself is a ⟨registerdef⟩. Define a control sequence to be a synonym for a \skip register.

\spacefactor ⟨special integer⟩ 1000 times the ratio by which the stretch component of the interword glue should be multiplied.

\spaceskip ⟨glue parameter⟩ Interword glue if non-zero.

\span ⟨primitive command⟩ Join two adjacent alignment entries, or (in preamble) expand the next token.

\special⟨general text⟩ ⟨primitive command⟩ Write a token list to the dvi file.

\splitbotmark ⟨expandable command⟩ The last mark on a split-off page.

\splitfirstmark ⟨expandable command⟩ The first mark on a split-off page.

\splitmaxdepth ⟨dimen parameter⟩ Maximum depth of a box split off by a \vsplit operation. Default 4pt in plain TeX.

\splittopskip ⟨glue parameter⟩ Minimum distance between the top of what remains after a \vsplit operation, and the first item in that box. Default 10pt in plain TeX.

\string⟨token⟩ ⟨expandable command⟩ Convert a token to a string of one or more characters.

\tabskip ⟨glue parameter⟩ Amount of glue in between columns (rows) of an \halign (\valign).

\textfont⟨4-bit number⟩ ⟨family member⟩; the control sequence itself is a ⟨font range⟩. Access the textfont of a family.

\textstyle ⟨primitive command⟩ Select the text style of math typesetting.

\the⟨internal quantity⟩ ⟨primitive command⟩ Expand the value of various quantities in TeX into a string of (character) tokens.

\thickmuskip ⟨muglue parameter⟩ Large amount of mu glue. Default value in plain TeX: 5mu plus 5mu.

\thinmuskip ⟨muglue parameter⟩ Small amount of mu glue. Default value in plain TeX: 3mu.

\time ⟨integer parameter⟩ Number of minutes after midnight that the current job started.

\toks⟨8-bit number⟩ ⟨register prefix⟩ Access a token list register.

\toksdef⟨control sequence⟩⟨equals⟩⟨8-bit number⟩ ⟨shorthand definition⟩; the control sequence itself is a ⟨registerdef⟩. Assign a control sequence to a \toks register.

\tolerance ⟨integer parameter⟩ Tolerance value for lines in a paragraph that does use hyphenation. Default 200 in plain TeX, 10 000 in IniTeX.

\topmark ⟨expandable command⟩ The last mark of the previous page.

\topskip ⟨glue parameter⟩ Minimum distance between the top of the page box and the baseline of the first box on the page. Default 10pt in plain TeX.

\tracingcommands ⟨integer parameter⟩ When this is 1, TeX displays primitive commands executed; when this is 2 or more the outcome of conditionals is also recorded.

\tracinglostchars ⟨integer parameter⟩ If this parameter is positive, TeX gives diagnostic messages whenever a character is accessed that is not present in a font. Plain TeX default: 1.

\tracingmacros ⟨integer parameter⟩ If this is 1, the log file shows expansion of macros that are performed and the actual values of the arguments; if this is 2 or more ⟨token parameter⟩s such as \output and \everypar are also traced.

\tracingonline ⟨integer parameter⟩ If this parameter is positive, TeX will write trace information also to the terminal.

\tracingoutput ⟨integer parameter⟩ If this parameter is positive, the log file shows a dump of boxes that are shipped to the dvi file.

\tracingpages ⟨integer parameter⟩ If this parameter is positive, TeX generates a trace of the page-breaking algorithm.

\tracingparagraphs ⟨integer parameter⟩ If this parameter is positive, TeX generates a trace of the line-breaking algorithm.

\tracingrestores ⟨integer parameter⟩ If this parameter is positive, TeX will report all values that are restored when a group level ends.

\tracingstats ⟨integer parameter⟩ If this parameter is positive, TeX reports at the end of the job the usage of various internal arrays.

\uccode⟨8-bit number⟩ ⟨internal integer⟩; the control sequence itself is a ⟨codename⟩. Access the character code that is the uppercase variant of a given code.

\uchyph ⟨integer parameter⟩ Positive if hyphenating words starting with a capital letter is allowed. Plain TeX default 1.

\underline⟨math field⟩ ⟨math atom⟩ Underline the following ⟨math field⟩.

\unhbox⟨8-bit number⟩ ⟨horizontal command⟩ Unpack a box register containing a horizontal box, appending the contents to the list, and emptying the register.

\unhcopy⟨8-bit number⟩ ⟨horizontal command⟩ The same as \unhbox, but do not empty the register.

\unkern ⟨primitive command⟩ Remove the last item of the list if this was a kern.

\unpenalty ⟨primitive command⟩ Remove the last item of the list if this was a penalty.

\unskip ⟨primitive command⟩ Remove the last item of the list if this was a skip.

\unvbox⟨8-bit number⟩ ⟨vertical command⟩ Unpack a box register containing a vertical box, appending the contents to the list, and emptying the register.

\unvcopy⟨8-bit number⟩ ⟨vertical command⟩ The same as \unvbox, but do not empty the register.

\uppercase⟨general text⟩ ⟨primitive command⟩ Convert the argument to its uppercase form.

`\vadjust⟨filler⟩{⟨vertical mode material⟩}` ⟨primitive command⟩ Specify in horizontal mode material for the enclosing vertical list.

`\valign⟨box specification⟩{⟨alignment material⟩}` ⟨horizontal command⟩ Vertical alignment.

`\vbadness` ⟨integer parameter⟩ Threshold below which overfull and underfull vertical boxes are not shown. Plain TeX default: `1000`.

`\vbox⟨box specification⟩{⟨vertical material⟩}` ⟨primitive command⟩ Construct a vertical box with reference point on the last item.

`\vcenter⟨box specification⟩{⟨vertical material⟩}` ⟨primitive command⟩ Construct a vertical box vertically centred on the math axis.

`\vfil` ⟨vertical command⟩ Vertical skip equivalent to `\vskip 0cm plus 1fil`.

`\vfill` ⟨vertical command⟩ Vertical skip equivalent to `\vskip 0cm plus 1fill`.

`\vfilneg` ⟨vertical command⟩ Vertical skip equivalent to `\vskip 0cm minus 1fil`.

`\vfuzz` ⟨dimen parameter⟩ Excess size that TeX tolerates before it considers a vertical box overfull. Plain TeX default: `0.1pt`.

`\voffset` ⟨dimen parameter⟩ Distance by which the page is shifted down from the reference point, which is one inch from the top of the page.

`\vrule` ⟨horizontal command⟩ Rule that spreads in vertical direction.

`\vsize` ⟨dimen parameter⟩ Height of the page box.

`\vskip⟨glue⟩` ⟨vertical command⟩ Insert in vertical mode a glue item.

`\vsplit⟨8-bit number⟩to⟨dimen⟩` ⟨primitive command⟩ Split off the top part of a vertical box.

`\vss` ⟨vertical command⟩ Vertical skip equivalent to `\vskip 0cm plus 1fil minus 1fil`.

`\vtop⟨box specification⟩{⟨vertical material⟩}` ⟨primitive command⟩ Construct a vertical box with reference point on the first item.

`\wd⟨8-bit number⟩` ⟨internal dimen⟩; the control sequence itself is a ⟨box dimension⟩. Width of the box in a box register.

`\widowpenalty` ⟨integer parameter⟩ Additional penalty for breaking a page before the last line of a paragraph. Default 150 in plain TeX.

`\write⟨number⟩⟨general text⟩` ⟨primitive command⟩ Generate a whatsit item containing a token list to be written to the terminal or to a file.

`\xdef` ⟨def⟩ Synonym for `\global\edef`.

`\xleaders` ⟨leaders⟩ As `\leaders`, but with box leaders any excess space is spread equally between the boxes.

`\xspaceskip` ⟨glue parameter⟩ Interword glue if non-zero and $\mathtt{\backslash spacefactor} \geq 2000$.

`\year` ⟨integer parameter⟩ The year of the current job.

CHAPTER 38
References

Appelt, W. (1988). *TEX für Fortgeschrittene*. Bonn: Addison-Wesley Verlag.
von Bechtolsheim, S. (1988). A tutorial on \futurelet. *TUGboat*, **9**(3), 276–278.
Beeton, B. (1988). Controlling <ctrl-M>; ruling the depths. *TUGboat*, **9**(2), 182–183.
Beeton, B. (1991). *Additional font and glyph attributes for processing of mathematics*. document N1174 Rev., of ISO/IEC JTC1/SC18/WG8.
Berry, K. (1990). Eplain. *TUGboat*, **11**(4), 571–572.
Braams, J., Eijkhout, V., and Poppelier, N.A.F.M. (1989). The development of national LaTeX styles. *TUGboat*, **10**(3), 401–406.
Braams, J. (1991). Babel, a language option for LaTeX. *TUGboat*, **12**(2), 291–301.
Downes, M.J. Line breaking in \unhboxed text. *TUGboat*, **11**(4), 605–612.
Eijkhout, V. (1990a). Unusual paragraph shapes. *TUGboat*, **11**(1), 51–53.
Eijkhout, V. (1990b). An indentation scheme. *TUGboat*, **11**(4), 613–616.
Eijkhout, V. (1990c). A paragraph skip scheme. *TUGboat*, **11**(4), 616–619.
Eijkhout, V. and Lenstra, A. (1991). The document style designer as a separate entity. *TUGboat*, **12**(1), 31–34.
Eijkhout, V. (1991). Oral TEX. *TUGboat*, **12**(2), 272–276.
Guenther, D. (1990). TEXT1 goes public domain. *TUGboat*, **11**(1), 54–55.
Hendrikson, A. (1991). *MacroTEX, A TEX Macro Toolkit*. Brookline, MA: TEXnology Inc.
Jeffrey, A. (1990). Lists in TEX's mouth. *TUGboat*, **11**(2), 237–245.
Knuth, D.E. (1984a). *The TEXbook*. Reading MA: Addison-Wesley, (reprinted with corrections 1989).
Knuth, D.E. (1984b). Literate programming. *Computer J.*, **27**, 97–111.
Knuth, D.E. (1984c). *A torture test for TEX*. Stanford Computer Science Report 1027, Stanford, California.
Knuth, D.E. (1986a). *TEX: the Program*. Reading MA: Addison-Wesley.
Knuth, D.E. (1986b). *Computer Modern Typefaces*. Reading MA: Addison-Wesley.
Knuth, D.E. (1989a). Typesetting Concrete Mathematics. *TUGboat*, **10**(1), 31–36.
Knuth, D.E. (1989b). The new versions of TEX and Metafont. *TUGboat*, **10**(3), 325–327.
Knuth, D.E. (1989c). The errors of TEX. *Software Practice and Experience*, **19**, 607–681.
Knuth, D.E. (1990). Virtual fonts: more fun for grand wizards. *TUGboat*, **11**(1), 13–23.
Knuth, D.E. and Plass, M.F. (1981). Breaking paragraphs into lines. *Software practice and experience*, **11**, 1119–1184.
Knuth, D.E. and Fuchs, D.R. (1986). *TEXware*, Stanford Computer Science report 86-1097.
Kuiken, G. (1990). Additional hyphenation patterns. *TUGboat*, **11**(1), 24–25.

Lamport, L. (1986). *LaTeX, a Document Preparation System*. Reading MA: Addison-Wesley.
Liang, F.M. (1983). *Word hy-phen-a-tion by com-pu-ter*. Ph.D. thesis, Stanford University Computer Science Department report 977.
Maus, S. (1990). Looking ahead for a ⟨box⟩. *TUGboat*, **11**(4), 612–613.
Maus, S. (1991). An expansion power lemma, *TUGboat*, **12**(2), 277.
Mittelbach, F. and Schöpf, R.(1989). With LaTeX into the nineties. *TUGboat*, **10**(4), 681–690.
Mittelbach, F. and Schöpf, R. (1991). LaTeX3, *TUGboat*, **12**(1).
Myers, E. and Paige, F.E. *TeXsis – TeX macros for physicists*. Macros and manual available by anonymous ftp from lifshitz.ph.utexas.edu (128.83.131.57).
Hart's Rules for Compositors and Readers at the Oxford University Press. Oxford: Oxford University Press, 39th edition, 1983.
Partl, H. (1988). German TeX. *TUGboat*, **9**(1), 70–72.
Rubinstein, Z. (1989). Printing annotated chess literature in natural notation. *TUGboat*, **10**(3), 387–390.
Salomon, D. (1990a). Output routines: Examples and techniques. Part I: Introduction and examples. *TUGboat*, **11**(1), 69–85.
Salomon, D. (1990b). Output routines: Examples and techniques. Part II: OTR Techniques. *TUGboat*, **11**(2), 212–236.
Salomon, D. (1990c). Output routines: Examples and techniques. Part III: Insertions. *TUGboat*, **11**(4), 588–605.
Sewell, W. (1989). *Weaving a Program: Literate Programming in WEB*. New York NY: Van Nostrand Reinhold.
Southall, R. (1984). Designing a new typeface with Metafont, in: *TeX for scientific documentation*. Lecture Notes in Computer Science 236, Berlin: Springer Verlag.
Spivak, M. (1986). *The Joy of TeX*. Providence RI: American Mathematical Society.
Spivak, M. (1989). *LAMS-TeX, the Synthesis*. The TeXplorators Corporation.
Thull, K. (1989). The virtual memory management of PubliC TeX, *TUGboat*, **10**(1), 15–22.
Tschichold, J. (1975). *Ausgewählte Aufsätze über Fragen der Gestalt des Buches und der Typographie*. Basel: Birkhäuser Verlag.
Tutelaers, P. (1991). A font and a style for typesetting chess using LaTeX or plain TeX. *TUGboat*, to appear.
Updike, D.B. (1937). *Printing Types*. Harvard University Press, (reprinted 1980, New York NY: Dover Publications).
Vox, M. (1955). *Caractère*, Christmas issue 1955.
Weinstein, M. (1984). *Everything you wanted to know about PHYZZX but didn't know to ask*. Stanford Linear Accelarator Publication, SLAC-TN-84-7.
White, J.V. (1988). *Graphic Design for the Electronic Age*. New York NY: Watson-Guptill.

CHAPTER 39

Tables

39.1 CHARACTER TABLES

ASCII CONTROL CODES

BITS				CONTROL		SYMBOLS NUMBERS		UPPERCASE		LOWERCASE	
b7 b6 b5				0 0 0	0 0 1	0 1 0	0 1 1	1 0 0	1 0 1	1 1 0	1 1 1
b4	b3	b2	b1								
0	0	0	0	NUL (0, 0, 0)	DLE (16, 10, 20)	SP (32, 20, 40)	0 (48, 30, 60)	@ (64, 40, 100)	P (80, 50, 120)	` (96, 60, 140)	p (112, 70, 160)
0	0	0	1	SOH (1, 1, 1)	DC1 (17, 11, 21)	! (33, 21, 41)	1 (49, 31, 61)	A (65, 41, 101)	Q (81, 51, 121)	a (97, 61, 141)	q (113, 71, 161)
0	0	1	0	STX (2, 2, 2)	DC2 (18, 12, 22)	" (34, 22, 42)	2 (50, 32, 62)	B (66, 42, 102)	R (82, 52, 122)	b (98, 62, 142)	r (114, 72, 162)
0	0	1	1	ETX (3, 3, 3)	DC3 (19, 13, 23)	# (35, 23, 43)	3 (51, 33, 63)	C (67, 43, 103)	S (83, 53, 123)	c (99, 63, 143)	s (115, 73, 163)
0	1	0	0	EOT (4, 4, 4)	DC4 (20, 14, 24)	$ (36, 24, 44)	4 (52, 34, 64)	D (68, 44, 104)	T (84, 54, 124)	d (100, 64, 144)	t (116, 74, 164)
0	1	0	1	ENQ (5, 5, 5)	NAK (21, 15, 25)	% (37, 25, 45)	5 (53, 35, 65)	E (69, 45, 105)	U (85, 55, 125)	e (101, 65, 145)	u (117, 75, 165)
0	1	1	0	ACK (6, 6, 6)	SYN (22, 16, 26)	& (38, 26, 46)	6 (54, 36, 66)	F (70, 46, 106)	V (86, 56, 126)	f (102, 66, 146)	v (118, 76, 166)
0	1	1	1	BEL (7, 7, 7)	ETB (23, 17, 27)	' (39, 27, 47)	7 (55, 37, 67)	G (71, 47, 107)	W (87, 57, 127)	g (103, 67, 147)	w (119, 77, 167)
1	0	0	0	BS (8, 8, 10)	CAN (24, 18, 30)	((40, 28, 50)	8 (56, 38, 70)	H (72, 48, 110)	X (88, 58, 130)	h (104, 68, 150)	x (120, 78, 170)
1	0	0	1	HT (9, 9, 11)	EM (25, 19, 31)	) (41, 29, 51)	9 (57, 39, 71)	I (73, 49, 111)	Y (89, 59, 131)	i (105, 69, 151)	y (121, 79, 171)
1	0	1	0	LF (10, A, 12)	SUB (26, 1A, 32)	* (42, 2A, 52)	: (58, 3A, 72)	J (74, 4A, 112)	Z (90, 5A, 132)	j (106, 6A, 152)	z (122, 7A, 172)
1	0	1	1	VT (11, B, 13)	ESC (27, 1B, 33)	+ (43, 2B, 53)	; (59, 3B, 73)	K (75, 4B, 113)	[(91, 5B, 133)	k (107, 6B, 153)	{ (123, 7B, 173)
1	1	0	0	FF (12, C, 14)	FS (28, 1C, 34)	, (44, 2C, 54)	< (60, 3C, 74)	L (76, 4C, 114)	\ (92, 5C, 134)	l (108, 6C, 154)	| (124, 7C, 174)
1	1	0	1	CR (13, D, 15)	GS (29, 1D, 35)	- (45, 2D, 55)	= (61, 3D, 75)	M (77, 4D, 115)	] (93, 5D, 135)	m (109, 6D, 155)	} (125, 7D, 175)
1	1	1	0	SO (14, E, 16)	RS (30, 1E, 36)	. (46, 2E, 56)	> (62, 3E, 76)	N (78, 4E, 116)	^ (94, 5E, 136)	n (110, 6E, 156)	~ (126, 7E, 176)
1	1	1	1	SI (15, F, 17)	US (31, 1F, 37)	/ (47, 2F, 57)	? (63, 3F, 77)	O (79, 4F, 117)	_ (95, 5F, 137)	o (111, 6F, 157)	DEL (127, 7F, 177)

TEX CHARACTER CODES

dec
CHAR
hex   oct

BITS				CONTROL		SYMBOLS NUMBERS		UPPERCASE		LOWERCASE	
b7				0	0	0	0	1	1	1	1
	b6			0	0	1	1	0	0	1	1
		b5		0	1	0	1	0	1	0	1
b4 b3 b2 b1											
0 0 0 0				0 ^^@ 0	16 ^^P 20	32 SP 40	48 0 60	64 @ 100	80 P 120	96 ` 140	112 p 160
0 0 0 1				1 ^^A 1	17 ^^Q 21	33 ! 41	49 1 61	65 A 101	81 Q 121	97 a 141	113 q 161
0 0 1 0				2 ^^B 2	18 ^^R 22	34 " 42	50 2 62	66 B 102	82 R 122	98 b 142	114 r 162
0 0 1 1				3 ^^C 3	19 ^^S 23	35 # 43	51 3 63	67 C 103	83 S 123	99 c 143	115 s 163
0 1 0 0				4 ^^D 4	20 ^^T 24	36 $ 44	52 4 64	68 D 104	84 T 124	100 d 144	116 t 164
0 1 0 1				5 ^^E 5	21 ^^U 25	37 % 45	53 5 65	69 E 105	85 U 125	101 e 145	117 u 165
0 1 1 0				6 ^^F 6	22 ^^V 26	38 & 46	54 6 66	70 F 106	86 V 126	102 f 146	118 v 166
0 1 1 1				7 ^^G 7	23 ^^W 27	39 ' 47	55 7 67	71 G 107	87 W 127	103 g 147	119 w 167
1 0 0 0				8 ^^H 10	24 ^^X 30	40 (50	56 8 70	72 H 110	88 X 130	104 h 150	120 x 170
1 0 0 1				9 ^^I 11	25 ^^Y 31	41) 51	57 9 71	73 I 111	89 Y 131	105 i 151	121 y 171
1 0 1 0				10 ^^J 12	26 ^^Z 32	42 * 52	58 : 72	74 J 112	90 Z 132	106 j 152	122 z 172
1 0 1 1				11 ^^K 13	27 ^^[33	43 + 53	59 ; 73	75 K 113	91 [133	107 k 153	123 { 173
1 1 0 0				12 ^^L 14	28 ^^\ 34	44 , 54	60 < 74	76 L 114	92 \ 134	108 l 154	124	174
1 1 0 1				13 ^^M 15	29 ^^] 35	45 - 55	61 = 75	77 M 115	93] 135	109 m 155	125 } 175
1 1 1 0				14 ^^N 16	30 ^^^ 36	46 . 56	62 > 76	78 N 116	94 ^ 136	110 n 156	126 ~ 176
1 1 1 1				15 ^^O 17	31 ^^_ 37	47 / 57	63 ? 77	79 O 117	95 _ 137	111 o 157	127 ^^? 177

39.2 COMPUTER MODERN FONTS

COMPUTER MODERN ROMAN FONT LAYOUT

	′0	′1	′2	′3	′4	′5	′6	′7	
″0x	Γ	ı	–	0	@	P	`	p	″16x
″1x	Δ	J	!	1	A	Q	a	q	″17x
″2x	Θ	`	"	2	B	R	b	r	″18x
″3x	Λ	′	#	3	C	S	c	s	″19x
″4x	Ξ	˘	$	4	D	T	d	t	″20x
″5x	Π	ˇ	%	5	E	U	e	u	″21x
″6x	Σ	¯	&	6	F	V	f	v	″22x
″7x	Υ	˚	'	7	G	W	g	w	″23x
″10x	Φ	¸	(	8	H	X	h	x	″24x
″11x	Ψ	ß	)	9	I	Y	i	y	″25x
″12x	Ω	æ	*	:	J	Z	j	z	″26x
″13x	ff	œ	+	;	K	[	k	–	″27x
″14x	fi	ø	,	¡	L	"	l	—	″30x
″15x	fl	Æ	-	=	M	]	m	"	″31x
″16x	ffi	Œ	.	¿	N	^	n	~	″32x
″17x	ffl	Ø	/	?	O	˙	o	¨	″33x
	″0	″1	″2	″3	″4	″5	″6	″7	

COMPUTER MODERN TYPEWRITER FONT LAYOUT

	´0			´1			´2			´3			´4			´5			´6			´7		
´00x	Γ	0	0	1	16	10	␣	32	20	0	48	30	@	64	40	P	80	50	`	96	60	p	112	70
´01x	Δ	1	1	J	17	11	!	33	21	1	49	31	A	65	41	Q	81	51	a	97	61	q	113	71
´02x	Θ	2	2	ˋ	18	12	"	34	22	2	50	32	B	66	42	R	82	52	b	98	62	r	114	72
´03x	Λ	3	3	ˊ	19	13	#	35	23	3	51	33	C	67	43	S	83	53	c	99	63	s	115	73
´04x	Ξ	4	4	ˇ	20	14	$	36	24	4	52	34	D	68	44	T	84	54	d	100	64	t	116	74
´05x	Π	5	5	˘	21	15	%	37	25	5	53	35	E	69	45	U	85	55	e	101	65	u	117	75
´06x	Σ	6	6	¯	22	16	&	38	26	6	54	36	F	70	46	V	86	56	f	102	66	v	118	76
´07x	Υ	7	7	˚	23	17	'	39	27	7	55	37	G	71	47	W	87	57	g	103	67	w	119	77
´10x	Φ	8	10	¸	24	18	(	40	28	8	56	38	H	72	48	X	88	58	h	104	68	x	120	78
´11x	Ψ	9	11	ß	25	19	)	41	29	9	57	39	I	73	49	Y	89	59	i	105	69	y	121	79
´12x	Ω	10	A	æ	26	1A	*	42	2A	:	58	3A	J	74	4A	Z	90	5A	j	106	6A	z	122	7A
´13x	↑	11	B	œ	27	1B	+	43	2B	;	59	3B	K	75	4B	[	91	5B	k	107	6B	{	123	7B
´14x	↓	12	C	ø	28	1C	,	44	2C	<	60	3C	L	76	4C	\	92	5C	l	108	6C	|	124	7C
´15x	'	13	D	Æ	29	1D	-	45	2D	=	61	3D	M	77	4D	]	93	5D	m	109	6D	}	125	7D
´16x	¡	14	E	Œ	30	1E	.	46	2E	>	62	3E	N	78	4E	ˆ	94	5E	n	110	6E	~	126	7E
´17x	¿	15	F	Ø	31	1F	/	47	2F	?	63	3F	O	79	4F	ˍ	95	5F	o	111	6F	¨	127	7F

COMPUTER MODERN ITALIC FONT LAYOUT

0 Γ 0 0	16 $\imath$ 10 20	32 ` 20 40	48 0 30 60	64 @ 40 100	80 P 50 120	96 ` 60 140	112 p 70 160
1 Δ 1 1	17 $\jmath$ 11 21	33 ! 21 41	49 1 31 61	65 A 41 101	81 Q 51 121	97 a 61 141	113 q 71 161
2 Θ 2 2	18 ` 12 22	34 " 22 42	50 2 32 62	66 B 42 102	82 R 52 122	98 b 62 142	114 r 72 162
3 Λ 3 3	19 ´ 13 23	35 # 23 43	51 3 33 63	67 C 43 103	83 S 53 123	99 c 63 143	115 s 73 163
4 Ξ 4 4	20 ˇ 14 24	36 £ 24 44	52 4 34 64	68 D 44 104	84 T 54 124	100 d 64 144	116 t 74 164
5 Π 5 5	21 ˘ 15 25	37 % 25 45	53 5 35 65	69 E 45 105	85 U 55 125	101 e 65 145	117 u 75 165
6 Σ 6 6	22 ¯ 16 26	38 & 26 46	54 6 36 66	70 F 46 106	86 V 56 126	102 f 66 146	118 v 76 166
7 Υ 7 7	23 ˚ 17 27	39 , 27 47	55 7 37 67	71 G 47 107	87 W 57 127	103 g 67 147	119 w 77 167
8 Φ 8 10	24 ¸ 18 30	40 (28 50	56 8 38 70	72 H 48 110	88 X 58 130	104 h 68 150	120 x 78 170
9 Ψ 9 11	25 β 19 31	41) 29 51	57 9 39 71	73 I 49 111	89 Y 59 131	105 i 69 151	121 y 79 171
10 Ω A 12	26 æ 1A 32	42 * 2A 52	58 : 3A 72	74 J 4A 112	90 Z 5A 132	106 j 6A 152	122 z 7A 172
11 ff B 13	27 œ 1B 33	43 + 2B 53	59 ; 3B 73	75 K 4B 113	91 [5B 133	107 k 6B 153	123 – 7B 173
12 fi C 14	28 ø 1C 34	44 , 2C 54	60 $\imath$ 3C 74	76 L 4C 114	92 " 5C 134	108 l 6C 154	124 — 7C 174
13 fl D 15	29 Æ 1D 35	45 - 2D 55	61 = 3D 75	77 M 4D 115	93] 5D 135	109 m 6D 155	125 " 7D 175
14 ffi E 16	30 Œ 1E 36	46 . 2E 56	62 $\jmath$ 3E 76	78 N 4E 116	94 ^ 5E 136	110 n 6E 156	126 ~ 7E 176
15 ffl F 17	31 Ø 1F 37	47 / 2F 57	63 ? 3F 77	79 O 4F 117	95 ˙ 5F 137	111 o 6F 157	127 ¨ 7F 177

COMPUTER MODERN SYMBOL FONT

0 — 0 0	16 ≍ 10 20	32 ← 20 40	48 / 30 60	64 $\aleph$ 40 100	80 $\mathcal{P}$ 50 120	96 ⊢ 60 140	112 √ 70 160
1 · 1 1	17 ≡ 11 21	33 → 21 41	49 ∞ 31 61	65 $\mathcal{A}$ 41 101	81 $\mathcal{Q}$ 51 121	97 ⊣ 61 141	113 ∐ 71 161
2 × 2 2	18 ⊆ 12 22	34 ↑ 22 42	50 ∈ 32 62	66 $\mathcal{B}$ 42 102	82 $\mathcal{R}$ 52 122	98 ⌊ 62 142	114 ∇ 72 162
3 ∗ 3 3	19 ⊇ 13 23	35 ↓ 23 43	51 ∋ 33 63	67 $\mathcal{C}$ 43 103	83 $\mathcal{S}$ 53 123	99 ⌋ 63 143	115 ∫ 73 163
4 ÷ 4 4	20 ≤ 14 24	36 ↔ 24 44	52 △ 34 64	68 $\mathcal{D}$ 44 104	84 $\mathcal{T}$ 54 124	100 ⌈ 64 144	116 ⊔ 74 164
5 ⋄ 5 5	21 ≥ 15 25	37 ↗ 25 45	53 ▽ 35 65	69 $\mathcal{E}$ 45 105	85 $\mathcal{U}$ 55 125	101 ⌉ 65 145	117 ⊓ 75 165
6 ± 6 6	22 ≼ 16 26	38 ↘ 26 46	54 / 36 66	70 $\mathcal{F}$ 46 106	86 $\mathcal{V}$ 56 126	102 { 66 146	118 ⊑ 76 166
7 ∓ 7 7	23 ≽ 17 27	39 ≃ 27 47	55 ∣ 37 67	71 $\mathcal{G}$ 47 107	87 $\mathcal{W}$ 57 127	103 } 67 147	119 ⊒ 77 167
8 ⊕ 8 10	24 ∼ 18 30	40 ⇐ 28 50	56 ∀ 38 70	72 $\mathcal{H}$ 48 110	88 $\mathcal{X}$ 58 130	104 ⟨ 68 150	120 § 78 170
9 ⊖ 9 11	25 ≈ 19 31	41 ⇒ 29 51	57 ∃ 39 71	73 $\mathcal{I}$ 49 111	89 $\mathcal{Y}$ 59 131	105 ⟩ 69 151	121 † 79 171
10 ⊗ A 12	26 ⊂ 1A 32	42 ⇑ 2A 52	58 ¬ 3A 72	74 $\mathcal{J}$ 4A 112	90 $\mathcal{Z}$ 5A 132	106 ∣ 6A 152	122 ‡ 7A 172
11 ⊘ B 13	27 ⊃ 1B 33	43 ⇓ 2B 53	59 ∅ 3B 73	75 $\mathcal{K}$ 4B 113	91 ∪ 5B 133	107 ∥ 6B 153	123 ¶ 7B 173
12 ⊙ C 14	28 ≪ 1C 34	44 ⇔ 2C 54	60 $\mathfrak{R}$ 3C 74	76 $\mathcal{L}$ 4C 114	92 ∩ 5C 134	108 ↕ 6C 154	124 ♣ 7C 174
13 ○ D 15	29 ≫ 1D 35	45 ↖ 2D 55	61 $\mathfrak{I}$ 3D 75	77 $\mathcal{M}$ 4D 115	93 ⊎ 5D 135	109 ⇕ 6D 155	125 ♦ 7D 175
14 ○ E 16	30 ≺ 1E 36	46 ↙ 2E 56	62 ⊤ 3E 76	78 $\mathcal{N}$ 4E 116	94 ∧ 5E 136	110 \ 6E 156	126 ♡ 7E 176
15 • F 17	31 ≻ 1F 37	47 ∝ 2F 57	63 ⊥ 3F 77	79 $\mathcal{O}$ 4F 117	95 ∨ 5F 137	111 ≀ 6F 157	127 ♠ 7F 177

COMPUTER MODERN MATH EXTENSION FONT

39.3 PLAIN TeX MATH SYMBOLS

39.3.1 Mathcharacter codes

The following characters have been defined in a

   \mathcode⟨8-bit number⟩⟨equals⟩⟨15-bit number⟩

assignment.

Character	\mathcode	Class	Family	Hex position
.	"013A	ordinary	1	3A
/	"013D			3D
\	"026E		2	6E
|	"026A			6A
+	"202B	binary operation	0	2B
*	"2203		2	03
−	"2200			00
:	"303A	relation	0	3A
=	"303D			3D
<	"313C		1	3C
>	"313E			3E
(	"4028	open symbol	0	28
[	"405B			5B
{	"4266		2	66
!	"5021	closing symbol	0	21
)	"5029			29
?	"503F			3F
]	"505D			5D
}	"5267		2	67
;	"603B	punctuation	0	3B
,	"613B		1	3B
␣	"8000			
'	"8000			
_	"8000			

39.3.2 Delimiter codes

The following characters have been defined in a

\delcode⟨8-bit number⟩⟨equals⟩⟨24-bit number⟩

assignment. They can be used with \left and \right.

Character	\mathcode	small variant		large variant	
		Family	Hex position	Family	Hex position
(	"028300	0	28	3	00
)	"029301	0	29	3	01
[	"05B302	0	5B	3	02
]	"05D303	0	5D	3	03
<	"26830A	2	68	3	0A
>	"26930B	2	69	3	0B
/	"02F30E	0	2F	3	0E
|	"26A30C	2	6A	3	0C
\	"26E30F	2	6E	3	0F

39.3.3 ⟨mathchardef tokens⟩: ordinary symbols

The following characters have been defined in a

$\quad$ \mathchardef⟨control sequence⟩⟨equals⟩⟨15-bit number⟩

assignment.

Symbol	Control Sequence	\mathcode	Family	Hex position
∂	\partial	"0140	1	40
$\flat$	\flat	"015B		5B
$\natural$	\natural	"015C		5C
$\sharp$	\sharp	"015D		5D
ℓ	\ell	"0160		60
$\imath$	\imath	"017B		7B
$\jmath$	\jmath	"017C		7C
$\wp$	\wp	"017D		7D
$\prime$	\prime	"0230	2	30
∞	\infty	"0231		31
$\triangle$	\triangle	"0234		34
$\forall$	\forall	"0238		38
$\exists$	\exists	"0239		39
$\neg$	\neg	"023A		3A
$\emptyset$	\emptyset	"023B		3B
$\Re$	\Re	"023C		3C
$\Im$	\Im	"023D		3D
$\top$	\top	"023E		3E
$\bot$	\bot	"023F		3F
$\aleph$	\aleph	"0240		40
∇	\nabla	"0272		72
$\clubsuit$	\clubsuit	"027C		7C
$\diamondsuit$	\diamondsuit	"027D		7D
$\heartsuit$	\heartsuit	"027E		7E
$\spadesuit$	\spadesuit	"027F		7F

39.3.4 ⟨mathchardef tokens⟩: large operators

The following characters have been defined in a

$\mathtt{\backslash mathchardef}\langle\text{control sequence}\rangle\langle\text{equals}\rangle\langle\text{15-bit number}\rangle$

assignment.

Symbol	Control Sequence	\mathcode	Family	Hex position
∫∫	\smallint	"1273	2	73
⊔⊔	\bigsqcup	"1346	3	46
∮∮	\ointop	"1348		48
⊙⊙	\bigodot	"134A		4A
⊕⊕	\bigoplus	"134C		4C
⊗⊗	\bigotimes	"134E		4E
ΣΣ	\sum	"1350		50
ΠΠ	\prod	"1351		51
∫∫	\intop	"1352		52
∪∪	\bigcup	"1353		53
∩∩	\bigcap	"1354		54
⊎⊎	\biguplus	"1355		55
∧∧	\bigwedge	"1356		56
∨∨	\bigvee	"1357		57
⊔⊔	\coprod	"1360		60

39.3.5 ⟨mathchardef tokens⟩: binary operations

The following characters have been defined in a

\mathchardef⟨control sequence⟩⟨equals⟩⟨15-bit number⟩

assignment.

Symbol	Control Sequence	\mathcode	Family	Hex position
▷	\triangleright	"212E	1	2E
◁	\triangleleft	"212F		2F
⋆	\star	"213F		3F
·	\cdot	"2201	2	01
×	\times	"2202		02
∗	\ast	"2203		03
÷	\div	"2204		04
⋄	\diamond	"2205		05
±	\pm	"2206		06
∓	\mp	"2207		07
⊕	\oplus	"2208		08
⊖	\ominus	"2209		09
⊗	\otimes	"220A		0A
⊘	\oslash	"220B		0B
⊙	\odot	"220C		0C
◯	\bigcirc	"220D		0D
∘	\circ	"220E		0E
•	\bullet	"220F		0F
△	\bigtriangleup	"2234		34
▽	\bigtriangledown	"2235		35
∪	\cup	"225B		5B
∩	\cap	"225C		5C
⊎	\uplus	"225D		5D
∧	\wedge	"225E		5E
∨	\vee	"225F		5F
\	\setminus	"226E		6E
≀	\wr	"226F		6F
⨿	\amalg	"2271		71
⊔	\sqcup	"2274		74
⊓	\sqcap	"2275		75
†	\dagger	"2279		79
‡	\ddagger	"227A		7A

39.3.6 ⟨mathchardef tokens⟩: relations

The following characters have been defined in a

\mathchardef⟨control sequence⟩⟨equals⟩⟨15-bit number⟩

assignment.

Symbol	Control Sequence	\mathcode	Family	Hex position
↼	\leftharpoonup	"3128	1	28
↽	\leftharpoondown	"3129		29
⇀	\rightharpoonup	"312A		2A
⇁	\rightharpoondown	"312B		2B
⌣	\smile	"315E		5E
⌢	\frown	"315F		5F
≍	\asymp	"3210	2	10
≡	\equiv	"3211		11
⊆	\subseteq	"3212		12
⊇	\supseteq	"3213		13
≤	\leq	"3214		14
≥	\geq	"3215		15
⪯	\preceq	"3216		16
⪰	\succeq	"3217		17
∼	\sim	"3218		18
≈	\approx	"3219		19
⊂	\subset	"321A		1A
⊃	\supset	"321B		1B
≪	\ll	"321C		1C
≫	\gg	"321D		1D
≺	\prec	"321E		1E
≻	\succ	"321F		1F
←	\leftarrow	"3220		20
→	\rightarrow	"3221		21
↔	\leftrightarrow	"3224		24
↗	\nearrow	"3225		25
↘	\searrow	"3226		26
≃	\simeq	"3227		27
⇐	\Leftarrow	"3228		28
⇒	\Rightarrow	"3229		29
⇔	\Leftrightarrow	"322C		2C
↖	\nwarrow	"322D		2D
↙	\swarrow	"322E		2E
∝	\propto	"322F		2F
∈	\in	"3232		32
∋	\ni	"3233		33
/	\not	"3236		36
⊢	\mapstochar	"3237		37
⊥	\perp	"323F		3F
⊢	\vdash	"3260		60
⊣	\dashv	"3261		61

	\mid	"326A	6A
∥	\parallel	"326B	6B
⊑	\sqsubseteq	"3276	76
⊒	\sqsupseteq	"3277	77

39.3.7 \delimiter macros

The following characters have been defined in a

$\quad$ \def⟨control sequence⟩{\delimiter⟨27-bit number⟩}

assignment.

Delimiters Symbol	Control Sequence	Hex code	Function
⎰	\lmoustache	"4000340	open symbol
⎱	\rmoustache	"5000341	closing symbol
⟮	\lgroup	"400033A	open symbol
⟯	\rgroup	"500033B	closing symbol
∣	\arrowvert	"33C	ordinary
∥	\Arrowvert	"33D	ordinary
∣	\bracevert	"33E	ordinary
∥	\Vert	"26B30D	ordinary
∣	\vert	"26A30C	ordinary
↑	\uparrow	"3222378	relation
↓	\downarrow	"3223379	relation
↕	\updownarrow	"326C33F	relation
⇑	\Uparrow	"322A37E	relation
⇓	\Downarrow	"322B37F	relation
⇕	\Updownarrow	"326D377	relation
\	\backslash	"26E30F	ordinary
⟩	\rangle	"526930B	closing symbol
⟨	\langle	"426830A	open symbol
}	\rbrace	"5267309	closing symbol
{	\lbrace	"4266308	open symbol
⌉	\rceil	"5265307	closing symbol
⌈	\lceil	"4264306	open symbol
⌋	\rfloor	"5263305	closing symbol
⌊	\lfloor	"4262304	open symbol

List of Examples

Change the meaning of the line end 20
Take a paragraph apart 53
Uppercase roman numberals 66
Change the default dimensions of rules 83
End a paragraph with leaders 87
Nested macro definitions 100
Hide counters from the user 101
Macros with an undetermined number of arguments 105
Examine a macro argument for the presence of some element 105
Macros with optional parameters 107
Take an input line as macro argument 108
Comment environment 108
Control expansion inside an \edef 122
Save and restore category codes 124
\vcenter outside math mode 126
Compare two strings 137
Compare two strings lexicographically 138
Stack macros 142
Control indentation systematically 152
Control vertical white space systematically 153
Prevent page breaks in between paragraphs 157
Centre the first/last line of a paragraph 161
Indent into the margin 162
Hang a paragraph from an object 162
Enable hyphenation of a word containing a hyphen 171
Specify exceptional hyphenations 173
Change fonts in a math formula 188
Adjust subscript lowering 200
Draw rules in an alignment 212
Specify page height in lines 215
Do tricks with headlines 227
Prevent indentation on top of page 229
Test whether a file exists 239
Input a file that was created in the same run of TeX 239

Index by Command

\- 170
\/ 36
\{ 92
\} 92
\␣ 11, 19, 176
\^ 192
_ 192

\above 197
\abovedisplayshortskip 202
\abovedisplayskip 202
\abovewithdelims 197
\accent 27
\active 10
\adjdemerits 168
\advance 67, 74
\afterassignment 114
\aftergroup 115
\allowbreak 197
\atop 197
\atopwithdelims 197

\badness 47
\baselineskip 145
\batchmode 247
\begingroup 90
\belowdisplayshortskip 202
\belowdisplayskip 202
\bgroup 91
\big etc. 183
\binoppenaly 197
\botmark 227
\box 40
\boxmaxdepth 43
\brokenpenalty 220
\bye 245

\c 28
\cases 213
\catcode 10
\centering 214
\char 25
\chardef 25
\cleaders 86

\closein 236
\closeout 237
\clubpenalty 219
\copy 40
\count 66
\countdef 67
\cr 213
\crcr 213
\csname 101

\day 254
\deadcycles 226
\def 96
\defaulthyphenchar 170
\defaultskewchar 185
\delcode 182
\delimiter 182
\delimiterfactor 183
\delimitershortfall 183
\dimen 73
\dimendef 73
\discretionary 170
\displayindent 202
\displaylimits 194
\displaystyle 193
\displaywidowpenalty 220
\displaywidth 202
\divide 67, 74
\doublehyphendemerits 168
\dp 45
\dump 248

\edef 96, 113
\egroup 91
\else 127
\emergencystretch 169
\end 245
\endcsname 101
\endgroup 90
\endinput 236
\endinsert 235
\endlinechar 8
\eqalignno 214

\eqno 203
\errhelp 263
\errmessage 263
\errorcontextlines 263
\errorstopmode 246
\escapechar 31
\everycr 213
\everydisplay 201
\everyhbox 48
\everyjob 245
\everymath 191
\everypar 151
\everyvbox 48
\exhyphenpenalty 170
\expandafter 112

\fam 187
\fi 127
\finalhyphendemerits 168
\firstmark 227
\floatingpenalty 233
\font 33
\fontdimen 35
\fontname 35
\frenchspacing 178
\futurelet 103

\gdef 96
\global 89, 95
\globaldefs 89

\halign 206
\hangafter 159
\hangindent 159
\hbadness 47
\hbox 41
\hfil 70
\hfill 70
\hfilneg 70
\hfuzz 47
\hglue 79
\hidewidth 212
\hoffset 215
\holdinginserts 234
\hrule 82

\hsize *159*
\hskip *76*
\hss *70*
\ht *45*
\hyphenation *173*
\hyphenchar *170*
\hyphenpenalty *170*

\if *127*
\ifcase *131*
\ifcat *128*
\ifdim *130*
\ifeof *130*
\iffalse *131*
\ifhbox *130*
\ifhmode *129*
\ifinner *129*
\ifmmode *129*
\ifnum *130*
\ifodd *130*
\iftrue *131*
\ifvbox *130*
\ifvmode *129*
\ifvoid *130*
\ifx *128*
\ignorespaces *17*
\immediate *238*
\indent *150*
\input *236*
\inputlineno *239*
\insert *231*
\insertpenalties *233, 234*
\interlinepenalty *219*

\jobname *245*

\kern *79*

\language *173*
\lastbox *41*
\lastkern *79*
\lastpenalty *219*
\lastskip *79*
\lccode *29*
\leaders *84*
\leavevmode *49*
\left *181*
\lefthyphenmin *173*
\leftskip *159*

\leqno *203*
\let *26, 102*
\limits *194*
\linepenalty *167*
\lineskip *146*
\lineskiplimit *146*
\llap *47*
\long *96*
\loop *104*
\looseness *168*
\lower *45*
\lowercase *29*

\mag *253*
\magnification *253*
\mark *226*
\mathaccent *184*
\mathbin *193*
\mathchar *181*
\mathchardef *181*
\mathchoice *193*
\mathclose *193*
\mathcode *180*
\mathinner *194*
\mathop *193*
\mathopen *193*
\mathord *193*
\mathpunct *193*
\mathrel *193*
\mathsurround *196*
\matrix *213*
\maxdeadcycles *226*
\maxdepth *216*
\meaning *259*
\medmuskip *195*
\message *239*
\midinsert *234*
\mkern *195*
\month *254*
\moveleft *45*
\moveright *45*
\mskip *195*
\multiply *67, 74*
\multispan *212*
\muskip *196*
\muskipdef *196*

\newbox *39*
\newcount *67*
\newdimen *74*

\newfam *187*
\newif *131*
\newinsert *231*
\newlanguage *242*
\newlinechar *240*
\newmuskip *196*
\newread *236*
\newskip *74*
\newtoks *141*
\newwrite *236*
\noalign *207*
\noboundary *37*
\noexpand *116*
\noindent *150*
\nointerlineskip *148*
\nolimits *194*
\nonfrenchspacing *178*
\nonscript *196*
\nonstopmode *247*
\nulldelimiterspace *183*
\nullfont *35*
\number *66*
\obeylines *20*

\offinterlineskip *148*
\omit *211*
\openin *236*
\openout *237*
\openup *149*
\or *131*
\outer *95*
\output *225*
\outputpenalty *217*
\over *197*
\overfullrule *48*
\overline *197*
\overwithdelims *197*

\pagedepth *219*
\pagefilllstretch *219*
\pagefillstretch *219*
\pagefilstretch *219*
\pagegoal *233*
\pageinsert *234*
\pageshrink *219*
\pagestretch *219*
\pagetotal *219*
\par *16*
\parfillskip *155*

\parindent *150*
\parshape *161*
\parskip *150*
\patterns *173*
\pausing *239*
\penalty *167, 220*
\postdisplaypenalty *202*
\predisplaypenalty *202*
\predisplaysize *202*
\pretolerance *169*
\prevdepth *147*
\prevgraf *168*
\protect *123*

\radical *184*
\raggedbottom *216*
\raggedright *159*
\raise *45*
\read *237*
\relax *117*
\relpenalty *197*
\removelastskip *80*
\right *181*
\righthyphenmin *173*
\rightskip *159*
\rlap *47*
\romannumeral *66*

\scriptfont *187*
\scriptscriptfont *187*
\scriptscriptstyle *193*
\scriptspace *192*
\scriptstyle *193*
\scrollmode *246*
\setbox *40*
\setlanguage *174*
\sfcode *177*
\shipout *225*
\show *259*
\showbox *259*
\showboxbreadth *260*
\showboxdepth *260*
\showlists *60*
\showthe *259*
\skew *184*
\skewchar *184*
\skip *73*
\skipdef *73*
\smash *45*

\spacefactor *175*
\spaceskip *175*
\span *209, 211*
\special *253*
\splitbotmark *227*
\splitfirstmark *227*
\splitmaxdepth *222*
\splittopskip *222*
\string *31*
\strut *212*

\tabskip *209*
\textfont *187*
\textstyle *193*
\the *119*
\thickmuskip *195*
\thinmuskip *195*
\time *254*
\toks *141*
\toksdef *141*
\tolerance *169*
\topmark *227*
\topskip *215*
\tracingcommands *258*
\tracinglostchars *258*
\tracingmacros *258*
\tracingonline *258*
\tracingoutput *259*
\tracingpages *258*
\tracingparagraphs *169*
\tracingrestores *258*
\tracingstats *261*

\uccode *29*
\uchyph *172*
\underline *197*
\unhbox *49*
\unhcopy *49*
\unkern *80*
\unpenalty *219*
\unskip *80*
\unvbox *49*
\unvcopy *49*
\uppercase *29*

\vadjust *59*
\valign *206*
\vbadness *47*
\vbox *42*
\vcenter *195*

\vfil *70*
\vfill *70*
\vfilneg *70*
\vfuzz *47*
\vglue *79*
\voffset *215*
\vrule *82*
\vsize *216*
\vskip *76*
\vsplit *221*
\vss *70*
\vtop *42*

\wd *45*
\widehat *185*
\widetilde *185*
\widowpenalty *220*
\write *121, 238*

\xdef *96*
\xleaders *86*
\xspaceskip *175*

\year *254*

Index by Topic

- *177*
^^ replacement *12*

accents *27*
  in math mode *184*
active character *103*
  and \noexpand *116*
alignment *206*
  alignment display *207*
  horizontal *206*
  rules in *212*
  tab *208*
  vertical *207*
arguments *96*
arithmetic *67*
  fixed-point *68*
  floating-point *68*
  on glue *74*
axis of math formulas *195*

badness
  calculation *78*
  and line breaking *166*
baseline distance *145*
box *38*
  dimensions *41*
  overfull and underfull *47*
  registers *39*
  text in *50*
braces *91*
breakpoints
  computation of *220*
  in horizontal lists *167*
  in math lists *197*
  in vertical lists *219*

code
  category *9*
  character *24*
  codenames *31*
  delimiter *182*
  space factor *177*

commands
  horizontal *57*
  primitive *103*
  vertical *57*
Computer Modern typefaces *255*
conditionals *127*
  evaluation of *133*
control
  sequence *11*
  space *11, 176*
  symbol *11*
cramped styles *192*

date *254*
delimiter *181*
  codes *182*
  group *90*
  sizes *182*
demerits *167*
device drivers *253, 255*
discardable items *55*
discretionary
  hyphen *170*
  item *170*
displays *201*
  non-centred *204*

equation numbering *203*
error
  overflow *264*
  patching *263*
escape character *13, 15*
expandable control sequences *111*
expansion *111*

files
  `dvi` *252*
  font *255*
  format *248*
  input *236*
  log *246*
  `tfm` *35*

font *33*
  dimensions *35*
  extension font *183*
  families *186*
  metrics *254*
  symbol font *198*
  tables *290*
  virtual font *254*

generalized fractions *197*
global statements *89*
glue *70*
  interline *145*
  mu *195*
  setting *78*
grouping *89*

hanging indentation *159*
hyphen
  character *170*
  discretionary *170*
hyphenation *171*

implicit characters *26*
IniTeX *248*
input
  files *236*
  lines *8*
  stack *104*
insertions *231*
integers *62*
internal states *11*
I/O *236*
italic correction *36*

job *245*

kerning *36*
keywords *268*

language
  current *173*
  natural *171, 173*
LaTeX *251*
leaders *83*
ligatures *37*

line
  empty *16*
  end of *8, 19*
  input *8*
  width of *159*
lists
  horizontal *55*
  token *140*
  vertical *56*
local statements *89*
Lollipop *252*
lowercase *29*

machine dependence *8, 203*
macro *94*
  definition *94*
  outer *95*
  prefix *95*
magnification *253*
marks *226*
math
  centring of formulas *195*
  characters *180*
  classes *193*
  modes *191*
  shift character *191*
  spacing *195*
  styles *191*
  symbols, lists of *295*
  unit *195*
migrating material *59*
modes *55*
  horizontal *55*
  internal *57*
  math *191*
  restricted *57*
  vertical *56*

numbers *62*
  conversion *66*

output routine *225*

page
  breaking *220*
  builder *217*
  current *217*
  depth *216*

length *218*
  numbering *228*
  positioning *215*
paragraph
  breaking into lines *169*
  end *155*
  shape *159*
  start *150*
parameter *96*
  character *14, 99*
  delimited *97*
  undelimited *97*
Pascal *256*
penalties
  in horizontal lists *167*
  in math mode *197*
  in vertical mode *219*
PostScript *254*

radicals *184*
recent contributions *217*
recursion *103*
registers, allocation of *242*
roman numerals *66*
rules *82*
  in alignments *212*
  leaders *84*
run modes *246*

save stack *89*
shrink *76*
space
  character *14*
  control space *11, 176*
  factor *175*
  factor code *177*
  funny space *18*
  optional space *17, 269*
  token *16, 18*
spacing *175*
  French *178*
  math *195*
specials *253*
statistics *258*
streams *236*
stretch *76*
subscript *192*
successors *182*
superscript *192*

tables
  ASCII *288*
  character codes *289*
  font *290*
  see also alignment
TeX *248*
  big TeX *266*
  Users Group, *see* TUG
  versions 2 and 3 *270*
tie *177*
time *254*
tracing *258*
TUG *257*
TUGboat *257*

unboxing *49*
units of measurement *75*
uppercase *29*

verbatim mode *109*
VirTeX *248*

WEB *256*
whatsits *238*